Withdrawn from
Davidson College Library

Library of
Davidson College

PHILOSOPHY, POLITICS AND SOCIETY
FOURTH SERIES

Philosophy, Politics and Society
FOURTH SERIES

*A collection edited by
Peter Laslett, W G Runciman
and Quentin Skinner*

BARNES & NOBLE BOOKS
10 East 53d St., New York 10022
(a division of Harper & Row Publishers, Inc.)

© in this collection
Basil Blackwell 1972

First published in the U.S.A. in 1972
by Harper & Row Publishers, Inc.
Barnes & Noble Import Division

ISBN 06-4940650

All rights reserved. No part of this publication may be reproduced, stored in a retrieval system, or transmitted, in any form or by any means, electronic, mechanical, photocopying, recording or otherwise, without the prior permission of Basil Blackwell & Mott Limited.

Printed in Great Britain

Contents

page 1   Introduction

1
page 8

Is a Science of Comparative Politics Possible?
Alasdair MacIntyre
PROFESSOR OF THE HISTORY OF IDEAS
BRANDEIS UNIVERSITY

2
page 27

The Political Theory of Scarcity
James Cornford
PROFESSOR OF POLITICAL SCIENCE
EDINBURGH UNIVERSITY

3
page 45

Obligation and Consent
Hanna Pitkin
PROFESSOR OF POLITICAL SCIENCE
UNIVERSITY OF CALIFORNIA, BERKELEY

4
page 86

'Normal' Science or Political Ideology?
Alan Ryan
FELLOW OF NEW COLLEGE
OXFORD

5
page 101

Coercion
Robert Nozick
PROFESSOR OF PHILOSOPHY
HARVARD UNIVERSITY

6
page 136

'Social Meaning' and the Explanation of Social Action
Quentin Skinner
FELLOW OF CHRIST'S COLLEGE
CAMBRIDGE

7
page 158
The Identity of the History of Ideas
John Dunn
FELLOW OF KING'S COLLEGE
CAMBRIDGE

8
page 174
Negative and Positive Freedom
Gerald C. MacCallum Jr.
PROFESSOR OF POLITICAL SCIENCE
UNIVERSITY OF WISCONSIN

9
page 194
Why is Authority such a Problem?
Richard Tuck
FELLOW OF JESUS COLLEGE
CAMBRIDGE

10
page 208
Collective Decisions and Collective Action
James Coleman
PROFESSOR OF SOCIOLOGY
JOHNS HOPKINS UNIVERSITY

Introduction

The introduction to each of the three previous volumes of *Philosophy, Politics and Society* has included a more or less anxious report on the health of theoretical reflection about social and political issues. The patient was at first taken for dead, and even though this announcement later came to seem a trifle premature, the introductions to both the succeeding volumes continued to voice considerable doubts about the prospect of any complete recovery.

It is arguable that we were never right to think in terms of such pathological metaphors, and it is clear in any case that they are no longer applicable. It has by now become a commonplace that both the intellectual movements prevailing at the time of our first introduction, in terms of which it looked plausible for sociologists to speak of 'the end of ideology' and even for philosophers to speak of 'the death of political theory' were themselves the masks of disputable ideological positions. It was a lack of critical awareness about the character of these movements rather than any genuine absence of ideological or theoretical reflection which gave rise to the always misleading and by now dramatically exploded sense that there might be nothing further to say.

It might seem most profitable at this point to turn away from the immediate past, and to consider instead the various directions in which the reanimated study of social and political philosophy has by now developed. Before attempting such a brief sketch, however, it seems right to yield to a somewhat sententious temptation—that of trying to see what lessons may perhaps be learnt from this immediate past, in the hope of avoiding any repetition of our mistakes.

The main lesson might perhaps be summarized as the need for greater self-awareness about the difficulty of giving any uncontentious and value-neutral statement of 'the facts' about moral and political issues. The end-of-ideology theorists took themselves simply to be examining and commenting on the most striking facts about the political structures of Western democracies at the time: their combination of a high degree of governmental stability with a high degree of popular apathy. Their equation of these undoubted facts, however, with 'the end of ideology' compromised their status as neutral observers in at least two ways. First, they failed to allow for the possibility (or rather the fact, as it has turned out) that the correct interpretation of the fact of widespread political apathy was that a number of minority groups could not see how to schedule their wants within the given political systems, rather than that they felt any very deep contentment with these systems themselves. Secondly, they failed to recognize the extent to which their own allegedly neutral reflections about the value of political stability and consensus were themselves the expression of a particular ideological commitment. As their shrewdest critics (such as Partridge)[1] noticed even at the time, it was the very fact of consensus amongst the pundits to the effect that (as Lipset notoriously put it) 'the good society itself' had already been achieved which gave them the comforting illusion that ideological debate was at an end, while allowing them at the same time, under the guise of offering value-free political analysis, to insist on the overriding value of a set of conservative political principles. In short, it is doubtful if ideology could end, and it certainly never did.

The strong belief of all these social and political analysts in the possibility of a wholly uncontentious examination of 'the facts' was in turn underpinned by, and in part derived from, the strongly positivist style of analysing moral and political concepts which then prevailed. The most widely influential authors here have of course been Weldon and Hare. It was the derivative but powerful work of the former, indeed, which was above all responsible for engendering the popular impression that ideology had not merely ended, but that all substantive social and political theory had died. Weldon and Hare fundamentally agreed in the accounts they gave of the behaviour of rational moral (or political) agents. Such an agent's point of departure is taken to be an examination of 'the facts of the case'. This in turn is taken to be both a logically isolated and a wholly unproblematical activity. These facts then refer the agent back to his underlying 'principles'. His grasp of the relations between the relevant principle and the relevant facts then shows him how to make the appropriate choice – the rational, unideological choice – of the appropriate course of action to adopt. The whole business of inculcating this sense of the proper relationship between principles and action is seen, as Hare put it in *The Language of Morals*, as very like the business of 'teaching African soldiers to drive'.

It is easy to see how this account of the agent's situation, in the hands of an enthusiast like Weldon, seemed to spell the death of any possibility of a substantive philosophical contribution to social and political debate. The agent's 'principles' are taken simply to be his own, and it is not for the philosopher to discuss their actual content, let alone their merits. The whole task of moral and political philosophy is thus reduced simply to that of attempting to elucidate the form in which a man's principles should relate to his actions. Not substantive moral issues but simply the language of morals, not substantive political issues but simply the

---

[1] P. H. Partridge, 'Politics, Philosophy, Ideology' first appeared in 1961, and has since been reprinted in A. Quinton, ed., *Political Philosophy* (Oxford, 1967), pp. 32–52.

vocabulary of politics, come to seem the sole appropriate subject-matter for general theoretical discussion. It is also easy to see, however, now that the spell cast by this account has been exorcized even in a number of textbook accounts of current moral philosophy,[2] how far it always depended on some extreme positivist assumptions about the facts of moral and political life. First there is the peculiarity, which Mrs Foot and others always stressed, that according to this account it is simply the agent's examination of 'the facts' which immediately yields him the reason for making his given moral choice. 'The facts' simply *are* his reasons. So moral and political arguments must always turn out either to be straightforwardly soluble arguments about 'the facts', or else to be liable to instant and total breakdown as arguments. The converse possibility, that 'the facts' might in themselves yield a normatively weighted description, has in turn been explored by Mrs. Foot, and has already been applied specifically to the discussion of political issues in an essay which Professor Charles Taylor contributed to our last volume, and which has since been extensively cited. Secondly, there is the more general implausibility, which Hampshire and others always stressed, of picturing the moral or political agent as nothing more than a man making *ad hoc*, empirical choices based on 'the facts', uncontaminated apparently by any prior conceptual scheme for viewing the facts, or even by any social commitment which might cause him to select and describe the facts in some particular and thus normatively weighted way.

There is no doubt, of course, that the lesson which a reaction against this sort of positivism teaches about the difficulty of talking uncontentiously about 'the facts' has by now been very thoroughly learnt. There is even a danger, indeed, that the recent influence of a rather wild neo-Hegelianism may now cause a contrary excess to develop: that of supposing that there can be no value-free social description at all. There is equally no doubt, however, that the final release from the positivist framework imposed by the sociologists and philosophers of the Fifties has had a largely fruitful effect on the theoretical study and appraisal of social and political issues. It is on the nature of these developments that we should now like very briefly to comment.

We have not of course been able, within the confines of this volume, properly to represent all these developments. Two in particular we have not managed to illustrate. We have included no discussion of the issues raised by the ideological debate which preoccupied a whole generation of students at the end of the Sixties, and which looked for a moment in

[2] One excellent example is G. J. Warnock, *Contemporary Moral Philosophy* (London, 1967), esp. Ch. IV.

1968 as though it might unseat a government. There can be no doubt, of course, of the importance of this movement both from a theoretical point of view – since it has generated a whole new vocabulary of social description and evaluation – and at the practical level – since it has had visible effects on policy-making, at least in the United States and in France. It is not surprising, however, that none of our efforts to commission a theoretical essay on these themes met with any success.[3] By the time we came to make the attempt, the movement itself had already become largely dormant. And even at its activist height there had been strikingly little attempt to formulate and justify a programme of aims and ends. Our failure might indeed be said to reflect two of the key features of the morality of the movement itself—the general suspicion of the value of argued reflection, and the specific rejection of all demands to talk about consequences.

The other major development we have not been able to reflect is the greatly increased interest, which has accompanied the rejection of purely 'linguistic' social theorizing and purely 'behavioural' political science, in the history of moral and political philosophy. This omission is due simply to the fact that the relevant issues tend in this case to be unsuitable for treatment at essay-length. But the nature of the development can readily be sketched. The historical study of social and political ideas has itself begun to develop in a more sociological direction, focusing less on the traditional canon of 'classic texts', and more on the study of the changing vocabularies which different societies have used to describe and justify their various social and political arrangements. An interesting example of this genre has just been published by Professor Pocock,[4] who contributed a methodological essay to our second volume which included a prediction that some such developments might take place. This renewed interest in, and the new focus of, such historical studies has in turn been associated with two further developments. The first has been an increased *rapprochement* with various schools of thought which had never ceased to take historical knowledge seriously. This can already be seen reflected in the recrudescence of the serious reputation of such philosophers as Collingwood, and in the increasing

---

[3] Several academic works have recently appeared, however, which argue for positions congenial to the New Left. See for example R. Miliband, *The State in Capitalist Society* (London, 1969) Michael Walzer, *Obligations* (Cambridge, Mass., 1970); R. P. Wolff, *In Defense of Anarchism* (New York, 1970).
[4] J. G. A. Pocock, *Politics, Language and Time* (New York, 1971).

availability in translation of works by such writers as Foucault, Habermas and others. The other development has derived from the fact that the intellectual historians have begun to produce the sort of information which makes it possible for them to add a missing dimension to purely 'behavioural' sociology and political science, and even to purely analytical social and political philosophy. The possibility of this latter type of dialogue can already be illustrated from the case of Professor MacIntyre's *Short History of Ethics*, with its insistence on the need for such an historical dimension to assure that 'our too narrow views of what can and cannot be thought, said, and done are discarded in face of the record of what has been thought, said, and done'. MacIntyre's book has the appearance of an ordinary historical textbook, but it also deploys its historical information in the service of a bold philosophical thesis concerning the relations between forms of social life and forms of moral argument. The history is thus a contribution to moral philosophy in itself, and as such the book has already given rise to considerable philosophical discussion.[5]

Our present volume does attempt, however, to represent each of the other main foci of interest in the current discussion of social and political issues. The most abstract but in some ways the most fundamental has been the continuing attempt to apply the methods and findings of the prevailing approaches to philosophical analysis. This is particularly evident in three main areas. First, the work of moral philosophers, which was to a considerable extent responsible for demolishing the positivist structures of the Fifties, continues to have an obvious impact on social and political theory. In this collection we publish two essays which particularly exhibit this influence, and might be said to stand on the borders of moral and political philosophy: Professor Pitkin's discussion of obligation (which also makes very illuminating use of historical examples) and Mr Tuck's discussion of authority. Secondly, the immense concentration of recent philosophical effort on the examination of human action and its explanation has had an important methodological as well as substantive impact on theory-construction in the social sciences. In this collection we publish several essays which reflect, and make critical use of, these current discussions of attitudes and beliefs, and motives and intentions, in relation to the explanation of social and political behaviour. Finally, perhaps the most fruitful of these applications, as we already noted in our last introduction, has proved to be in legal philosophy. Here the newest tools from the philosophy of action

---

[5] See for example the essay by Peter Winch on 'Human Nature' in *The Proper Study*: Royal Institute of Philosophy Lectures IV, 1969–1970 (London, 1971), pp. 1–13.

have been used to re-open the discussion of some of the most fundamental concepts, notably those of causation and responsibility. The most significant recent contributions to both these discussions have been made by Professor H. L. A. Hart, whose work (with A. M. Honoré) on *Causation in the Law* appeared just before the publication of our second volume, and whose collection of essays on *Punishment and Resonsibility* has appeared since our last volume was published. In our present volume we publish two essays which might be said to stand on the borders of legal and political philosophy: Professor MacCallum's essay on liberty, and Professor Nozick's on coercion.

A second major focus of interest which we have represented has been the attempt to apply some current techniques of philosophical analysis to reconstruct the methodological foundations of the social sciences. This current preoccupation with methodology is perhaps a reflection of the new directions being mapped in these disciplines. It is attested by the remarkably widespread influence of such works as Kuhn's *Structure of Scientific Revolutions*, and by the very recent appearance of such collections as Emmet and MacIntyre's on theoretical and methodological questions in sociology,[6] and Bryan Wilson's on similar questions chiefly as they arise in social anthropology.[7] One of us has just published a study of Max Weber's philosophy of social science which is principally concerned with these same themes.[8] And in our own collection we publish several essays which reflect these methodological preoccupations. Mr Dunn is concerned with the method and the rationale of studying the history especially of social and political thought in a more sociological spirit, conceiving of it as the history of an activity. Mr Ryan is concerned with the redrawing of the line betwen science and ideology which Kuhn's work has suggested, but in a spirit markedly critical of Kuhn's conclusions.

The third major focus of interest which we have represented is the attempt to apply models derived from economics to the study of social and political behaviour. At one level, the value of this approach has become a subject of energetic debate. Professor Brian Barry, whose book on *Political Argument* we cited in our last introduction for its useful attempt to treat political issues in the current idiom of analytical philosophy, included in that work a very sharp attack on Buchanan and Tulloch and the other so-called economic theorists of democracy. His more

[6] Dorothy Emmet and Alasdair MacIntyre, eds., *Sociological Theory and Philosophical Analysis* (London, 1970).
[7] Bryan R. Wilson, ed., *Rationality* (Blackwell, Oxford, 1970).
[8] W. G. Runciman, *A Critique of Max Weber's Philosophy of Social Science* (Cambridge, 1972).

recent book, however, on *Sociologists, Economists and Democracy* includes a much more appreciative account of the results which might follow from treating political man as a rational and egoistic bargainer. As a contribution to this controversy we publish Professor Cornford's inaugural lecture, in which he comments critically on these invocations of the spirit of Hobbes in current political science. There is another level, however, at which the application of economic models has yielded results of unquestioned value. This has been the very abstract level at which the techniques of game-theory analysis have been applied to elucidate the problem of social choice. In our last volume we published an essay by Professor Arrow on this theme, and in our present volume we publish an essay in the same genre by Professor Coleman, which is in part critical of Professor Arrow's results.

We make no pretence that any central theme unifies each of the topics we have been concerned to represent. On the contrary, our aim has rather been to survey the variety of developments which are now taking place in discussions about philosophy in relation to politics and society. If there is any one undercurrent, however, which might be said to run through many of these developments, it might be characterized as a recognition of the fact that the study of ideologies, and the problem of distinguishing ideological from genuinely philosophical or even 'scientific' social analysis, has become central to social and political science. The irony here needs no emphasizing: our first introduction was written at a time when it seemed that ideology might be ending; our present introduction comes at a time when the phenomenon, and the awareness of it, seem to have become extremely widespread, and when even the most confidently dispassionate observers have come either to fear or to embrace the process of 'politicization'.

1 Is a Science of Comparative Politics Possible?[1]

Alasdair MacIntyre

There was once a man who aspired to be the author of the general theory of holes. When asked 'What kind of hole – holes dug by children in the sand for amusement, holes dug by gardeners to plant lettuce seedlings, tank traps, holes made by roadmakers?' he would reply indignantly that he wished for a *general* theory that would explain all of these. He rejected *ab initio* the – as he saw it – pathetically common-sense view that of the digging of different kinds of holes there are quite different kinds of explanations to be given; why then he would ask do we have the concept of a hole? Lacking the explanations to which he originally aspired, he then fell to discovering statistically significant correlations; he found for example that there is a correlation between the aggregate hole-digging achievement of a society as measured, or at least one day to be measured, by econometric techniques, and its degree of technological development. The United States surpasses both Paraguay and Upper Volta in hole-digging. He also discovered that war accelerates hole-digging; there are more holes in Vietnam than there were. These observations, he would always insist, were neutral and value-free. This man's achievement has passed totally unnoticed except by me. Had he however turned his talents to political science, had he concerned himself not with holes, but with modernization, urbanization or violence, I find it difficult to believe that he might not have achieved high office in the APSA.

I

The ultimate aim of this paper is constructive; the scepticism which infects so much of my argument is a means and not an end. I do not want to show that there *cannot* be a general science of political action, but only to indicate certain obstacles that stand in the way of the founding

[1] From *Against the Self-Images of the Age, Essays on Ideology and Philosophy* by Alasdair MacIntyre, London, Duckworth and New York, Schocken Books, © 1971. Reprinted by permission.

of such a science and to suggest that the present practice of so-called political science is unlikely to overcome these obstacles. In writing more specifically of *comparative* political science I do not wish to suggest that there could be any other sort of political science; this the APSA recognized when it merged what was its section devoted to comparative politics into the general body. It is with the claim to be using legitimate *comparative* methods which could enable us to advance and to test genuine law-like *cross-cultural* generalizations that I shall initially be concerned. I shall not be concerned to question the possibility of genuine and relevant comparison and even of cross-cultural comparison for other purposes: to exhibit the march of the *Weltgeist* through history, for instance, or to draw moral lessons about the respective benefits of barbarism and civilization. These may or may not be reputable activities; I shall not argue for or against them here. I shall be solely interested in the project of a political *science*, of the formulation of cross-cultural, law-like causal generalizations which may in turn be explained by theories, as the generalizations of Boyle's Law and Dalton's Law are explained by the kinetic theory of gases; all that I say about the problem of comparability must be understood in this particular context. Moreover, my scepticism about any alleged parallel between theorizing about politics and theorizing about gases will not initially be founded on the consideration of the character of human action in general. I shall not argue, for example, that human actions cannot have causes, not just or even mainly because I believe that this proposition is false, but because I believe that, even if its falsity is agreed, we still have substantial grounds for scepticism about comparative political science. My method of proceeding in the first part of my argument will be as follows: I shall examine in turn the claim to have formulated law-like generalizations about political attitudes, about political institutions and practices, and about the discharge of political functions. I shall then in the second part of my argument suggest an alternative strategy to that now customarily employed, although the change in strategy will turn out to also involve a change in aim.

II

The study of political culture, of political attitudes, as it has been developed, seems to rest upon the assumption that it is possible to identify political attitudes independently of political institutions and practices. There are at least two reasons for thinking this assumption false. The first derives from Wittgenstein, who pointed out that we identify and define attitudes in terms of the objects toward which they are directed, and not vice versa. Our understanding of the concept of fear depends upon our understanding of the concepts of harm and danger and not vice versa. Our understanding of the concept of an aesthetic attitude depends upon our understanding of the concept of a work of art. It follows that an ability to identify a set of attitudes in one culture as political, and a set of attitudes in some second culture as political, with a view to comparing them must depend upon our having already identified as political in both cultures a set of institutions and practices toward which these attitudes are directed. In other words, the ability to construct comparative generalizations about attitudes depends on our already having solved the problem of how to construct comparative generalizations about institutions and practices. The notion of political culture is secondary to and parasitic upon the notion of political practice.

It follows that a necessary condition of a comparative investigation of political cultures is that the argument about the comparability of political institutions should have a certain outcome; but this is only a necessary end not a sufficient condition. It is also necessary if political attitudes are to be the subject of comparative inquiry that other attitudes shall be susceptible of comparison of a certain kind. I can explain what I mean by this by citing an example from *The Civic Culture* (Chapter IV, pp. 102–5) where Almond and Verba argue that Italians are less committed to and identified with the actions of their government than are Germans or Englishmen, offering as evidence the fact that the Italian respondents, as compared with the English and German respondents to their survey, placed such actions very low on a list of items to which they had been asked to give a rank order in terms of the amount of pride they took in them. At no point do Almond and Verba pause to ask whether the concept of pride is the same in the three different national cultures, that is, to ask whether the different respondents had after all been asked the same question. But in fact the concept of pride (' . . . si sente piu' orgoglioso . . .') in Italy is not the same as that pride in England. The notion of taking pride in Italian culture is still inexorably linked, especially in the South but also in the North, to the notion of honour. What one takes pride in is what touches on one's honour. If asked to list the subjects which touched their honour, many Italians would spontaneously place the chastity of their immediate female relatives high on the list – a connection that it would occur to very few Englishmen to make. These notions of pride and honour partially specify and are partially specified by a notion of the family itself importantly, if imperfectly, embodied in the actualities of Italian family life. Hence we cannot hope to compare an Italian's attitude to his government's acts with an Englishman's in respect of the pride each takes; any comparison would have to begin from the different range of virtues and emotions incorporated in the different social institutions. Once again the project of comparing attitudes independently of institutions and practices encounters difficulties. These particular difficulties suggest that a key question is: what are the units in each culture which are compared to be? To this question I shall of course return; but let me note that the difficulty which I have exemplified in the preceding argument is contingent on Almond and Verba's particular procedures. It does not arise from the project of comparison as such. For the difficulty which arises over any comparison between English and German culture on the one hand, and Italian on the other, from relying on the in fact false assumption that these cultures agree in their concept of pride would not arise in the same way if Italian attitudes were to be compared with Greek, for example. Not that there would not be other and perhaps more subtle pitfalls, but these would not arise merely because concepts of pride and honour are not shared.

We can now pose our problem in the following way: we wish to find identifiable units in different societies and cultures about which we may construct true causal generalizations. Political attitudes, for the two reasons I have given, are implausible candidates; what about political institutions and practices? The first point to be made here is that in turning to the discussion of political institutions and practices we have not left behind the topic of political attitudes. For attitudes to and beliefs about institutions and practices may sometimes be purely external phenomena; that is, the institution or the practice is what it is and does what it does independently of what certain people think and feel about it. But it is an obvious truism that no institution or practice is what it is, or does what it does, independently of what anyone whatsoever thinks or feels about it. For institutions and practices are always partially, even if to differing degrees, constituted by what certain people think and feel about them.

Consider the example of a currency system: a given type of piece of paper or of metal has the value that it has not only because it has been issued by a duly constituted authority, but because it is accepted as having that value by the members of a particular currency-using population. When this condition is not generally satisfied, as in Germany and Austria in 1923, the currency ceases to have value, and thus ceases to be currency. So also with an army: an officer has the authority that he has not only because his commission has been issued by a duly constituted authority, but because he is accepted as having that status by the men serving under him. When this condition is not generally satisfied, as in Russia in 1917, an officer ceases to have authority, and thus ceases to be an officer. Since such beliefs about social institutions are partially constitutive of social institutions, it is impossible to identify the institution except in terms of the beliefs of those who engage in its practices. This fact is ignored in general by those who wish to define political science as the study of political *behaviour*, with a view to thereby providing a public, neutral subject matter for scientific enquiry. But if we identify behaviour except in terms of the intentions and therefore of the beliefs of the agents we shall risk describing what they are doing as what we would be doing if we went through that series of movements or something like it rather than what they are actually doing. Nor do we avoid this difficulty merely by finding *some* description of the behaviour in question which both the agents themselves and the political scientist would accept. For clearly both agents and political scientist might apply the description 'voting behaviour' to what they do, but yet have a quite different understanding of what it is to vote. But now what bearing does all this have upon the project of comparing political institutions and practices?

III

I take it that if the generalizations which political scientists construct are to be part of a science, then among the conditions which must be satisfied is this: that we shall be able to distinguish between genuine lawlike generalizations and mere *de facto* generalizations which hold only of the instances so far observed. I understand by this distinction, as many others have understood by it, the difference between a generalization the assertion of which commits one to the assertion of a set of corresponding counterfactual conditionals and a generalization which does not so commit one. In the natural sciences the ground for treating a generalization as a law is generally not merely that as a matter of fact no plausible counter-examples have yet been produced. It is also normally required that it be supported by a body of theory. But what then of these generalizations which we wish to assert as genuine law-like generalizations before we have any well-established theory? What about the generalizations of Kepler or of Galileo before Newton formulated his laws? What about Boyle's Law or Dalton's Law before the establishment of the kinetic theory? At this point the problems of confirmation theory become real.

The particular finding of confirmation theory that is relevant is that the degree to which a positive instance does genuinely confirm a generalization is in part a matter of the kind of environment in which it is found. For the greater the extent of the radically different environments in which confirmatory instances of a generalization are found, the less likely it is that the generalization is only confirmed in certain contingent environmental circumstances. Now it is a matter of contingent fact that nature is so structured that this condition is normally realizable. For nature could have been otherwise. If black ravens on being taken into laboratories for pigmentation tests, or if black ravens on being observed in the Arctic – in the course of our seeking confirmation or otherwise of the generalization that all ravens are black – promptly turned into philosophers of science or clouds of dust, generalizations about ravenly nigritude could not be as well founded as they are. But in fact the character of social life is such that in some respects it resembles this imaginary nature rather than nature as it – fortunately for natural scientists – is.

Consider for example the alleged generalization that in two-party electoral systems the two parties will tend to move together in their policies and the alleged explanation for this generalization, that this is because neither party can hope to win those voters attracted by the furthest opposed wing of the other party, but only those nearest to it. Hence where, for example, the parties and their wings can be placed on a Left-Right dimension, each party tends to move its policies toward the centre, having no hope of winning votes from the extreme Right or Left. Now consider two different kinds of attempts to provide counter-examples to this generalization. An example of the first would be Greece before the coup d'état of the colonels. This seems to be a straightforward refutation of the generalization, even if we remember that a single counter-example in the natural sciences is never adequate to refute a well-established theory or a generalization with a huge weight of evidence supporting it, such as the generalization that all solids except bismuth, cast-iron, ice, and type-metal expand when heated. For here we have nothing like a well-supported theory or generalization; it is rather as if the seventh raven we were to come across was coloured magenta.

Now consider a quite different kind of attempt to provide a counter-example.

Suppose that someone were to point to the rival parties in Sierra Leone immediately before the army seized power there, and to offer them as a counter-example. We ought at once to remember what Ruth Schachter wrote of African mass parties: 'They and their cultural affiliates were interested in everything from the cradle to the grave – in birth, initiation, religion, marriage, divorce, dancing, song, plays, feuds, debts, land, migration, death, public order – and not only electoral success.' At once the question cannot but be framed: 'Why do we think of these as parties, rather than as, say, churches?' The answer, that they have some of the marks of American political parties, and that they call themselves parties, does nothing to show that in fact the meaning of 'party' is not radically changed when the cultural context is radically changed, or that even if it is not changed the description has not become inapplicable. The intentions, the beliefs, the concepts which inform the practices of African mass parties provide so different a context that there can be no question of transporting the phenomena of party to this context in order to provide a suitably different environment for testing our generalization. Where the environment and where the culture is radically different the phenomenon is viewed so differently by those who participate in it that it is an entirely different phenomenon. In just this respect does society differ from nature. That is to say, the provision of an environment sufficiently different to make the search for counter-examples interesting will normally be the provision of an environment where we cannot hope or expect to find examples of the original phenomenon and therefore cannot hope to find counter-examples.

Note that my thesis is not that to transplant a phenomenon such as party is to subject it to causal influences which transform it. That is doubtless true. But the difficulty of studying political parties in alien social environments to test a generalization constructed about political parties in familiar social environments is not like the difficulty of studying viruses: that their own causal properties and/or those of the environment cause them to mutate too rapidly and too often. If this were the type of difficulty that we encountered in formulating cross-cultural generalizations about politics, then we might well ask if we could not insulate the object of study in its new environment from the disturbing causal influences at work. To ask this would be to mistake my point which is not about casual interference with the phenomenon of party, but with the absence of the same concept of party, or perhaps of any concept of party, as we understand it, in the alien culture.

Let me now consider a possible objection to this thesis which would base itself upon my choice of examples. A quite different choice of examples might provide us with more plausible candidates for cross-cultural generalization. Consider the alleged (and quite possibly false) generalization that in the government of cities, if a single non-transferable vote for single members is the method of election, then there will be over a certain time span a tendency for a two-party system to flourish. This seems to hold in the United States. But it might hold in other alien environments, even environments of an exotic kind, where we could identify the system as two-party, even if unclear in what sense the parties were parties. But this is surely therefore an example of at least a possible cross-cultural comparison which provides us with a law-like generalization and is therefore lethal to my entire thesis. Let me at once concede that I take this generalization to be law-like in that it does indeed entail counter-factual conditionals, and let me further concede that the counter-factuals in question might be true. But I do not concede that it injures my thesis. Why not?

The reason for not conceding that this example, if true, would injure my thesis is intimately connected with the fact that I should not be extremely surprised if the generalization in question did turn out to be true of cities outside North America as well as in North America. For what could make the generalization true, if true, is that voters prefer in general not to waste their votes in voting on matters that concern the administration of their daily lives; and it requires only a minimal and a very untheoretical understanding of the electoral system produced by such a voting procedure to understand that in the majority of cases votes for a third party will be wasted. The considerations from which we can deduce *this* particular generalization are thus concerned with human rationality in general; they do not have any specific connection with politics and they do not belong to political science, but to our general understanding of rationality. This will be true of all generalizations which concern the formal structures of human argument, even if they appear in political clothing, furnishing us with explanations of particular political choices and actions. So it must be, for example, with all applications of the theory of games to politics.

My thesis about the legitimacy or otherwise of the project of accumulating a stock of cross-cultural generalizations about political behaviour to furnish the empirical foundation for a political science, as I have developed it so far, can now be stated disjunctively: *either* such generalizations about institutions will necessarily lack the kind of confirmation they require *or* they will be consequences of true generalizations about human rationality and not part of a specifically political science.

To complete this part of my argument I must now make three further observations. The first is that my statement of the difficulties in constructing true and warranted cross-cultural generalizations about political institutions is obviously akin to the arguments which some anthropologists – notably Edmund Leach and Walter Goldschmidt – have developed about cross-cultural generalizations in their discipline. But Goldschmidt has then argued that it is not institutions, but functions, or rather institutions only as serving certain functions, which we ought to aspire to compare; and this contention has already been advanced by some political scientists. We are, that is to say, to begin by identifying the same function in different societies and then to inquire how quite different institutions have this same effect; for I take it that to say that X performs, serves, or discharges a given function always entails that X is the cause of a particular effect, even if this does not exhaust the meaning of the statement in which function was ascribed. It is certainly not a final objection to this project that most political scientists who have tried to specify the functions in question have produced nothing but statements about institutions and their effects in which the word 'function' may appear, but could be replaced not only without loss, but with gain. 'Wherever the political party has emerged, it appears to perform some common functions in a wide variety of political systems . . . the organization called the party is expected to organize public opinion and to communicate demands to the centre of governmental power and decision . . . the party must articulate to its followers the concept and meaning of the broader community . . . the party is likely to be involved in political recruitment . . . These similarities of function . . . suggest that the political party when the activities of a political system reach a certain degree of complexity, or whenever the notion of political power comes to include the idea that the mass public must participate or be controlled.'[2] In a passage like this, the notion of function can be replaced entirely by either the notion of effect or the notion of purpose. When we so replace it, we notice also that the transition from previous to tentative conclusion requires no reliance on any factual generalizations anyway; it is merely a matter of drawing out the consequences of definition. But even if in the writing of political scientists as sophisticated as LaPalombara and Weiner the function of the use of 'function' is unclear, it does not follow that this has to be so. But the condition of its not being so is that we should have some criteria for identifying the functions served by political institutions which is other than, and independent of, the aims and purposes of political agents and the effects of political institutions.

---

[2] J. LaPalombara and M. Weiner, eds., *Political Parties and Political Development* (Princeton, N.J.: Princeton University Press).

The provision of such a criteria would require the identification of a system, using the word 'system' precisely, so that concepts of feedback and equilibrium are applicable on the basis of quantitative data which will provide values for variables in differential equations. I scarcely need stress the remoteness of this goal from the present state of all political science; if we match the requirements that have to be satisfied to identify such a system – which would involve, for example, being able to distinguish between change that is part of the movement of items through the system, change that is itself part of the structuring of the system, and change that is the system decaying by providing ways of measuring rates of change for all three – then a work like David Easton's *A Systems Analysis of Political Life* looks like a mad, millenarian dream. I therefore take it that any attempt to answer my argument by suggesting that cross-cultural generalizations about institutions may be provided by means of a prior account in terms of functions is bound to fail.

My second observation is that my argument does not imply any undervaluation of the importance of the work done by political scientists in establishing both the facts about particular institutions and the very limited generalizations they do establish. That the conditions under which these generalizations hold necessarily remain unclear to us for the kind of reason that I have given does not mean that we do not need the best that we can get in this case, which is what they give us; only this kind of accumulation of data in no way leads toward the construction of a science. I shall later suggest an alternative context in which these empirical labours could perhaps be viewed more constructively. For the moment I note that it is Machiavelli who ought to be regarded as the patron saint of political studies and not Hobbes, and for this reason: Hobbes believed – as presumably Almond and LaPalombara and Easton (although Easton, in ways that I do not entirely understand, tries to distinguish his enterprise from that of Hobbes (believe – that the fortuitous, the surprising, the unpredicted, arise in politics only because our knowledge of political motions is less adequate than our knowledge of planetary motions. Given time, labour, and foundation grants – the contemporary version of royal patronage – an unpredicted revolution – but for the sheer complexity of human affairs – ought to be as disgraceful to political scientists as an unpredicted eclipse to astronomers. But Machiavelli realized that in political life *fortuna*, the bitch goddess of unpredictability, has never been dethroned. To any stock of maxims derived from empirically founded generalizations the student of politics must always add one more: 'And do not be surprised if in the event things turn out otherwise.' The need to include this maxim follows from my argument, just as it follows from Machiavelli's.

My third observation is that in the history of political theory we have more than once been here before, and notably in the dispute between James Mill and Macaulay. James Mill argued, although in the interests of a quite different conclusion, even more that we cannot find reliable empirical generalizations about political behaviour: 'Absolute monarchy under Neros and Caligulas . . . is the scourge of human nature. On the other side, the public of Denmark . . . under their absolute monarch are as well governed as any people in Europe . . . the surface of history affords, therefore, no certain principles of decision.' Mill then proceeded to argue from this that we ought to turn instead to the type of psychology favoured by the utilitarians for our explanations, that there is no specifically political science. Against him Macaulay argued that the empirical facts about government *do* yield genuine law-like generalizations, not least generalizations of a kind which enable us to predict future actions with great confidence. And it is clear that this practical use of law-like generalizations provides Macaulay with a crucial motive. The claim to technical expertise on the part of the political scientist is closely bound up with the defence of the possibility of formulating law-like generalizations. If the latter fails, the former is gravely impaired. When in our time on the basis of *his* generalizations Lipset predicts totalitarian horrors as the outcome of widespread political participation, he turns out to be the true heir of Macaulay who, on the basis of *his* generalizations, predicted cultural ruin if 'the great number' were allowed to participate in government; 'they will commit waste of every sort in the estate of mankind, and transmit it to posterity impoverished and desolate,' so that 'in two or three hundred years, a few lean and half naked fishermen may divide with owls and foxes the ruins of the greatest of European cities . . .' In both Macaulay and Lipset the claims of political science are closely linked to a claim about the political status of the political scientist, to a claim about the possession of political expertise, which entitles the political scientist to advise government. This claim too demands inquiry; but a prerequisite for such inquiry is a further development of my central argument.

IV

My doubts about identifying institutions in different cultures as 'the same' and therefore as interestingly different are of course compatible with a recognition of the massive fact that the same actions are regularly performed in quite different cultures. One class of such actions are those that derive from implicit imitation. It is of course not necessarily or always the case that if one person imitates another he does what the other does. Indeed it is sometimes the condition of successful imitation that he who imitates shall not do what the other does precisely in order to seem to do what the other does. But when the intention to perform the same action as another *is* present, we always have an intelligible question as to why, if the corresponding action or its consequences or both are not the same as those produced by the agent imitated, they are not so. Of course it may be that even a particular intention to perform certain actions cannot be intelligibly embodied in some cultures; *Don Quixote* is the classical example. But we do have clear cases where the same intention is embodied in two different cultures, such intentions as to apply Roman Law or the Code Napoléon, or to bring about some particular course of economic development. What we shall achieve if we study the projects springing from such intentions are two or more histories of these projects, and it is only after writing these histories that we shall be able to compare the different outcomes of the same intention. We shall not, that is to say, begin by collecting data in the hope of formulating causal generalizations; we shall begin by looking at cases where a will to achieve the same end was realized with greater or lesser success in different cultural contexts.

There is of course a notable formula which seems to prescribe this approach: 'Men make their own history, but they do not make it just as they please. They do not make it under circumstances chosen by themselves, but under circumstances directly encountered, given and transmitted from the past.' But when Marx wrote these words he did not discriminate what was implied by this approach from a search for causal generalizations, and he does not do so at least in part because he treats what he calls the circumstances of action only as a causally effective and limiting environment and not in addition, or rather primarily, as a context of meaning-conferring symbols and rules. So Marx speaks of 'the burden of history' in the very next sentence and Engels speaks of history as a 'series of parallelograms of forces', and it is this model of Engels which creates for Plekhanov the problem of the role of the individual in history (since an individual can be no more than a point at which some force operates). But the question with which Marx began in the *Eighteenth Brumaire* does not require an answer in terms of causal generalizations and parallelograms of forces. For what Marx asks then is why, when someone aspires to perform the same actions as a predecessor in some earlier cultural period – as the English Puritans aspired to be Old Testament Israelites or the French Revolutionary Roman republicans or Louis Napoléon to do the deeds of Napoleon I – the actions should be so different. A full answer to Marx's question would provide a genuine starting point for historical comparison, but such an answer could only be provided by first writing a history of each of these episodes.

I therefore take it that if we wish to have a science of comparative politics, one first step is the writing of a series of comparative histories; that comparative history is a more fundamental discipline than comparative politics. But then the crucial question arises: what can we legitimately expect the study of comparative history to yield? And one of the best ways of answering this question is to ask what the study of comparative history has in fact yielded. Consider for example Isaac Deutscher's thesis about revolutions. Deutscher asserted that in the English, French, and Russian revolutions the same 'broad scheme of revolutionary development' could be discerned. This scheme involves three stages: a first stage in which 'popular energy, impatience, anger and hope' burst out, and 'the party that gives the fullest expression to the popular mood outdoes its rivals, gains the confidence of the masses and rises to power'; a second stage in which during the war on behalf of the revolution the leaders of the revolutionary party and the people are so well in accord that the leaders 'are willing and even eager to submit their policies to open debate and to accept the popular verdict'; and a third stage in which weariness and ruthlessness divide party and people, so that the revolutionary party cannot listen to, but must indeed suppress the voice of the people, thus in consequence splitting itself between the holders of revolutionary power and the caretakers of the purity of revolutionary doctrine. This pattern holds of 'any party of the revolution, whether it be called Independent, Jacobin or Bolshevik'.

That there are such patterns revealed by the rare studies of comparative history that we already possess and that there will be more is clear. But how are we to understand them? When we assert the recurrence of such a pattern, what are we asserting? Deutscher himself, following Engels and Plekhanov, understood this pattern of revolutionary behaviour deterministically. Hence followed his very different assessment of Trotsky's relation to Stalin from Trotsky's own non-deterministic assessment of that relationship. Deutscher treats each stage, as he specified it, as satisfying both a necessary and a sufficient condition for the occurrence of the next stage, as he specified it; hence he takes it that Trotsky, the caretaker of revolutionary purity, could not but have failed to hold power, since maintaining the revolutionary doctrine and holding power are causally incompatible.

The evaluation of Deutscher's specific contentions about revolution is not relevant to my present argument; but the contention Deutscher almost takes for granted, namely that the discernment of recurring patterns in history has as its end-product the formulation of law-like generalizations, is precisely what I want to question. For when I suggested that the study of comparative politics would certainly benefit from, and perhaps require, a prior writing of comparative history, I did not intend to imply that what comparative history will provide us with is merely a stock of more adequate materials for the construction of these cross-cultural, law-like generalizations which the present methods of orthodox political science aspire to but in fact fail to provide; that the comparative history is not so much an alternative, as merely a necessary prelude to proceeding as before. What I want to suggest is that it is characteristic of the causal knowledge which history does provide us with that the antecedent conditions in terms of which we explain historical outcomes are sometimes necessary conditions for the occurrence of some specific outcome, but are never sufficient. If this is so, then the patterns which we discern in comparative history will always be *de facto* guides yielding Machiavellian maxims, rather than Hobbesian laws. But is it so? Is comparative political science, even when based on comparative history, precluded from formulating law-like generalizations?

To cast light on this, compare the situation of the political scientist with that of the political agent. The political agent confronts a situation in which he wishes to produce certain outcomes. He wishes, for example, to maintain two-party democracy in a new state, or he wishes to overthrow that state by revolutionary action. The situation he confronts consists of other political agents: party politicians, soldiers, trade union leaders, trade union rank and file, and so on. Some of each of these groups are keen readers of such works as *Political Man*, *Voting*, *Permanent Revolution*, and so on. Each of these derives certain inductively grounded maxims from these works; in an earlier age the maxims had different sources – Livy, Plutarch, what Napoleon did, or political folk wisdom – but the situation was essentially the same. The difficulty in applying the maxims is that the factors in the situation confronting the agent include the beliefs of every other agent about what each agent other than himself will do in applying the maxims, including the beliefs of every agent about what every other agent believes about his beliefs. 'I know you know I know you know I know' is a crucial piece of poetic wisdom for political as well as for sexual behaviour. The perception of any pattern or regularity in the behaviour of the other actors, or in the behaviour characteristic of this particular type of situation, is what particularly invites deviation from the pattern. 'They all knew what Napoleon would have done,' said Grant of the Union generals. 'The trouble was that the rebel generals didn't know about Napoleon.'

The key part that beliefs play in defining political situations, and the fact that beliefs are always liable to be altered by reflection upon the situation, including reflection about the beliefs of other agents, has a crucial consequence: that we cannot ever identify a determinate set of factors which constitute the initial conditions for the production of some outcome in conformity with a law-like regularity. To claim that we could identify such regularities and such sets of factors would be to claim that we can understand what occurs in politics independently of a knowledge of the beliefs of the agents, for it would be to claim that the beliefs do not play a causal role in political outcomes.

It makes no difference at this point if the alleged law-like regularity is framed in probabilistic terms: when the alleged probability of an outcome is .7, the prediction is as vulnerable to reflection by agents as when the alleged probability of an outcome is 1. The conclusion that political agents are bound to be prone to error in their predictions of what other agents will do, and hence of political outcomes, has one important merit other than that of following validly from my premises: it would appear to be true. Nor is its truth incompatible with the fact that some political agents produce more correct predictions than others. It would perhaps be cynical to explain this latter fact by pointing out that given an entirely random relationship between prediction and outcome in a sufficiently large population of predictors, predictions, and outcomes, certain predictors would consistently predict correctly, just as certain predictors would consistently predict incorrectly. But without resorting to either cynicism or the theorems of statistics one can point out that success at prediction in practical affairs, including political affairs, can never be embodied into a method which can be taught, precisely because the maxims relied upon are open-textured and open-ended, and the sense of when which maxim is relevant cannot itself be unpacked into a set of maxims.

It may be asked: when I conclude that political agents cannot find law-like generalizations to aid them in their actions (other of course than those crucial and rock-like law-like generalizations of the physical senses which are available to us all, that such a bullet accelerates in the way that all moving bodies do, and that when a man's skull is crushed by an ice pick he dies), what is the force of 'cannot'? Do I mean only that we have at the moment no technique for identifying determinate sets of antecedent conditions of the relevant kind, but that such a technique might well be discovered? Or do I mean that there is some confusion in the nature of such a technique? Am I saying what the limits of inquiry are *as of now*, or what the limits *as such* are?

I am strongly inclined to say that at the moment we have no grounds for answering this question as it stands in either way. We lack even the most minimal theoretical background against which to raise such questions. To say this is not to ignore the empirical work done by both psychologists and sociologists on such topics as prejudice, cognitive dissonance, and the relation of roles to beliefs; it is to say that the results of empirical studies in this field (which are not always obviously consistent with each other) are exceptionally difficult to interpret and to assess, in part just for the type of reason that I have given.

What I have been arguing in this latter part of my essay is that the political agent cannot rely on law-governed regularities in his activities. But just those premises, which entail that conclusion, entail that the political scientist is in no better position in this respect than the political agent. The political scientist may claim to know more (quantitatively, as it were) than many political agents; but his knowledge is not of a different kind, and there seems no reason to believe that the chances that he will be able to apply the inductively grounded maxims which he derives from his studies in the course of political action successfully are any higher than they are for any other political agent.

If this is so, then the case for Machiavelli against Hobbes rests not merely on the impossibility of testing these law-like generalizations to which a true science of comparative politics would have to aspire; it derives also from the nature of the subject matter of political science. For the most that any study of comparative politics based upon comparative history can hope to supply us with in the foreseeable future is *de facto* generalizations about what has been an obstacle to or has facilitated certain types of course of action. There is available for the formulation of this type of generalization no vocabulary for political scientists which is essentially more sophisticated than the vocabulary of political agents themselves. And the advice given by political scientists turns out to be simply the advice given by a certain genre of political agent, agents as partial, as socially conditioned, as creative and as wayward as any others.

To this the defender of orthodox political science might well feel bound to reply as follows. *Qua* scientist, he may claim, he has a vocabulary that is not available to political agents; and he has this neutrality precisely because he restricts himself to the facts and to theorizing about them in an uncommitted way. Your redefinition of the tasks of political studies would, he might complain, destroy this neutrality. For the model of explanation implicit in your view of the relation of comparative history to comparative politics is as follows: Men in two different cultures seek to implement the same intention in action. Either their actions or the consequences of their actions may differ. If they do, by examining what was present in the one case and absent in the other, you make inferences as to what the obstacles or diversions were in either or both cases. You then explain in terms of the presence or absence of these obstacles or diversions the success or failure of the respective projects. But this is in fact a model of explanation familiar in our everyday understanding of action; and when we apply it in everyday life we cite as explanations for the success or failure of men's projects, not merely the external obstacles which they faced or the lack of such obstacles, but such factors as their reasonableness or unreasonableness, their courage or their weakness, their willingness or reluctance to commit injustice and so on. That is to say, your model of explanation is that used by ordinary men in their political and other actions to assess themselves and each other and it is of the essence of this mode of explanation that we may cite in explanation evaluations both of intelligence and of moral character. The strength of orthodox comparative political science, this objector will go on, is that it has broken decisively with the evaluative commitments of the world of action. Just because it aspires to study these scientifically, it cannot share them. It must instead be objective in a sense that requires that it be neutral and value-free.

I accept from this objection the characterization of my own standpoint. It would certainly be an open empirical question whether it ever was in fact true that this or that project failed because of the unreasonableness or the injustice of the agents; but a priori nothing could rule out the possibility of these being true and relevant explanations. Political science would become in a true sense a moral science. But I do not take this to be in any way an objection. For what is the alternative, as it is exemplified in comparative political science as it is now usually practiced?

The type of comparative political science of which I have been highly critical is indeed generally and deeply committed to the view that its inquiries and explanations are indeed value-free. This results in an attempt to allow evaluative expressions into political life only in intentional contexts, in oratio obliqua, or in quotation marks. Hence, as John Schaar has pointed out,[3] such notions as those of legitimacy are in fact defined in terms of belief. Lipset says that 'Legitimacy involves the capacity of the system to engender and maintain the belief that the existing political institutions are the most appropriate ones for the society' (*Political Man*, p. 77) and Robert Bierstedt writes that 'In the tradition of Weber, legitimacy has been defined as the degree to which institutions are valued for themselves and considered right and proper.'[4]

---

[3] 'Legitimacy in the Modern State,' in Green and Levison, eds., *Power and Community*.

[4] 'Legitimacy,' in *Dictionary of Social Sciences*, p. 386.

These definitions are clearly mistaken in any case; not only would there be no contradiction in holding that a government was entirely legitimate, but that its institutions were morally ill-suited to a particular society, but in a society where this latter was widely believed, it would not follow either that the government was, or that it was considered, illegitimate. But it is not mere definitional ineptitude that I am concerned with here. Suppose that we define, as Lipset and the Weberian tradition according to Bierstedt do, evaluation in terms so that where 'X' is an evaluative expression it is always defined so that 'A is X' is equivalent in meaning to an expression of the form 'A is believed by some class of persons to be Y' where 'Y' is another evaluative expression. Suppose further that, as both Lipset and some Weberians do, we try to explain legitimacy in terms of stability or vice versa. What is clear is that the original definitional move has preempted on a crucial causal and explanatory question: is it only beliefs about what is legitimate, what is appropriate, what is right which can be causally effective, or can the legitimacy of an institution, the appropriateness of an institution or an action, or the rightness or the justice of an action, themselves be causally effective? The definitional move of Lipset and Bierstedt removes a priori the possibility of a certain class of characteristics of intention and urgency being relevant in giving causal explanations.

Lipset and Bierstedt are thereby taking sides in an ancient philosophical argument: is it important for the ruler to be just, or is it only important for him to be thought to be just? What Lipset and Bierstedt do in defining legitimacy is not unlike what Thrasymachus did in defining justice and what Glaucon and Adeimantus did in developing Thrasymachus' case. We may now recall that Thrasymachus too claimed to be merely reporting how the world went, to be a neutral and value-free observer. My thesis on this last point can indeed be summarized as follows: to insist that political science be value-free is to insist that we never use in our explanations such clauses as 'because it was unjust' or 'because it was illegitimate' when we explain the collapse of a policy or a regime; and to insist on this is to agree with Thrasymachus – even if for different reasons – that justice plays no part and can play no part in political life. The insistence on being value-free thus involves the most extreme of value commitments. Hence I take it to be no objection to the methodology which I propose that it is clearly not able to purge its explanations of evaluative elements.

Note that I have offered no arguments at this point for believing that Thrasymachus is, as a matter of fact, mistaken; what I have done is to suggest that those who maintain the stance of orthodox comparative political science are committed by their starting point and not by the empirical findings to the view that he was right. And this raises one more kind of doubt about their view. For the response to my parable about the man who aspired to be the author of the general theory of holes might well have been that such a man is intellectually misguided, but practically harmless. When, however, one has to recognize that this kind of intellectual mistake is allied to a Thrasymachean attitude to morality, it becomes clear that if this type of enterprise is to be ranked as a joke, it must be classed with the more dangerous kinds of practical jokes.

2 The Political Theory of Scarcity[1]

James Cornford

For thirty odd years Political Science has suffered what one might call a moral paralysis. It is perhaps more sensitive to the public mood than most disciplines and equally liable to the curse of professionalism. At any rate, whether from diffidence, conviction, fear, complacency, weariness, or whatever, political scientists have been reluctant to get involved with the perennial questions of political philosophy: the questions of justice, obligation, liberty, equality and so forth – the questions of the good society. Political theory at this level, which is at once an explanation of how things work and a guide to right conduct, may be a hopelessly ambitious enterprise. It is, however, one we are bound to attempt. And things are not so bad now as they were in the dark days of the fifties. In the wake of philosophers, economists, strategists and sociologists, political scientists are gradually being drawn back into ethical debate.

In the *American Political Science Review*, a journal much devoted to professional interior monologue and displays of technical virtuosity, an article recently appeared entitled 'If, as Verba says, the state functions as a religion, what are we to do then to save our souls?'.[2] The impetus for this return to prescriptive questions is clear enough. Public events, especially in the United States, have posed in immediate personal terms the classic problems of political obligation, and a new generation has inconveniently chosen to take at face value the standards proclaimed but not respected by its elders. And, of course, among an articulate minority those standards are themselves called in question and the values of liberal democracy rejected. In Britain, we have had only faint premonitions of these disturbances, but enough perhaps to justify a brief examination of some of the defences of liberal democracy currently on offer, the assumptions on which they rest, the possible objections that may be made to them, and what these suggest about the nature of a satisfactory political theory.

[1] This is a version of an inaugural lecture delivered before the University of Edinburgh in April 1969. I have removed purely local references but the smell of the pulpit is ineradicable. I am particularly grateful to Dr. J. R. S. Wilson and Dr. H. M. Drucker for their comments on the original.
[2] Lewis Lipsitz in *The American Political Science Review*, Vol. LXII, June 1968, No. 2, pp. 527–535.

The arguments I propose to discuss are contemporary, but not new. They represent current versions of arguments about popular, representative, or republican government that have been going the rounds in one form or another for the past three hundred years. They have thus the double advantage of being at once fashionable and familiar. Beyond dropping the occasional household name, I shall not provide pedigrees for these arguments but talk about recent contributions and present them in bare outline or, as it may appear, in caricature, under two general headings: first, distributive theories of democracy concerned with the problems of constitution-making and the allocation of goods: here we have a revival both of the ideas of social contract and of utilitarianism; and, second, participatory theories of democracy concerned with the political activities of citizens as a condition of freedom and with the control of the institutions of government.

As far as distributive theory is concerned, I shall concentrate directly on two fairly recent contributions – the articles by the philosopher John Rawls on the concept of justice and its relation to constitutional government,[3] and the somewhat different approach to the logical foundations of constitutional democracy taken by two economists, James Buchanan and Gordon Tulloch, in their book *The Calculus of Consent*.[4] I have chosen them to illustrate the distributive or individualist approach, because they are among the boldest, most ambitious, ingenious and influential statements of an increasingly influential intellectual genre. The language of participatory theory partakes more of rhetoric than of logic, and here, beyond acknowledging the parental status of John Stuart Mill, I shall not attempt to unravel specific arguments but state the general position taken by its advocates and examine its implications and consequences.

Now all democratic theory appears to have in common two fundamental assumptions. The first is the notion of the value of social peace: that it is *a priori* desirable to achieve a means of resolving conflicts of interest or opinion without the use of force. This assumption is not peculiar to democrats. The second assumption is the assumption of political equality, whether based on a doctrine of natural rights or some form of Kantian imperative. This is where the difficulties begin, for

---

[3] In particular 'Justice as Fairness' in *Philosophy, Politics and Society*, 2nd series, Oxford, 1962; 'Distributive Justice' in *Philosophy, Politics and Society*, 3rd series, Oxford, 1967; and 'Constitutional Liberty and the concept of Justice' in *Nomos* VI, 1963, ed. C. J. Friedrich and J. W. Chapman.

[4] J. M. Buchanan and G. Tullock, *The Calculus of Consent* (Ann Arbor Paperbacks, University of Michigan Press, 1965).

any assumption of inherent rights immediately raises the question whether there are indefeasible rights, and hence whether there are bounds or limits upon governmental or collective action. Political equality involves, therefore, not merely equal rights in the process of making collective decisions, but also the proper limits of those decisions as regards the individual. Democratic theorists have not been agreed on three questions to which these connected problems, equality in decision-making and the scope of decision-making, give rise: first, whether there must be agreement on anything else besides political equality; second, what is to be the character of the institutions, procedures or rules for giving effect to political equality – what are the guarantees of political equality; third, how are the rights of the individual to be protected– what is to be the scope of collective decision-making?

We must, I think, rule out from the start any simple majoritarian view of democracy. In the first place it cannot deal with the problem of individual rights. In the second, the problems of arriving at any procedures which guarantee the rule of the majority appear insuperable, if, as I think must be the case, democratic principle demands equality of influence and not simply formal procedural equality: by formal procedural equality I mean simply the right to vote in free elections; by equality of influence I mean an equal chance for each individual that the results of decisions will be the ones he favours.

Studies of voting and committee procedure have demonstrated the logical difficulties. Of course, the conditions laid down in these studies of voting and of the welfare function are somewhat restrictive and one might argue that though majoritarian procedures may not be fool or mathematician proof, they give a near enough approximation to the requirements of democratic principle. This is in part an empirical argument with which I shall try to deal later on. But I think if one has read, for instance, Robin Farquharson's elegant demonstration that two different but widely used methods of taking an amendment in committee would under quite plausible circumstances produce contrary results, one would accept that majoritarian procedures in themselves provide an insecure foundation for democracy.[5]

Must we therefore abandon any attempt to define democracy in terms of some basic decision-making rules or constitution? What I have called the distributive theorists of democracy would argue not. Rawls, and Buchanan and Tullock, revive or rework the ideas of the social contract and of the market society to demonstrate that given the assumption of a

[5] 'The Application of Game Theory to Committee Procedure' in *Operational Research and the Social Sciences*, ed. R. J. Lawrence (Tavistock Publications, London, 1966).

state of nature in which men are political equals (an equivalent assumption to that of inherent rights) a constitutional rule and the proper scope of its application can be deduced. This process of deduction requires only one further assumption, albeit a large one, that in the state of nature men are not only free, but also rational and self-interested. They exhibit the familiar character of *homo economicus*. Rawls leaves it at that. Buchanan and Tullock attempt some justification of the assumption by arguing that they have not in fact assumed any particular psychological character: they leave open the question of what a person's self-interest may be: in their system it is a matter of personal definition. But they do suppose that whatever this self-interest may be it will be pursued or maximized on the basis of individual calculation in a world of other individuals likewise concerned, with all operating on the basis of uncertainty of outcomes and of individual and, therefore, anonymous behaviour. This is the analogy with the perfect market, which at the moment the constitution is formed, denies any knowledge of how others are likely to behave and, therefore, denies the ability to act deceptively or strategically in such a way as to manipulate the rules contrary to their ostensible purpose.

For Rawls this condition of ignorance, like the social contract itself, is a necessary fiction which allows him to put the essential question about the justice of any inequality: would the persons subject to this inequality have assented to its existence if they had not known beforehand whether they were to suffer or benefit from it? Or to put it another way: what political arrangements would a rational man assent to if he knew that his own position would be assigned to him by an enemy? Rawls is primarily concerned with justice but the principles which he argues would be accepted by free rational self-interested men in setting up a political society for their mutual benefit turn out to be close to the essential ideas of liberal democracy: namely, first, each person has an equal right to the most extensive liberty compatible with a like liberty for all, and, second, inequalities are arbitrary (or unjust) unless it is reasonable to expect that they will work out for everyone's advantage, and unless the positions and offices to which they attach, or from which they may be gained, are open to all. 'These principles', says Rawls, 'express justice as a complex of three ideas: liberty, equality and reward for services contributing to the common good'.[6]

These principles appear both attractive and compelling, and Rawls is able to argue from them for the protection of the fundamental rights of liberty of person and conscience under any constitution. 'For a man to

---

[6] 'Justice as Fairness', pp. 133-4.

face his children he must insist on the two principles of justice.'[7] To this extent at least he answers the question about the scope of collective decision-making. The difficulties arise when it comes to the application of the principles to the problems of government itself. First, these principles do not specify how the necessary or justified positions of inequality should be allocated among individuals; and, second, they do not indicate how one is to judge between generally beneficial but differentially unequal arrangements. To meet these difficulties Rawls advances two further propositions: that the selection for especially favoured positions should be on the basis of merit; and that in choosing between two arrangements which involve different degrees of inequality, the interests of the less well off should always prevail. The second principle then takes on a redistributive element since no existing inequality can be justified if any redistribution would make those less well off better off. Again this is an attractive proposition, but it is hard to see why free rational self-interested men should assent to it. Whilst Rawls's original argument, that such men would reject a society in which they might be slaves, has much force, it cannot be extended to argue that rational men would seek to minimize other degrees of inequality simply because they themselves might not enjoy the best positions. Their calculations would presumably turn on the chances of being successful and the degree of deprivation entailed by failure. But this difficulty is less serious than the restricted way in which Rawls deals with the question of public office. It is all right to say that inequalities can be justified if they work to everyone's advantage, but it is clear that what Rawls means by 'inequalities' has little to do with any notion of participation in decision-making. 'By "inequalities" it is best to understand not any differences in the institutional structure between offices and positions and the rules defining their rights, duties, powers and privileges, but differences in the benefits and burdens attached to them either directly or indirectly, such as prestige, wealth and liability for taxation and compulsory service.'[8] That is to say that Rawls looks upon the inequalities arising from the holding of public office in terms of the perquisites, the individual rewards of a material kind, attaching to them, and not upon the activity of holding office as in itself valuable and therefore a source of inequality. One can only in justice object to some holding more important positions than others on the grounds of the perquisites deriving from those positions, not because of the enjoyment of office itself nor the unequal influence those positions give on decisions of policy within the minimum framework which justice, according to

[7] 'Constitutional liberty and the Concept of Justice', p. 114.
[8] *Ibid.*, p. 101.

Rawls, requires. That is to say that Rawls does not address himself to the question of political equality at all. The original compact may require a certain liberty as long as that liberty is regarded as a limited freedom from interference, but in return for the benefits of inequalities it may rationally entail the absence of citizenship in the sense of influence over future policy.

While Rawls thus addresses himself to the possibility of rational men preferring a caste society and effectively dismisses it, he does not confront the serious problem that even in his open society, where political positions are earned by merit, the inequalities of position accepted for the general advantage include not simply personal reward but the constitutional power to decide for the future the definition of the general advantage itself, and hence not only the future distribution of inequalities but the extent of liberty. We may perhaps conclude that even if one accepts that free rational self-interested men would unanimously agree to the two principles of justice, these principles in themselves provide little guidance to the forms of government necessary to maintain in the future that liberty and equality without which no free man would give his assent to be governed.[9]

This problem, of trying to give specific content or consequences to the terms of the contract, is avoided by Buchanan and Tullock, since they make a clear distinction between the rules governing the original social contract, or constitution, and the subordinate rules which operate once the constitution is established. They agree with Rawls on the necessity of unanimity in the social contract, that is, they argue that individuals will agree on a constitution on the basis of uncertainty about the position they will occupy when the constitution has been established. And they argue, apparently as a matter of fact, that this uncertainty seems likely to be present at any constitutional stage of discussion. This may be regarded as a convenient self-delusion. However, having concluded that unanimity is the only satisfactory rule for establishing the constitution, Buchanan and Tullock proceed to consider the grounds for departing from unanimity in subordinate rules and they do this in terms of the costs attached to various kinds of action. Most people have argued that representative institutions are necessary because direct democracy outside the face-to-face community is simply impossible. Buchanan and Tullock argue a little differently: for them, majority rules and representative institutions will be adopted not because anything else is impossible, but because it would be prohibitively expensive. I suppose that in this

[9] For a thorough critique, see Michael Lessnoff, 'John Rawls' Theory of Justice', *Political Studies*, Vol. 19, March 1971, No. 1, pp. 63–80.

electronic age one can just about imagine every citizen sitting at home in front of his two-way T.V. set and voting machine taking part in every decision. But clearly this would be time-consuming, especially when every proposal could be vetoed by a single individual. In order to get on with other things, rational men would settle for majority decisions and representative institutions in order to limit their personal intervention to once a week, once a month, once a year, once every five years. The essential point is that most forms of action impose costs on the individuals who take them and, indeed, collective action, or the constitution would only be adopted in the first place because of the high costs individuals imposed on themselves and others by individual action: collective action is adopted only to avoid the diseconomies of individual action. But collective decision-making also imposes costs and the application of various subordinate rules depends on the extent of these costs as compared with the costs of individual action. With this cost/benefit approach, Buchanan and Tullock make short work of any majoritarian principles. If there were no decision-making costs, then the unanimity rule would always be the rational one for the individual to support. Since there are costs, he may on grounds of utility accept some form of majority rule, but this acceptance does not depend on the rightness of the majority principle; it depends on the fact that some dilution of the unanimity principle may be agreed unanimously in specific collective choices if individuals perceive that the expected costs of achieving unanimity in these choices exceed the damage to them of being in a minority. This formulation has two advantages. First, such decisions do not have to work for the benefit of all: decisions which do not work for the benefit of all are admissible because of the factor of decision costs. And, second, these calculations do not involve any comparison between the preferences of individuals (the Serbonian bog of Welfare Economics) but involve only an individual estimate in terms of personal priorities of the costs of individual action, the costs imposed by collective action, and the costs of decision-making itself.

Buchanan and Tullock, therefore, draw a clear distinction between what is optimal in choosing a single rule or constitution and what is optimal in considering the allocation of resources at a particular time. At the constitution-making stage the individual is in a state of uncertainty as to his preferences and position when the rule comes to be applied; where particular choices are involved, the individual's interest and preference in relation to others is clearly defined. In the first instance the individual must regard himself as representative and must, therefore, choose as if for all members of the potential society. In this case there will be no difference between altruism and selfishness.

Unanimity will therefore be the basic rule: subsequently every individual has a veto over the introduction of variants, which will, in fact, be rationally chosen not because they will produce better collective decisions, but because the sheer weight of the decision costs of unanimity dictate some departure from the ideal.

Both in their argument for the unanimity rule as the constitution and in their elaboration of personal calculation of cost in the choice of subordinate rules, Buchanan and Tullock attempt to avoid the problems of personal preferences and their summation which are inherent in the assumptions of majoritarian theories of democracy. And they succeed – at a cost.

The first problem is one of credibility, a problem common to contract theory in general: the system rests on a social contract but there is no explanation of its origin, and the conditions in which it might be used appear to be as restricted as those which Buchanan and Tullock lay down for the use of the majority principle: 'Our analysis of the constitution-making process', they write, 'has little relevance for a society that is characterized by a sharp cleavage of the population into distinguishable social classes or separate racial, religious, or ethnic groupings sufficient to encourage the formation of predictable political coalitions and in which one of these coalitions has a clearly advantageous position at the constitutional stage.'[10] The contract then is not only fictitious but historically improbable.

The second problem arises from the premise of individualism, by which Buchanan and Tullock simply ignore one of the major problems of social theory: – whether and in what ways society is greater than the sum of its part – and consequently can abandon any attempt to define the common good or general welfare. In doing this they even ignore the long established distinction between public and private goods from which another economist has drawn the interesting conclusion that no rational self-interested man will voluntarily contribute to the provision of any public good which will be provided whether he contributes or not.[11] This gives rise to arguments about the necessity for coercing free rational self-interested men in the common or public interest which go clean against Buchanan and Tullock's voluntaristic model.

There is also a problem about the personal calculation of costs necessary for departures from the principle of unanimity. To make the constitutional system work, individuals must be able to assess the costs to themselves of various courses of action. This implies at least an accurate

---

[10] *The Calculus of Consent*, p. 80.
[11] Mancur Olson Jr: *The Logic of Collective Action* (Harvard University Press, Cambridge, 1965).

knowledge of the probabilities of the results of these actions; that is to say, in the technical sense, a situation of risk if not of certainty. But how are individuals to act in a situation of uncertainty? It is only by limiting their examples to simple cases involving taxation, the provision of services and so forth, that Buchanan and Tullock avoid the problem that the consequences of many government decisions are impossible to predict and the benefits to be derived from them incalculable (defence policy comes readily to mind). This also serves to draw attention to two further, more general points about the importation of notions of rationality from economic into political theory. In the first place there seems to be no good reason why it should be assumed that rational men always know exactly what they want: it is possible to conceive of rational uncertainty as to preferences. Secondly, it is doubtful that choice among a finite set of goods is a satisfactory analogy for the process of governmental decision. Indeed, one economist has argued for a distinction between choice and decision, which he conceives as an act of creative imagination from which comes the possibility of innovation.[12] All of which is introduced by way of throwing doubt on the possibility of calculating personal costs, without which, in Buchanan and Tullock's system, there can be no departure from the unanimity rule. One is then either left with a constitution which gives every individual a right of veto over every collective decision; or the acceptance of the unanimity rule must involve further substantive agreements about its subsequent application. The basic decision rule is then no better than the majority rule, and, in fact, worse because it is a virtual guarantee of political immobility. That is to say, Buchanan and Tullock have not avoided the necessity for collective decisions to be based on certain agreed values beyond the basic assumption of political equality.

Why is it worth bothering with a theory which lacks credibility and results in constitutional absurdities? The reason is that Buchanan and

[12] G. L. S. Shackle, *Decision Order and Time*, Cambridge, 1961, p. 6: 'Decision ... is creative and is able to be so through the freedom which uncertainty gives for the creation of unpredictable hypotheses. Decision is not choice amongst the delimited and prescribed moves in a game with fixed rules and a known list of possible outcomes of any move or sequence of moves. There is no assurance that anyone can in advance say what set of hypotheses a decision-maker will entertain concerning any specified act available to him. Decision is thought and not merely determinate response.'
Shackle's view of decision bears a resemblance to recent theories of perception; cf. Richard Gregory, *The Intelligent Eye*.

Tullock put forward in extreme form and with refreshing lucidity and candour a point of view which is widely held in a less articulate form as the recent car sticker 'Happiness is the free market society' attests. It is a point of view which assumes that life consists of unlimited competition for limited goods, and it might be dignified with the title 'The political theory of scarcity'. A work such as Buchanan and Tullock's *The Calculus of Consent* gives the theory intellectual cachet: it has the aura of hard-nosed unsentimental realism, which has made the application of game theory to strategic doctrine so attractive and so dangerous; and it is mistaken for much the same reason – the divorce between rationality and morality implicit in the notion of the free rational self-interested man. To assume that the only basis on which rational men could form a political society is by the calculation of individual self-interest is also to assume that all goods in the world may be regarded as finite and divisible commodities. We are all familiar with the hold which the analogy between money and other goods exercised in the heyday of classical economics: it remains fundamental to the political theory of scarcity. As Buchanan and Tullock engagingly state: 'if love is the most precious thing in the world, there could be no stronger ethical argument in support of an attempt to minimize the necessity of its use in the ordering of the political activity of men'.[13]

Historically, the attraction of this sort of theory has been its apparent ability to solve the constitutional problem of democracy from the single assumption of political equality. And within its own terms this assumption may be easily defensible and thought of as a sufficient condition where other forms of inequality are not serious. In this sense democracy may be seen as an anachronistic ideal from the eighteenth century when technology was relatively simple, governments small in size and limited in role, property meant the actual control of resources and there was some prospect of its being widely diffused: where, in fact, the market appeared a fair mechanism of exchange, and voting might be considered a parallel mechanism for the exercise of political influence. In this kind of society the extension of collective decision-making is not required beyond a certain minimum provision of rules and their enforcement – guarantees of legal tender, sanctity of contract, property rights, physical integrity and so forth – and other social relations can be left to individuals because they are roughly equal in their resources anyway. Such a society may never have existed but it was at least conceivable.

But of what use is political equality if the actual situation bears no relation to the eighteenth-century Utopia of freeholders? This is where

---

[13] *The Calculus of Consent*, p. 28.

the concept of rationality in the political theory of scarcity comes in. C. B. Macpherson has pointed out that the fundamental change in attitudes to economic resources in the seventeenth and eighteenth centuries – that equality was not in itself desirable and that unlimited individual accumulation is a rational pursuit – has justified a minimum collective intervention not on the grounds that anything else is unnecessary, but on the grounds that the overall aim of society should be to increase wealth, irrespective of its distribution – and that this would be best achieved through a minimum collective intervention: in effect, the liberal idea of the nightwatchman state.[14] And thus the aim of society, or of collective action, is defined as increasing certain kinds of goods – primarily material ones – and not others – primarily psychological ones – which are not the finite and divisible commodities which a rational man can pursue, but which may be equally important to the good life. The question we have to put to the political theorists of scarcity is: how is it possible to justify or defend as democratic societies like our own in which formal political equality is accompanied by great inequalities in other resources, many of which are, in fact, relevant to politics? These inequalities may be defended on the grounds that they have raised the general level of material welfare further than other means of organizing economic and social life could have done, but they cannot be defended in terms of the psychological inequalities in personal autonomy or self-development or the meaningfulness of people's lives, which they may also create.

Minimizing the occasions for the use of love is then not only an unattractive defence of a political theory, it is also biased and mistaken. For I think we might say with equal conviction that certain goods such as confidence, trust and affection – goods essential to the existence of a political or any other society – are not finite, are not divisible and do not diminish with use, but, on the contrary, grow with their exercise. And it seems to me that any theorist who starts from individualist, contractarian or distributive assumptions takes on the difficulties implicit in this mistaken analogy. For he becomes committed to the view that political societies exist only for the satisfaction of individual wants, that these wants are of the limited kind that can be satisfied individually, and in the end to the equation of human progress with the infinite elaboration of material culture. Finally, he assumes that the citizen only undertakes political activity as a necessary evil. As Buchanan and Tullock have it: 'The costs of reaching agreement, of bargaining are . . . wasteful'.[15]

[14] 'The Maximization of Democracy', *Philosophy, Politics and Society*, 3rd Series, Oxford, 1967.
[15] *The Calculus of Consent*, p. 112.

This negative view of political activity runs clear against the second sort of justifying theory of liberal democracy, what I have called participatory theories of democracy. On this view, expressed in its classic form by John Stuart Mill, but also vigorously championed today, popular government presents an opportunity to the citizen not to satisfy his wants but to realize his potential: participation and self-government are goods in themselves because of their capacity to develop the moral qualities of independence, responsibility and care for others. Thus the citizen is not looked upon primarily as a consumer who enters politics only to protect his established interests, but as an actor realizing his moral potentialities and indeed his freedom through public life. In a sense, this argument comes close to the ideas of anarchists in its concern not for what people want but for what will make them good, and perhaps also in its notion of freedom. Anarchists especially oppose the rationality of scarcity and refuse to equate progress with the accumulation of material wealth and greater complexity of living. They believe in the virtues of simplicity, and in the abolition of authority, inequality and economic exploitation as the way to moralize society. With these aims it seems to me that participatory democrats might agree. Where they would part company with the anarchists is over the desirability of political action: for the liberal it is the condition of freedom, for the anarchist it is a corrupting delusion. It is easy to make a practical case against the doctrines of anarchism. Even if one believed possible a spontaneous uprising that would sweep away all institutions of formal authority, one can hardly see how the informal consensual authority and communal solidarity, on which anarchist society must rely, would arise in a society characterized by the minute division of labour, the diversity and insulation of social roles and the non-place urban realm: it is hard to see how the values of the Andalusian pueblo could be re-created in Megalopolis. But it does seem to me that anarchist criticisms are relevant to the participatory theory of democracy: first in questioning the value and achievements of representative institutions and, secondly, in questioning the assumption of the primacy of politics in achieving the good life. I am not against the view that over the last hundred years we have made some moral progress in our everyday life, but I am reluctant to attribute this to the benign influence of representative institutions or self-government. What I think is clear is the failure of the institutions of representative government to involve the vast majority of citizens in active political life and to overcome their sense of frustration with and alienation from the characteristic forms of authority in the modern bureaucratic state. Most recent institutional innovations have appeared to undermine the representative element in government, while the growth in the range and complexity of government activity has made it both more important and less comprehensible, and hence less controllable.

The representative system as a means of control seems, in fact, to be on the point of breakdown. On many issues there is little relation between the views of voters and those of their representatives, little enough between the views of representatives and those of governments, and governments themselves seem only precariously in control at the centre. Policy appears to emerge from a permanent poker game among public and private bureaucracies – a game whose stakes are too high for many citizens to enter save as the clients of organizations as unresponsive to individual pressure as the political institutions themselves. The political system of liberal democracy looks more and more like a mixture of plebiscitory dictatorship and corporate oligarchy. Participatory theorists are, of course, intensely aware of this situation and are prominent amongst the protagonists of institutional reform: there are numerous suggestions for increasing the opportunities for control and participation by ordinary citizens in the activities of government: greater use of referenda, devices to ensure more answerability by representatives, changes of structure which will bring the point of decision physically closer to the citizen or that will make the process of decision-making more open to scrutiny, and proposals to limit the discretion of the bureaucracy through the law, and even to change the style of the bureaucracy itself. The question is: are these more than variations on liberal solutions already proved inadequate, which can have little effect without at least equal attention being directed to the reform of private government?[16] It remains doubtful whether the representative element can reassert control, and doubtful too whether any such control would be directed to or result in greater participation by citizens as opposed to some form of increased efficiency.

The failure of representative institutions to rise to the challenge of bureaucratic government threatens a cardinal article of the liberal democratic faith: the belief that political equality is some guarantee that if other inequalities are insupportable, or the development of governmental institutions is unsatisfactory to a majority, then that majority has the political power to alter the balance of resources, to change the institutions and to redirect government action to the pursuit of alternative values. Some critics have always dismissed this belief out of hand. Even the sympathetic have recognized the shortcomings of any system of representation which reduces electoral democracy to the choice

[16] Cf. Stein Rokkan 'Norway: Numerical Democracy and Corporate Pluralism' in *Political Opposition in Western Democracies*, ed. Robert A. Dahl, etc. (New Haven, 1966).

between teams of leaders; leaders who necessarily enjoy a fair degree of autonomy though subject to their own anticipations of the periodic veto of the electorate. It is a system in which initiative lies largely with the politicians and it is difficult to envisage the circumstances in which it would suit the politicians to have a fundamental redistribution or change of direction. And, of course, the equality of voters in periodic judgment does not preclude inequalities in other political resources such as information, access to government, or control of the means of persuasion.

In the end, this brings democratic theory down to an argument about the amount of popular control in Western politics. Here a relatively optimistic and influential recent apologist, Robert Dahl, appears to have beaten a retreat from a feeling that fairly rigorous requirements for equality of influence are within reach of fulfilment to a much weaker belief that nobody in the United States at least is without some political resources.[17]

In arguing that in a liberal democracy everybody has some political resources, or potential political influence, Dahl is really concerned to refute the view that there is a single ruling class, or élite, on two grounds: first, that everybody has access at some point in the decision-making process; and second, that different people have different amounts of influence over different issues: there may be inequalities but they are not cumulative because a person who is powerful in one respect may lack any influence in another, and *vice versa*. There are at least two difficulties with this attempt to defend the effectiveness of formal political equality: the fact that everybody has access to the decision-making process at some point is no guarantee of any substantial equality, because access at different points can mean very different things: being consulted in the formulation of policy is preferable to having the right to vote on the end product. Secondly, in regard to the argument that such inequalities are not cumulative – people will occupy more or less favourable positions on different policies – it is very difficult to know what significance we can attach to this unless we can distinguish the relative importance of areas of decision and explain who has the initiative on the relatively more important decisions. The justification of any particular political system on Dahl's grounds would seem to demand not only that different people should have influence on different issues (and that each of these issues should be equally important to the distribution of inequalities) but also that everybody should have an equal

---

[17] Dahl's recessional can be followed in *A Preface to Democratic Theory* (Chicago, 1956), *Who Governs* (New Haven, 1961) and *Political Oppositions in Western Democracies* (New Haven, 1966).

chance of making any issue a matter for collective action. These seem to me to be rather good empirical tests of the claims of liberal democracy, but I can't think of any existing system which could pass them.

Satisfaction with the diluted proposition that everybody has some political resources stems in part from a certain complacency about the institutions of one well-known democracy, but it stems also in part from a concern with historical or empirical questions as well as prescriptive ones: in particular how to reconcile conflict arising from legitimate differences with the consensus necessary to maintain the constitution: how much conflict can a political system contain without breakdown? Dahl's so-called pluralist theory is in a sense an answer to the question: how has the American Constitution survived the manifest inequalities which have grown up under its wing? It is a good question and it is worth putting in a more general form: what are the conditions for the survival of democratic politics? Can the liberal democratic apparatus of free elections, competing parties, freedom of association and speech be maintained without, shall we say, agreement on the fundamentals of the economic system, so that inequalities resulting from it are seen to be legitimate? Can there be no democracy without prior agreement of the kind implicit in the model of free rational self-interested men? Or, alternatively, can there be agreement to differ on the economic system so long as the difference is manifested in practice over the division of an increasing surplus? This would mean no democracy without economic growth. And perhaps neither of these would be sufficient without a common education in the norms of democracy. No democracy, in effect, without a compulsory education in liberal values.

The trouble with a great deal of the literature at this level is that it takes for granted the democratic character of societies possessing these institutions and proceeds to explain by examination of their traditions how this beatific state is arrived at – and how others may develop themselves to some approximation of it. It does not, in fact, examine whether the consequences or results of liberal democratic institutions are satisfactory: the literature of political development is the last outpost of Whiggism.

It would be unfair to lumber John Stuart Mill, or the other participatory theorists, with the failures of lesser apologists, but their ideas must be measured, to some degree, against the performance of representative institutions. If representative institutions are supposed to have good results, we must know whether the results are good or not. Unfortunately this raises a problem which is found embarrassing by political and other social scientists, who aspire to a value-free scientific discipline: they are not happy about measuring performance against some vision of the good society. I do not myself see how this is to be avoided, nor indeed what the objection to it is as long as the test is explicit. This seems especially important at a time when the defenders of liberal democracy are apt to dismiss much criticism of our institutions as unrealistic. Dissent is often characterized as irrational because it appears to demand the impossible. What the liberal democrats fail to consider sufficiently is whether their own conception of the possible is not restricted by the assumption of scarcity. Are the critics demanding the impossible or do our present social arrangements reinforce the conception of human nature on which they are based? Would not the 'facts of life' which radical dissenters are accused of ignoring be better described as the artefacts of life? Participatory democrats especially ought to pay more attention to alternative social arrangements when and if they recognize the contrast which exists between the claims they make for political equality and the subordination most people experience in their everyday lives. If, as Adam Smith put it, 'the understandings of the greater part of men are necessarily formed by their ordinary employments', how can you expect him to develop as a free citizen who is required to be a biddable cipher in his work? I do not pretend that it is easy to say what the facts of life are. That alternative systems are possible in the sense that they exist is obvious, but I remain to be convinced that their peculiar virtues are any more transferable than our own (I am not a supporter of the general proposition that they manage these things better in Polynesia). Though it may be difficult to see what historical possibilities are open to ourselves, nevertheless I am convinced that this is what political theory ought to be about: and in particular, it ought to emphasize the distinction between affluence and abundance, between deciding how to get more and deciding when you have got enough. Political theory ought to be directed to the question of how much is enough and what else might we do than get more of what we have already. It is in this sense that I would advocate a political theory of abundance.

To recapitulate, I have suggested that certain justifying theories of liberal democracy may be said to be deficient on three grounds. First, that there can be no axiomatic justification of liberal democratic institutions and values, least of all when based on assumptions about rationality which restrict and distort human possibilities and ignore the importance of the social virtues. The distributive approach is at once ahistorical in method and bound to a particular political morality whose motto might read, 'Fear thy neighbour as thyself'. Second, that liberal democracy has failed to make good in practice or in theory the disparities of political power which arise from inequalities outside formal political institutions. Third, that there is a gap between the opportunities which liberal democracy is supposed to afford for the citizen to achieve freedom through public life and the experience of most citizens under the bureaucratic state.

And perhaps one final, more personal observation: it seems to me that liberal democracy requires a commitment to the risks of freedom in all aspects of life and that this commitment is missing. In striking the balance between hope and fear, in the home, at school, at work, we come down more often on the side of restraint, caution, obedience and conformity than on that of adventure, initiative, independence and experiment. Where liberal democracy fails most of all perhaps is in the want of practical faith among those who profess its principles.

It is not too difficult to suggest the connections between these various failures. The historical link between the rationality of unlimited acquisition, economic inequalities and disparities of political power is obvious. One might also say that in any contest between them this rationality has generally defeated the values of participation. And this in turn may help to explain the defeat of representative institutions, which embody at least the promise of self-government for all, by bureaucracies, which embody at least the promise of efficiency.

It should be clear already that I do not have any alternative system up my sleeve. But I shall at least try to do what I promised at the beginning – to suggest, in the light of these criticisms, the essential characteristics of a more satisfactory political theory.

I start from the assumption that the aim of political theory is to make the connection between morality and action; between what ought to be done and how to do it; between the good society and the means to achieve it. Here I support the participatory theorists who would be prepared to say what they mean by a good man, a satisfactory human being, against those who would have us pursue the infinitely receding prospect of some undefined individual happiness.

So the first suggestion I have to make is that any satisfactory political theory cannot be based on intellectually convenient fictions, but must be historically concerned with a unique situation and its possibilities.

Secondly, it should consider the range of human as well as institutional possibilities: it should not ask only what set of institutions is consonant with a particular view of human nature, but what institutions make for what human nature.

Following from this it should not confine itself to the political, as such, but be concerned with all aspects and institutions of society, especially with those experiences which go to form the habits of obedience – child-rearing, education and the various disciplines and examples through which people come to define themselves and their relations with each other.

Finally, it is the peculiar duty of political theory to be public. A political theory which is comprehensible to a select band of initiates only may have all the virtues except the saving grace of relevance. A satisfactory political theory must, therefore, avoid both the barbarous neologisms of contemporary social science and the tedious obsession with the antiquated gymnastics of Hegelian philosophy. Its aim must be to help people to make their political choices conscious of all the possibilities; and in the particular parochial context of liberal democracy of which I have been speaking to enable them to recognize the existence of a choice between what is efficient in any measurable sense and what is not, and to recognize also that it may be both meaningful and rational to choose the latter.

3 Obligation and Consent[1]

Hanna Pitkin

One might suppose that if political theorists are by now clear about anything at all, they should be clear about the problem of political obligation and the solution to it most commonly offered, the doctrine of consent. The greatest modern political theorists took up this problem and formulated this answer. The resulting theories are deeply imbedded in our American political tradition; as a consequence we are already taught a sort of rudimentary consent theory in high school. And yet I want to suggest that we are not even now clear on what '*the* problem of political obligation' is, what sorts of 'answers' are appropriate to it, what the consent answer really says, or whether it is a satisfactory answer. This essay is designed to point up the extent of our confusion, to explore some of the ground anew as best it can, and to invite further effort by others. That such effort is worthwhile, that such political theory is still worth considering and that it can be made genuinely relevant to our world, are the assumptions on which this essay rests and the larger message it is meant to convey.

I The Problem of Political Obligation

The difficulties begin with the formulation of the problem itself. What exactly is the 'problem of political obligation'? It is characteristic that we take it for granted there is a single problem to be defined here, and that nevertheless a dozen different formulations clamour for our attention. The classical theorists on the subject have treated it in varying ways; and even within the writings of a Hobbes, Locke or Rousseau it is difficult to say what the theorist's 'basic problem' is, or indeed whether he has one. We tend, I think, to suppose that it does not matter very much how you phrase the problem, that the different formulations boil down to the same thing. But my first point will be that this attitude of arbitrariness or indifference should not be trusted. It is not, in fact, true that any formulation of the problem is equivalent to any other. Rather, this supposed single problem is a whole cluster of different questions – questions of quite various kind and scope. And though their

[1] Reprinted with trifling amendments from the *American Political Science Review*, Vol. LIX, no. 4, 1965; and Vol. LX, no. 1, 1966.

answers *may* turn out to be related, so that an answer to one provides answers to the others also, it is by no means obvious that this must be so. Specifically, I suggest that most of the familiar answers to the problem are satisfactory responses to some of its questions but not to others, and that the answer adopted depends a good deal on the question stressed.

For the purpose of this essay it will be useful to distinguish four questions, or rather, four clusters of questions, all of which are part of what bothers theorists about political obligation. They range from a relatively concrete and practical political concern with what is to be done, through increasing theoretical abstractness, to a philosophical concern with the meanings of concepts and the paradoxes that arise out of them. Because we are used to treating them all as different versions of one problem, the reader may not at first see any significant differences among them; but the differences should emerge in the course of the discussion. No doubt the problem encompasses more than these four questions, and could be divided up in a number of different ways. Indeed, some aspects of it not covered by these four questions will emerge in the course of this discussion.

We are told often enough that the theorists of political obligation were not merely philosophers, but also practical men writing about the political needs of their times. They produced 'not simply academic treatises, but essays in advocacy, adapted to the urgencies of a particular situation. Men rarely question the legitimacy of established authority when all is going well; the problem of political obligation is urgent when the state is sick, when someone is seriously contemplating disobedience or revolt on principle.[2] Thus we may begin with a cluster of questions centred around the *limits* of political obligation, the more or less practical concern with *when*, under what circumstances, resistance or revolution is justified. The theorist wants to promote or prevent a revolution, or he lives in a time when one is taking place, or he contemplates one in the recent past. So he seeks some fairly general, but still practically applicable principles to guide a man in deciding when (if ever) political obligation ends or ceases to bind. They must have a certain degree of generality in order to be principles rather than *ad hoc* considerations in one particular situation, in order to be recognized by us as *theory*. But they are also fairly directly tied to what Tussman has called the question 'what should I do?'[3] They are guidelines to action.

---

[2] S. I. Benn and R. S. Peters, *Social Principles and the Democratic State* (London, George Allen & Unwin, 1959), pp. 299-300.
[3] *Obligation and the Body Politic* (New York, Oxford University Press, 1960), p. 12.

At other times the same practical concern tends to take a slightly different form: 'Whom am I obligated to obey? Which of the persons (or groups) claiming to command me actually has authority to do so?' Put this second way, the problem seems to be one of rival authorities, sometimes identified in political theory as the problem of the locus of sovereignty. The former question tends to arise in situations of potential civil disobedience or nascent revolution, where the individual is relatively alone in his confrontation of a government. The latter question is more likely to come up in situations of civil war or when a revolution is more advanced, when the individual is already confronted by two 'sides' between which he must choose.

But as the theorist tries to formulate general principles to guide such a choice, he may be led to a more abstract version of his problem. He may be struck by the seeming arbitrariness or conventionality of human authority: how is it that some men have the right to command, and others are obligated to obey? And so the theorist looks for the general difference between legitimate authority on the one hand, and illegitimate, naked coercive force on the other. He begins to wonder whether there is really any difference in principle between a legitimate government and a highway robber, pirate, or slave-owner. He begins to suspect that terms like 'legitimate', 'authority', 'obligation' may be parts of an elaborate social swindle, used to clothe those highway robbers who have the approval of society with a deceptive mantle of moralistic sanctity. Essentially, he begins to ask whether men are ever truly obligated to obey, or only coerced. 'Strength is a physical attribute,' says Rousseau, 'and I fail to see how any moral sanction can attach to its effects. To yield to the strong is an act of necessity, not of will. At most it is the result of a dictate of prudence. How, then, can it become a duty?' Such questions are no longer merely guides to action; they are attempts to describe and classify parts of the social world. Instead of focussing on the individual's 'what should I do?' they focus outward, on the (real or alleged) authority: 'what is legitimate authority like?'

Finally, behind even this more abstract question, lies what is essentially a philosophical problem, a cluster of questions centering around the *justification* of obligation: *why* are you obligated to obey even a legitimate government? Why is anyone ever obligated to obey any authority at all? How can such a thing be rationalized, explained, defended, justified? What can account for the binding nature of valid law and legitimate authority? I call these questions philosophical problems because they no longer seek distinctions or guides to action, but arise out of puzzlement over the nature of law, government, obligation as such. They are categorical questions to which the theorist is led, characteristically, after an extended abstract contemplation of the concepts he has been using. They are reminiscent of other philosophical puzzles, like 'do we ever really know anything?' or 'do other people really exist?'

We have, then, four clusters of questions, any or all of which are sometimes taken to define the problem of political obligation:

(1) The limits of obligation ('*When* are you obligated to obey, and when not?')

(2) The locus of sovereignty ('*Whom* are you obligated to obey?')

(3) The difference between legitimate authority and mere coercion ('Is there *really* any difference; are you ever *really* obligated?')

(4) The justification of obligation ('*Why* are you ever obligated to obey even a legitimate authority?')

Obviously the answers to these questions may be connected. If, for example, one answers question three in terms of the reductionist realism of a Thrasymachus or of vulgar Marxism: 'there is no difference,' then the other questions become essentially irrelevant. But we should not take it for granted that any answer to one of these questions will automatically provide consistent answers to the rest; we should look to see how familiar answers in fact perform. Our prime interest is, of course, the consent answer, but before examining it, we might look briefly at very abstract, ideal-typicalized versions of some of its major rivals. Their brief treatment here would not allow, and is not meant to be a balanced assessment of their merits. It is meant only to explore a little of the complexity of political obligation, and the difficulty of providing a consistent treatment of it.

Theories of Divine Right or the will of God, for example, seem much better designed to cope with some of our questions than with others. Saying, with St Paul, that 'the powers that be are ordained of God,' seems a decisive answer (at least for a believer) to our question four. Granted only that there is a God (in the full sense of the word), the fact that he commands certain actions is surely a decisive justification for our obligation to perform them. But applied to our other questions the doctrine is ambiguous. Taken one way, it seems to imply that there is no difference between mere coercive force and legitimate authority, since all power comes from God. Then resistance is never justified, even against a heretical ruler who attacks religion. For times when power is in flux, as in cases of civil war, this version of the theory seems to provide very little guidance for action. Taking the doctrine a different way, some divine right theorists have wanted to argue that there is nevertheless a distinction to be made between divinely ordained power and illegitimate power, and that there are times when certain kinds of power must be resisted.

Prescription, another familiar response to the problem of obligation, seems more directly designed to give an unequivocal answer to questions one and perhaps three. It teaches that old, established power is legitimate in every case, and there are no limits on our obligation to obey it. But this again is no guide in times of successful revolution; is it obedience or counterrevolution that is then required? And what of occasions when an old, established government begins to act in new and tyrannical ways? Even Burke was sympathetic to the American Revolution. Further, this doctrine has real difficulties with our question four; a government's age, and our habitual obedience to it, do not seem to *justify* an obligation to obey. At most the connection can only be made through a number of additional assumptions concerning human reason and the nature of society, and adding up to the thesis that old, accepted government is most likely to be good government.

A third, equally well known response to our problem, that of Utilitarianism, is perhaps an even better illustration of the complexities involved. The utilitarian theorist argues that you are obligated to obey if and only if the consequences of obedience will be best on the whole, in terms of a calculus of pains and pleasures. There are, of course, familiar difficulties over the manner of calculation and whether all pains and pleasures are to count equally. But even beyond these, there is a fundamental question left unclear, namely, *whose* pains and pleasures are to count: your own personal ones, or those of the (majority of) people in your society. Bentham himself says that it is

> allowable to, if not incumbent on every man . . . to enter into measures of resistance . . . when the probable mischiefs of resistance (speaking with respect to the community in general) appear less to him than the probable mischiefs of obedience. (Jeremy Bentham, *Fragment on Government*, ch. IV, par. 21).

But the phrase in the parentheses is, of course, the crux of the matter. The Utilitarians are notoriously inconsistent on precisely this point, saying one thing when they speak of personal ethics and personal decision, and quite another on the subject of legislation and public policy. So it will be well for us to consider both possibilities.

First, there is what might be called individualistic utilitarianism. Such a theory argues that you are obligated when the consequences of obedience are best on the whole in terms of your personal pleasure and pain. As a response to our question four, this argument has a certain appeal: you are obligated *because* it is best for you in terms of your own pleasure and pain. But the implications for the other questions are more strange. For they are that each individual is obligated to obey only while it is best for him, and becomes obligated to resist when that would promote his personal welfare. Thus the same government will be a legitimate authority for some of its subjects but naked illegitimate power to others. And anyone is free to disobey or resist whenever it benefits him to do so; he can have no obligation to the contrary. Indeed, the sum total of such a doctrine is that you have no obligation at all, or none except the pursuit of your own welfare. If that happens at one point to entail obeying the law, you should do so; if not, not. And in precisely the same way, if it happens at one point to entail obeying a highway robber, you are 'obligated' to do that. Thus, as an answer to question three, individualistic utilitarianism essentially denies the existence of authority altogether.

The second alternative is what we might call social utilitarianism. This position argues that you are obligated to obey if and only if the consequences of your doing so will be best on the whole, in terms of the pains and pleasures of the people in your society – in terms of the greatest good for the greatest number. Unlike individualistic utilitarianism, this seems a fairly reasonable, conventional answer to questions one and two. You must obey while that promotes the welfare of society, even if it hurts you; and you must resist when that is socially best, even if it hurts you. The answer to question three is less obvious but not, on the face of it, irrational. A legitimate government is one that promotes the greatest good for the greatest number; and if a highway robber does that, then he becomes thereby a legitimate authority entitled to your obedience. A selfish or (on the whole) harmful robber or government may or must be resisted. But as an answer to question four, social utilitarianism seems less successful. For it teaches that you are obligated *because* your obedience will promote the greatest good for the greatest number. But if you are bothered about political obligation, *that* is just the problem: why should that criterion mean anything to you? Why should it be any easier to accept *that* obligation than to accept the obligation to obey law and authority?

Sometimes, of course, the utilitarians assume that there is no problem about individualistic *versus* social utilitarianism, that the two criteria are essentially the same because of the invisible hand, because individual welfare is (in sum) social welfare. When they write about economics, particularly, this solution tempts them. But in political life, concerning legislation or concerning political obligation, they are fairly well aware that this is not the case. Private interest must be *made* to coincide with public interest by wise legislation. And instructions to resist when it is best for society will often produce quite different results than instructions to resist when it is best for you personally. There are bound to be occasions when the public welfare requires serious sacrifices (perhaps even of life) by some individuals. To suppose otherwise seems incredibly unrealistic.

The theorist founding political obligation in consent responds to our four questions in this way: you are obligated to obey if and only if you have consented. Thus your consent defines the limits of your obligation as well as the person or persons to whom it is owed. Legitimate authority is distinguished from mere coercive power precisely by the consent of those subject to it. And the justification for your obligation to obey is your own consent to it; because you have agreed, it is right for you to have an obligation. But the seeming harmonious simplicity of these answers is deceptive; when consent theory is worked out in detail, its answers to some of our questions begin to interfere with its answers to others.

In the first place, there is the problem of exactly whose consent is to count. We have all known, at least since Hume – if it was not already obvious before him – that the historical origins of society are essentially irrelevant to the consent argument. The consent of our ancestors does not settle the problem about our obligation today. Or rather, someone who seriously argues that the consent of our ancestors does settle this problem, is arguing more from prescription than from consent, and is probably not very troubled about political obligation anyway.

But even if it is the consent of those now subject to power (or authority) that matters, there are still several alternatives: is it to be the individual's personal consent that determines his obligation, or the consent of all (or most) of those subject to the government? And is it to be his or their present consent, or consent given in the past? Let us consider the possibilities.

(1) You are obligated only insofar as you personally consent right now. Where your consenting ends, there ends also your obligation. What this presumably means is that as long as you accept the government it is wrong for you to disobey it, and right for it to punish any disobedience by you. But as soon as you withdraw your consent, you become free to disobey, and no attempt to punish you can be justified. This doctrine would have the peculiar consequence that you can never violate your obligation; for as soon as you decide the time has come for revolution (withdraw your consent), your obligation disappears. It also means that you can never be mistaken about your obligation, for what you think defines it. This answer comes to much the same thing as individualistic utilitarianism, except that it demands no rational calculation, looking to your will rather than to your welfare.

(2) You are obligated only insofar as you personally have *in the past*

consented. This is closer to traditional contract theory. You gave your word, and so you are bound for the future, unless (of course) the government changes and becomes tyrannical. But this position seems to allow the possibility of becoming obligated to a tyrannical government, if you expressly consent to one that was already corrupt. One can avoid that problem by saying such promises are invalid, that you *cannot* expressly consent to become a slave; but then the argument is already moving away from a consent theory. Then your obligation is no longer merely a matter of your having consented (tried to consent, intended to consent).

Further, there seems to be a real problem about why and whether your past promise should bind you now. The classical contract theorists provide a law of nature to take care of this difficulty: it is a law of nature that promises oblige. But why should it seem so obvious and 'natural' and self-evident that your promises oblige you, when it is so doubtful and problematic and un-'natural' that law and authority oblige you?

(3) You are obligated only insofar as your fellow-subjects consent. One consequence of this position is that the matter is no longer left up to you; you can sometimes be obligated to obey even against your will and your private judgment, and without ever having consented or been consulted. But, if so, how many of your fellow-subjects must consent? All? That is surely impossible. A majority? But that implies that the way to decide whether you are obligated, or whether you should start a revolution, is to take a public opinion poll. And can majorities never be wrong? Are there no occasions in the history of mankind when it was right for a dedicated minority to begin agitating for a revolution, or even to lead or make a revolution? And finally *why* should what the majority (or any other proportion) of your fellow-subjects think be binding on you? What justification is there for that? Why should that obligation seem more basic or natural or self-evident than the obligation to obey laws and authority? Because you have consented to majority rule? But then the whole cycle of difficulties begins again.

Besides the matter of whose consent is to count, consent theory is also much troubled by the difficulty of showing that you, or a majority of your fellow-citizens (as the case may be) have in fact consented. Most of us have not signed any contract with our government or our society or our fellow-citizens. There is no such contract for us to sign. And while we political theorists may be enlightened about our obligations, we realize that the largest proportion of our fellow-citizens has never contemplated this sort of question at all. If they have consented, it comes as news to most of them. Of course, these facts need not invalidate the consent argument. Perhaps most of us are not really obligated in modern, apathetic mass society; perhaps our government is not really legitimate.

But such conclusions seem to fly in the face of common sense. Surely, one feels, if the present government of the United States is not a legitimate authority, no government has ever been. [This was written in 1964. I leave it as a historical relic. H.P.] And surely it is absurd to adopt a theory according to which only those people who are most educated and aware of their obligations, most moral and sensitive, are obligated to obey the law. Surely it is absurd to suppose that all the rest are free to do whatever they please, whatever they can get away with. A more common move at this stage in the argument is the introduction of some notion of 'tacit consent', demonstrating that even the unaware masses have consented after all. But it appears to be extremely difficult to formulate a notion of tacit consent strong enough to create the required obligation, yet not so strong as to destroy the very substance and meaning of consent.

Let us now examine in more detail how these difficulties are encountered and treated in two consent arguments: the most famous one of the tradition, made by John Locke, and a recent attempt at revision by Joseph Tussman. What should emerge from a review of their arguments is a somewhat unexpected and different doctrine of political obligation: perhaps a new interpretation of consent theory, perhaps a new rival to it.

II *Locke on Consent*

Locke tells us in the preface to his *Two Treatises* that he wants both to 'make good' the title of William III to the English throne 'in the consent of the People' and also 'to justifie to the World, the people of England, whose love of their Just and Natural Rights, with their Resolution to preserve them, saved the Nation when it was on the very brink of Slavery and Ruine.' Apart from the exegetic problems of how much of the *Treatises* may have been written before the Glorious Revolution and for quite other purposes, the thrust of Locke's argument makes clear enough that this dual orientation does pervade the work.[4] He seeks both to defend the obligation to obey legitimate authority (which is authority based on consent), and to defend the right to resist coercive force in the absence of authority. But Locke moves easily, and seemingly without awareness, from one to another of our four questions about obligation and back again. Often when the going gets difficult on one, he switches to another.

[4] For a discussion of the evidence on when the *Treatises* were written, see Peter Laslett, Ed., *John Locke, Two Treatises of Government*, Introduction, esp. part III.

Legitimate authority, for Locke, comes from the consent of those subject to it, never from mere conquest (force); and even a consent extracted by coercion is invalid. Thus the limits of a government's authority are defined by the social contract on which it is based. Strictly speaking, of course, Locke's contract sets up *society* and government is established by society as a trust. There is no contract with the government. But the government gets its powers (in trust) from 'the society', acting by majority vote. And 'the society' has only such powers to give, as it has itself received from the separate contracting individuals. Thus, even for Locke, it is the contract which ultimately determines what powers the government can have. He himself makes this assumption and I shall follow suit, since it simplifies the argument.

Although Locke sometimes seems to take contract seriously as an account of the historical origins of society, he is nevertheless quite explicit about the requirement that no person is obligated to obey today unless he has himself consented. Most of us have not consented expressly? Ah, but there is tacit consent, and its scope turns out to be very wide indeed. Although a father may not consent for his son, he can make consent to the community a condition on inheritance of the property he leaves behind: then in accepting the property the son tacitly consents to obey the government. But the final definition of tacit consent is even wider, for land is not the only form of property, and property not the only form of right that men enjoy:

> Every man that hath any possession or enjoyment of any part of the dominions of any government doth thereby give his tacit consent, and is as far forth obliged to obedience to the laws of that government, during such enjoyment, as any one under it, whether this his possession be of land to him and his heirs forever, or a lodging only for a week; or whether it be barely travelling freely on the highway; and, in effect, it reaches as far as the very being of anyone within the territories of that government.

Just as Locke maintained earlier in the *Treatise* that men have tacitly consented to all inequalities in property, simply by accepting and using money as a medium of exchange; so in the political realm he argues that men have tacitly consented to obey a government, simply by remaining within its territory. But now there no longer seems to be much power in the concept of consent, nor any difference between legitimate government and mere coercion. Being within the territory of the worst tyranny in the world seems to constitute tacit consent to it and create an obligation to obey it. Only physical withdrawal – emigration – and the abandoning of all property frees you from that obligation; there is no such thing as tacit *dissent*.

At this point we are likely to feel cheated by Locke's argument: why all the stress on consent if it is to include everything we do; why go through the whole social contract argument if it turns out in the end that everyone is automatically obligated? It seems that in his eagerness to save the consent answer to our question four (because only your own consent *can* justify your obligation), Locke has been forced so to widen the definition of consent as to make it almost unrecognizable. He has been forced to abandon his answers to our other questions as well as one of his own initial purposes: the justification of an (occasional) right of revolution.

But clearly this is not Locke's real position. I have developed it this way only because the corrections we must now make are so revealing about consent theory. For despite his doctrine of tacit consent, Locke does not want to abandon either the right of revolution or the distinction between legitimate authority and coercive power. His position is not, in fact, that living within the territory of a tyrannical government or holding property under it constitutes tacit consent to it.

Suppose that we ask: *to what* have you consented when you live in a country and use its highways? Unfortunately, Locke is less than clear on this question. What he says explicitly in the crucial section on tacit consent is that you have 'consented', period; he does not say to what. But apparently, what you consent to is a kind of associate membership in the commonwealth. Full membership, achieved only by express consent, is an indissoluble bond for life. The obligation of a tacit consenter, however, terminates if he leaves the country and gives up his property there. Locke also variously describes tacit consent as a joining oneself to a society, putting oneself under a commonwealth and submitting to a government. Sometimes he simply equates its 'joining up' aspects with submission to a government; at other times he regards submission as an immediate consequence of joining.

But in the context of the problems we have encountered, a better interpretation of Locke's intention here would be this: what you consent to tacitly is *the terms of the original contract which the founders of the commonwealth made*, no more and no less. You append your 'signature', as it were, to the original 'document'. Then if you live or use the roads or hold property under a government which is violating its trust, exceeding its authority, taking property without due compensation, 'altering the legislative', or generally acting in a tyrannical manner, you have consented to none of these things. You are not obligated to obey one inch beyond the limits of the original contract, any more than its original signatories were. You retain the right of revolution, as they did, in case the government oversteps the limits of its authority.

So we seem to be led to the position that you are obligated to obey not really because you have consented; your consent is virtually automatic. Rather, you are obligated to obey because of certain characteristics of the government – that it is acting within the bounds of a trusteeship based on an original contract. And here it seems to me that interpreters of Locke have given far too little attention to the degree to which he regards the terms of the original contract as inevitably determined. In truth, the original contract could not have read any otherwise than it did, and the powers it gave and limits it placed can be logically deduced from the laws of nature and conditions in the state of nature. Not only does Locke himself confidently deduce them in this way, sure that he can tell us what the terms of that original contract were, *must* have been; but he says explicitly that they could not have been otherwise. For men had to give up sufficient of their rights to make an effective government possible, to allow a government to remedy the 'inconveniences' of the state of nature. Nothing short of this would create a society, a government. 'There, and there only, is political society, where every one of the members' has given up the powers necessary to a society:

> Whosoever therefore out of a state of nature unite into a community, must be understood to give up all the power necessary to the needs for which they unite into society . . .

More power than this, on the other hand, men cannot be supposed to have given; and, indeed, they are forbidden by the law of nature to give more. When the limits of authority are to be defined, Locke invokes the purpose for which the contract was made, the intention which those making it must have had:

> But though men when they enter into society give up the equality, liberty and executive power they had in the state of nature into the hands of the society, to be so far disposed of by the legislative as the good of society shall require, yet it being only with an intention in everyone the better to preserve himself, his liberty and his property (*for no rational creature can be supposed to change his condition with an intention to the worse*), the power of the society or legislative constituted by them *can never be supposed to extend farther* than the common good, but is obliged to secure everyone's property by providing against those three defects above-mentioned that made the state of nature so unsafe and uneasy. (italics mine)

Thus men cannot sell themselves into slavery 'for nobody has an absolute arbitrary power over himself' to give to another; he '*cannot* subject himself to the arbitrary power of another'. Arbritary or absolute power can never be legitimate, consented to, because 'God and Nature' do not allow 'a man so to abandon himself as to neglect his own preservation'. 'Thus,' says Locke, 'the law of nature stands as an eternal rule to all men, legislators as well as others.'

If the terms of the original contract are, as I am arguing, 'self-evident' truths to Locke, which could not be or have been otherwise, then the historical veracity of the contract theory becomes in a new and more profound sense irrelevant. For now the Lockean doctrine becomes this: your personal consent is essentially irrelevant to your obligation to obey, or its absence. Your obligation to obey depends on the character of the government – whether it is acting within the bounds of *the* (only possible) contract. If it is, and you are in its territory, you must obey. If it is not, then no amount of personal consent from you, no matter how explicit, can create an obligation to obey it. No matter how often you pledge allegiance to a tyranny, those pledges *cannot* constitute a valid obligation, because they violate the law of nature. So, not only is your personal consent irrelevant, but it actually no longer matters whether this government or any government was really founded by a group of men deciding to leave the state of nature by means of a contract. As long as a government's actions are within the bounds of what such a contract hypothetically *would have* provided, would have *had* to provide, those living within its territory must obey. This is the true significance of what we have all learned to say in political theory: that the historical accuracy of the contract doctrine is basically irrelevant – that the contract is a logical construct. The only 'consent' that is relevant is the hypothetical consent imputed to hypothetical, timeless, abstract, rational men.

III   *Tussman on Consent*

A more modern version of the story is told by Joseph Tussman in his excellent and provocative book, *Obligation and the Body Politic*. Tussman, too, seeks to found political obligation in the consent of the governed. Only on that basis, he maintains, is political obligation 'distinguishable from captivity', for 'obligations are, or even must be voluntarily assumed'.[5] Tussman acknowledges the rarity of express

---

[5] *Op. cit.*, pp. 24, 8. I hope it is clear, in spite of all the criticisms I make of Tussman's argument, how greatly this essay is indebted to his work.

consent except in the case of naturalized citizens who take an oath of citizenship. But, like Locke, he introduces a notion of tacit consent. Unlike Locke's, however, Tussman's tacit consent does not include merely walking on a country's highway; he insists that even tacit consent must be 'knowing', made with awareness of what one is doing and of its significance. A great many different actions, done with awareness and intent, can constitute such tacit consent: pledging allegiance to the flag, voting in an election, and so on. But even this doctrine, as Tussman admits, produces only a relatively small number of persons who can be said to have consented. Reluctantly he accepts this conclusion, which he calls the notion of 'shrinkage'.

> If it is insisted that only those who have consented are members of the body politic then the body politic may shrink alarmingly . . . [But] any description of a body politic, like the United States, would have to recognize that there are some, or many, 'citizens' who could not be described as having consented. There is no point to resorting to fiction to conceal this fact.

Thus it is Tussman's position that only those who have consented (perhaps tacitly, but knowingly) are truly members, and that these may be a relatively small proportion of the population. But, of course, he is not willing to conclude that only those few consenting members are bound to obey the laws and accept the actions of the government as authoritative. He takes it for granted that everyone must obey, is obligated to obey, ought to be punished for disobeying – even the man who has never given government or obligation a single thought. Tussman allows for the possibility of withdrawal, emigration, as an express refusal to consent; but (as with Locke) there is no such thing as tacit dissent. The clods who merely live in a country without ever being sufficiently aware of public life to consent even tacitly, are not members of the body politic, but they are nevertheless bound to obey the law. The clods are obligated, Tussman says, like children. 'Non-consenting-adult citizens are, in effect, like minors who are governed without their own consent. The period of tutelage and dependence is unduly prolonged.'

The interesting thing is that this doctrine does not seem to bother Tussman; he sees no inconsistency in it. He is not disturbed by saying on the one hand that membership in a body politic can only be distinguished from mere captivity if it is voluntary, and on the other hand that large masses of people must obey though they have not consented and are consequently not members. He does not seem to be bothered by saying that great masses of adults are obligated like children; he does not discuss why or how children are obligated, how their obligation – let alone its continuation into adult life – can be *justified*. To be sure, he obviously regrets the state of affairs that makes so large a proportion of our population clods who are not truly members. In a sense his whole book is written to advocate a more adequate system of political education, which would make more people aware of morality and public life, so that they would truly consent.

This is his ideal; but we have a right to ask what happens in the meantime, and how satisfactorily Tussman's account explains political obligation in the meantime. And when we do, we have the same feeling of betrayal as with Locke: why all the liberal protestations at the outset about the need for voluntary consent, if the net result in the end is that everyone has to obey anyway? In Locke the betrayal seems to centre in the way he stretches the notion of tacit consent; Tussman avoids this, but instead introduces a second, childlike kind of obligation.

Now, there are good reasons why Tussman's argument proceeds as it does, why he does not seem to see these difficulties. For, although his book purports to be about obligation (as the title indeed indicates) the primary thrust of its argument, the question Tussman really seems to have asked himself, is about *membership* in a body politic. He takes it for granted that exploring the nature of membership will also produce answers about political obligation. At the outset of the book, confronting the question of what membership in a body politic is like, Tussman suggests three alternative possibilities: that membership be construed as subordination to a single coercive power; or as sharing in a common set of habits or customs; or as being party to (consenting to) a system of agreements on the model of a voluntary association. Given these three alternatives, he opts for the last one, because only if membership rests on consent can it be related to concepts like legitimacy and obligation. ' "I have a duty to . . . " seems to follow from "I have agreed to" in a way that it does not follow from "I am forced to" or "I am in the habit of." '

In terms of our classification, Tussman directs his inquiry at question three, the difference between legitimate authority and coercive power. As an answer to that question, as an account of membership, his theory surely is very compelling. Confronted with unaware, non-consenting clods, it seems reasonable then to say that not everyone is truly a member; that no body politic is entirely legitimate, based on the consent of every single subject; that political education might make our nation a better, truer political association in the future. But approached from our question four, for instance, the theory seems arbitrary and inadequate. If 'obligations are, or even must be voluntarily assumed', then how can one consistently maintain that children or the non-consenting clods are obligated to obey the law? How is their situation different from captivity, and how can it be justified? Tussman is not interested in our question four. Or perhaps that statement is not strong enough; he refuses to consider the question, because he regards it as 'a symptom of moral disorder'.

Tussman is right to be suspicious of the question; there is something strange about it, as we shall later see. But it is a symptom less of moral disorder than of philosophical disorder; and it needs to be considered, not rejected. For although Tussman explicitly rejects the question, he is already profoundly committed to one particular answer to it: that only consent can justify obligation, distinguish it from captivity. And this commitment conflicts with his treatment of the clods in society. As a result, Tussman's theory also has difficulties with our questions one and two, concerning the limits and location of authority.

For Tussman wants to maintain that all persons in a country – consenting members and clods alike – are obligated to obey law and government, *except when occasions for revolution arise*. He recognizes that there are occasions and situations when revolution is justified, that there is a right of revolution. He talks about the need to 'exhaust the remedies' available within a system, about what happens when there are only 'corrupt tribunals' left to appeal to; and he says 'where government is based on force, forceful opposition needs no special permit'. Thus we may legitimately ask him, *who* has the right to revolt when the occasion for revolution arises. The members presumably do. Surely they never consented to tyranny, and a tyrannical government is acting *ultra vires*, beyond any consent they have given. But surely, too, the clods, who have never consented, ought also to be morally free to resist a 'government' that has become a tyranny. Though they may ordinarily be obligated to obey as children are, yet surely Tussman cannot mean that they continue to be obligated no matter what the government does or how it degenerates. Surely a clod who suddenly awakens to moral awareness under a Hitler government is right to resist it.

But why, when, how does their childlike obligation come to an end? Tussman does not tell us, because he does not consider the question. He seems, thus, to be saying: you are obligated to obey a government that is legitimate authority, *whether you personally consented to it or not*. If you have consented, you are obligated as a member; if not, as a child. In either case your obligation ends if the government abuses its power or ceases to be a legitimate authority. And what defines a legitimate authority? Why, consent, of course. Then we are all of us obligated to obey a government based on our consent, whether or not we have consented to it.

Though he never makes it explicit, the position that Tussman really seems to want to take is that we are all obligated to obey a government based on the consent *of the aware elite*, the true members, whether or not we ourselves have consented. A government is legitimate when those who are aware consent to it, and it then becomes legitimate for *all* its subjects; a government is tyrannical if it lacks this consent of the aware ones, or oversteps the limits of it. And then *all* its former subjects are released from their obligation. Some evidence for the contention that this is what Tussman means to say may be drawn from his treatment of the child's obligation. For he says, 'Non-consenting adult citizens are, in effect, like minors who are governed without *their own* consent.'

But again Tussman fails to tell us who does consent for minors, how and why the consent of some can legitimately be taken to bind others. Thus saying that the aware few consent for the rest is by no means a satisfactory answer, but from it I believe a more satisfactory answer can be reached by one further step. We must ask Tussman whether the aware few *could conceivably* consent to a tyranny, whether such consent would *count*, would be binding on them or the clods. I think clearly Tussman would want to say no, that such an action would not be a genuine consent, that an attempt to consent to tyranny does not create valid obligation either for the aware few or for the many clods for whom they are said to act. Thus a different doctrine begins to emerge between the lines of Tussman's book, as it did with Locke. It is not so much your consent nor even the consent of a majority of the aware few in your society that obligates you. You do not consent to be obligated, but rather are obligated to consent, if the government is just. Your obligation has something to do with the objective characteristics of the government – whether, for example, its 'tribunals' are or are not 'corrupt'. Again the relevant consent seems to be best interpreted as hypothetical or constructive – the abstract consent that would be given by rational men. Like Locke, Tussman can be pushed back to this position: you are obligated neither by your own consent nor by that of the majority, but by the consent rational men in a hypothetical 'state of nature' would have to give. A government acting within the bounds of such a hypothetical consent is legitimate and we are all obligated to obey it. A government systematically violating those limits is tyrannical, and we are free to resist it.

Both Locke's and Tussman's argument, then lead us to a somewhat surprising new doctrine: that your obligation to obey depends not on any special relationship (consent) between you and your government, but on the nature of that government itself. If it is a good, just government doing what a government should, then you must obey it; if it is a tyrannical, unjust government trying to do what no government should, then you have no such obligation. In one sense this 'nature of the government' theory is thus a substitute for the doctrine of consent. But it may also be regarded as a new interpretation of consent theory, what we may call the doctrine of *hypothetical* consent. For a legitimate government, a true authority, one whose subjects are obligated to obey it, emerges as being one to which they *ought to consent*, quite apart from whether they have done so. Legitimate government acts within the limits of the authority rational men would, abstractly and hypothetically, have to give a government they are founding. Legitimate government is government which *deserves* consent.

I do not mean to suggest that the 'nature of the government' theory which thus emerges is really Locke's and Tussman's secret doctrine, which they hide from the casual reader and which has only now been unearthed. Probably neither of them saw that his argument was moving in this direction. Rather I suggest that this theory is a better response to the problem of political obligation from their own premises – that it is the truth toward which they were striving, but which they saw only indistinctly. Only in that sense is it 'what they really meant to say', and of course both of them also say other things incompatible with it.

IV The Theory Applied

Our new doctrine seems most obviously satisfactory as a response to question three, concerning the difference between legitimate authority and mere coercion. For it teaches that legitimate authority is precisely that which *ought* to be obeyed, to which one ought to consent, which deserves obedience and consent, to which rational men considering all relevant facts and issues would consent, to which consent can be justified. Anything or anyone else who tries to command us is then merely coercing, and is not entitled to our obedience. This answer to the question is essentially what Wittgenstein calls a 'point of grammar'; it reminds us of the way concepts like 'authority', 'legitimacy', 'law' are related in our language (and therefore in our world) to concepts like 'consent' and 'obedience'.[6] To call something a legitimate authority is

[6] Ludwig Wittgenstein, *Philosophical Investigations* (Oxford, Blackwell and New York, Macmillan, 1953). See also Stanley Louis Cavell, 'The Claim to Rationality' (Unpublished Ph.D. dissertation, Harvard University, 1961), esp. Chapter I.

normally to imply that it ought to be obeyed. You cannot, without further rather elaborate explanation, maintain simultaneously *both* that this government has legitimate authority over you *and* that you have no obligation to obey it. Thus if you say that you consent to it (recognize it as an authority), that statement itself is normally a recognition of the obligation to obey, at least at the moment it is uttered. Part of what 'authority' means is that those subject to it are obligated to obey. As an answer to question three, then, this doctrine tells us (something about) what legitimate authority *is* by reminding us of something about what 'legitimate authority' *means*. But of course that is not yet to provide criteria for telling apart the two species – legitimate authority and mere coercion – when you encounter them in reality.

Thus, insofar as our *real* need is for a practical way of deciding whether to obey or resist this government right now, or which of two rival authorities to follow, our new theory seems less adequate. Its response to our question three does not seem immediately helpful with questions one and two; and surely those are of the most concern to real people confronted with decisions about action. It just does not seem very helpful to tell a man considering resistance to authority: you must obey if the government is such that you ought to obey. But neither is traditional consent theory very helpful to this man; indeed, one of its weaknesses has always been this matter of detailed application. Perhaps it is even a mistake to assume that a theory of political obligation is supposed to tell a man directly what to do in particular cases.[7]

One might argue, however, that such a theory should at least tell him what sorts of considerations are relevant to his decision, direct his attention and tell him where to look.[8] And in that regard, I suggest that traditional consent theory is defective, for it directs such a man's attention to the wrong place. It teaches him to look at himself (for his own consent) or at the people around him (for theirs), rather than at the merits of the government. Where it demands obedience, consent theory does so on the grounds that he or the majority have consented; where it justifies resistance, it does so on the grounds that consent was never given or has been exceeded. Thus the man who must choose is directed to the question: have I (we) consented to this? The new doctrine formulated in this essay seems at least to have the virtue of pointing such a man in the right direction. For it tells him: look to the nature of the government

---

[7] See, for example, Margaret Macdonald, 'The Language of Political Theory', in A. Flew, ed., *Logic and Language: First Series* (Oxford: Basil Blackwell, 1960), pp. 167–186.

[8] This suggestion is advanced, against Miss Macdonald's argument in Benn and Peters, pp. 299–301.

– its characteristics, structure, activities, functioning. This is not much of a guide, but it is a beginning much more usefully related to what men need to think about when they make such choices.

Let us consider seriously what sorts of things people really think about when they confront a genuine decision about obedience and resistance, and what sorts of things they ought to think about. But anyone who undertakes to do that is immediately overwhelmed by the complexity and multiplicity of what seems relevant, and by the many different imaginable cases. We need to consider a list of specific cases at least as diverse as these:

Socrates, as presented in the *Crito* and the *Apology*.
An ordinary criminal.
An American student engaging in civil disobedience.
A Mississippi Negro who decides to join a revolutionary group.
A South African Negro who decides to join a revolutionary group.
A minor official in Nazi Germany, who continues to carry out his functions.

Even a brief review of such cases teaches at least this much: the occasions for contemplating and possibly engaging in disobedience are extremely varied; and a great many kinds of non-obedience are available, from flight through crime to attempted revolution.[9] Some forms of non-obedience are violent, others not; some are personal and others organized; some are isolated actions and others a systematic programme of action; some are directed against a particular law or decree and others against an entire system of government. To a person confronted with a real decision about resistance or obedience, it makes an enormous difference what kind of action is contemplated. Circumstances that may justify escape or isolated refusal to obey a particular law may not suffice to justify revolution; indeed, some forms of resistance (like civil disobedience) may even be provided for within a political system.

Next, we may notice that all of our examples are, or could reasonably be, people in conflict. Socrates may never have been in doubt as to what he would do, but his friends certainly disagreed with him at first; and he cast his own argument in the form of a confrontation between the desire 'to play truant' and the admonitions of the laws. All of our examples (with the exception of the criminal?) might have good, serious reasons for resistance. None of them ought to feel entirely free to pursue those reasons without first weighing them against something else – his *prima facie* obligation to obey. One might say: all these men ought

[9] Something like this point is suggested by Tussman, *op. cit.*, p. 43.

to feel a certain tie to their governments, their societies, in the sense in which Socrates feels such a tie, but some of them might nevertheless be justified in disobeying or resisting. That he does not sufficiently feel such a tie, that he has no (good) reason, no justification for disobedience, is precisely what makes the case of an 'ordinary' criminal different from the rest. This is at least in accord with the formula offered by our new theory: normally law, authority, government are to be obeyed and resistance requires justification. You are not morally free to resist as a matter of whim.

The real person confronted by a problematic situation about obedience needs to know that, but he obviously needs to know much more. He needs to know much more specifically when resistance is justified and what might count as a justification. Does he learn this by thinking about his own past consent or that of his fellow-citizens, as traditional consent theory would suggest? Or does he learn it by assessing the nature and quality of the government?

Our cases of potential disobedience show an interesting division in this respect. Three of them – the student and the two Negroes – seem quite unlikely to think much about their own past consent – when and whether they consented, how often and how seriously, expressly or tacitly, and so on. What they are likely to think about is the 'outrageous' conduct and 'oppressive, unjust' structure of the government, and of the possible consequences of resistance. The criminal (since we have defined him as 'ordinary') is not likely to think about either obligations to obey or justifications for his action. The Nazi might well cite his consent to the Fuehrer, his oath of office, pledges of absolute obedience despite 'certain unpleasant government measures that perhaps ought not to have been taken'. And Socrates is passionately aware of his ties to the Athenian laws, the gratitude he owes them for past favours, the power of his past consent to them.

Thus both Socrates and the Nazi do seem to look to past consent rather than to the nature of the government. But the significance of this fact has yet to be assessed; for on closer examination, each of their cases reveals an important weakness in traditional consent theory. From the case of the Nazi we can learn that even express consent may not be enough; and from that of Socrates, the difficulties of applying past consent as a guide to action.

It might be tempting to say that of our six cases, only Socrates is truly moral, for only he thinks about his obligations and commitments to the laws. But the example of the Nazi saves us from this simplistic response, by showing that sometimes past promises and oaths are not enough to determine present obligations. Sometimes a man who cites even an express oath to obedience, is being not admirable but hypocritical, refusing to recognize where his real duty lies. We would not want to say that past oaths and promises count for nothing, that they can be ignored at will. We all feel the power of the argument that you ought to be consistent, that it isn't fair to pick up your marbles and go home just because it's your turn to lose under the rules you have accepted so far. But that is partly because such a partisan assessment of the rules is likely to be biased. If you can in fact show that the rules are really unfair, then any time is a good time to change them. Again, normally rules and authorities are to be obeyed; when occasions for questioning this obligation arise, what is ultimately needed is an assessment of the rules or authorities. Mere reference to your 'going along with them' in the past is not enough.

No doubt if a man had no political obligation he could acquire one by a promise or contract. But that by no means proves that political obligation can be acquired *only* by promise or contract; it may be that a quite independent political obligation is sometimes reinforced by an oath to obey, at other times (partly) countered by a promise to resist. A personal past commitment to obey need not settle the matter.

Indeed, the case of the Nazi calls attention to something traditional consent theory seems to have overlooked: the duty to resist. There are times in human history when men are not merely free(d) from an obligation to obey, but positively obligated to oppose the powers that be. The authors of the Declaration of Independence recognized this, despite their heavy reliance on Locke; for they saw resistance to tyranny not merely as man's right but as his duty. Locke, and traditional consent theory in general, make no provision for such a duty, nor can it be easily accommodated within their framework. There is provision in Locke's system for majority resistance to a tyrannical government, and a duty to follow such a majority. But *individual* resistance has a highly ambiguous status at best, and is certainly *not* a duty. For if political obligation arises from contract, the violation or overstepping of this contract leaves each individual free to do as he likes with regard to the tyranny. True, the individual is still then bound by natural law; but natural law does not command the punishment of offenders, it only permits it. And amending the Lockean system on this score would obviously require fundamental changes in its individualistic presuppositions.

Similarly, traditional consent theory teaches that at times of civil war or successful revolution, when an old authority structure collapses, each individual is free to place his consent anew wherever he wishes and thinks best for himself. If he thinks fit to follow a highway robber then, he is free to do so. But when we contemplate real cases, would we not rather want to maintain that even in chaos there is responsibility, that even then the individual has some obligation to think of others as well as himself, the welfare of society or mankind as well as his own?

It seems that insufficient attention has been given to the failure of traditional consent theory to provide for any obligation to resist, or any obligation to choose responsibly when new authorities must be chosen. Indeed, divine right, prescription and utilitarianism can accommodate such obligations far more easily than a contract theory can. As for the 'nature of the government' or 'hypothetical consent' doctrine developed in this essay, it too would presumably require amendment on this score. An enlarged version might hold: your obligation is to obey what deserves obedience and consent, and to resist what deserves resistance and rejection (leaving the important possibility that many persons or agencies deserve neither obedience nor resistance). But it is not obvious to me whether the obligation to resist tyranny should be construed as a part of political obligation at all, or as an occasional alternative to it. The question seems related to that of whether revolution is a special part of political life or a breakdown of the political.

V The Case of Socrates

Though the Nazi may continue to obey on the grounds that he has sworn to do so, we may find that he thereby fails to perform his true obligations. Why, then, does Socrates' position – equally founded on past personal consent – strike us as so exemplary and moral? I would suggest that the distinguishing thing about Socrates' situation is this: he can find no fault with the Athenian laws, nor even with the Athenian way of administering them. Only his own particular conviction and sentence are (almost fortuitously) unjust. And his dialogue with the laws is essentially a way of expressing or establishing this fact. Socrates' past consent is not so much compelling in its own right, as it is a way of expressing and reinforcing his present judgment that there is nothing basically wrong with the system, no justification for resistance. What amazes us about him is not this judgment, nor the refusal to accept a single case of injustice as a justification for disobedience. These are relatively ordinary positions to take. What amazes us about him is that he construes disobedience so widely, to include even flight; and that he is willing to perform his obligation down to the minutest detail, even at the cost of his life.[10]

[10] Plato, *Crito* [50]: 'are you not going by an act of yours to

The suggestion is, then, that Socrates' focus on his past acceptance of the laws and his gratitude to them is in fact an evaluation of the Athenian government (or the expression of such an evaluation). We need to recall that this same moral Socrates refused to carry out an 'authoritative' order given him in the time of the Thirty Tyrants, because it was unjust, and would apparently have refused to carry out injustice voted by a democratic majority as well.[11] In those earlier situations, one may suppose, what Socrates thought about was the injustice of what he had been ordered to do, and of those who issued the order, not his own (tacit?) consent to them.

To this line of argument a traditional consent theorist might respond: Socrates looks to his own past consent in order to find and determine its limits, in order to see whether this new governmental action does not exceed what he had consented to. But if we take that seriously as a model of what the moral man must do when he contemplates resistance, we set him an extremely difficult task. How is Socrates to know *to what* he has consented, particularly if his consent has been tacit? Surely it is not enough to say that he has consented only to those precise things the government did in the past, so that any new or unprecedented action is automatically *ultra vires*. But if not that, then to what does one give tacit consent? Is it to the particular people then in authority, or to the authority of the office they hold, or to the laws that define and limit that office, or to the body that makes those laws, or to the Constitution that lays down rules and procedures for the making of laws, or to the principles behind that Constitution, or to the fellow-members of the society, or even to all of mankind? In particular cases, these various foci of loyalty may come into conflict; then knowing that one has consented to them all at a time when they were in agreement is no help for deciding what to do.

In short, though two of our examples do look to their own past consent in deciding what to do, one of them thereby fails to perform his true obligation, and the other seems to be using the language of consent to express a favourable assessment of the government. Furthermore, we have noted at least two disadvantages of personal consent as a criterion: the difficulty of knowing *to what* you have consented (especially if consent was tacit), and the fact that even an express oath to obey may sometimes be outweighed by an obligation to resist.

Besides an individual's personal consent, traditional consent theory offers as an alternative criterion the 'consent of the governed', the consent

---

overturn us – the laws, and the whole state, as far as in you lies?' Jowett translation.

[11] Plato, *Apology*, 32.

of all, or a majority of one's fellow-citizens. Of such consent, too, we would have to say that it cannot simply be dismissed as irrelevant. Even our Negro in Mississippi or South Africa might think about how widely shared his grievances are. But again, the consent or dissent of the majority cannot by itself be decisive for defining your obligation. Majorities are sometimes wrong, and have been known to do evil. Resistance might be justified in Athens under the Thirty Tyrants or in Nazi Germany despite the majority.

But majority consent does enter the argument at another level, in a way quite different from the relevance of personal consent. Majority consent may be relevant as a *way* of assessing, as *evidence about* the nature of the government, given that the nature of the government bears on political obligation. In fact, a variety of considerations each of which we might want to call 'consent of the governed' can be used in the process of evaluating a government. They may come into conflict with each other, and their relative weight and importance will be a matter of one's political values, of what kind of government he thinks desirable or even tolerable.

It is useful to distinguish here between the 'procedural' criteria yielded by the consent of the governed for assessing a government, and the 'substantive' ones. Procedural criteria are those which concern the institutional structure and political functioning of the government, the way in which it makes decisions and takes actions. To assess its nature, we want to know about the way a government functions in relation to the governed – whether it is responsive to them or forces its policies on them. Thus we look for machinery for the expression of popular desires; we look for the degree of popular participation in or control over decisions, for channels for the redress of grievances, for access to power. At the same time we look also for signs of repression, of propaganda, of coercion. We look, of course, not merely at the institutions defined on paper, but at their actual functioning in the largest social sense. Denial of suffrage to Negroes in South Africa is very different from denial of suffrage to women in Switzerland (and theorists would do well to think about why this is so). But roughly speaking, a government is likely to seem to us deserving if it is open to the governed, reprehensible if it rules them against their will. This general criterion may well be expressed by some formula like 'the consent of the governed'; but that formula must not be taken too simply, and that criterion must not be regarded as our only one.

Besides this vague cluster of procedural criteria, we have in addition substantive ones. We may look also at the substance of what the government does – whether it pursues good, benevolent, justifiable policies. A government that systematically harms its subjects, whether out of misguided good intentions or simply for the selfish gain of the rulers, is to that extent illegitimate – even if the subjects do not know it, even if they 'consent' to being abused. But even here 'the consent of the governed' is *relevant* as important evidence, for one of the main ways we estimate whether people are being well treated is by whether they seem to like what they get. Only we may sometimes need to consider other evidence as well; the consent or dissent of the governed need not be decisive as to the goodness or justness of a government's policies.

It is the relationship between at least these two kinds of criteria that is likely to determine our assessment of a government, whether it deserves support or opposition. Thus we may all agree that a government pursuing very bad policies and forcing them on its subjects, so that it is obviously doing great harm to them and other countries, and doing so despite their attempts at protest and without their consent – such a government clearly is the occasion for resistance. Conversely, if we find a government that truly has the consent of its subjects although they have wide sources of information and true opportunities to dissent and criticize, and if that government pursues only the most praiseworthy policies, then few of us would urge revolution or resistance to it. The problematic cases are, of course, the ones in between, where procedure and substance are partly good, partly bad, and you need to make evaluations and decisions. Here it begins to be a matter of your metapolitics – how you think of men and societies, what positions you are willing to take and defend, and take responsibility for.

Suppose, for example, that a government is procedurally open, with genuine channels for controlling policy from below, but it engages in vicious policies. Then, one might want to say, the citizen is not free to engage in revolution; he has channels available and it is his duty to use them, to change the policy. But what if he tries to do so, and fails because the majority continues to approve of the wickedness? What if he is a member of a permanent minority group, being systematically abused and exploited by an eager, consenting majority? Then the seemingly open channels of consent are not truly open to him. Might there not come a point when violent minority resistance of some sort is justified?

Or suppose that a government is benevolent, so no one can criticize its actions, but in procedure it is simply autocratic and dictatorial. Is revolution justified against a benevolent dictatorship? This might be the case, for example, if men need political participation in order to be really well, in order to reach their full human potential. Then bad procedure would itself become a substantive grievance.

The theoretical complications possible here are legion, but at least this much seems clear: evaluating a government in order to decide whether it deserves obedience or resistance, requires attention both to the way it works and to what it does. In both cases something like consent is relevant; it may be a formula for expressing some rather complex requirements concerning opportunities for dissent and participation, or it may be evidence of good policies. Thus even if we adhere to the doctrine of hypothetical consent or the nature of government, majority consent may still be relevant in a subordinate capacity for assessing a government, for working out more detailed answers to our questions one and two about consent, the specific practical 'when' and 'whom' of obedience. But here 'the consent of the governed' is not one simple thing, decisive for obligation; rather, it is relevant in a number of different, potentially conflicting ways.

And all of these ways put together differ, in turn, not merely from personal consent, but also from the doctrine of hypothetical consent developed in this essay.[12] That legitimate authority is such that one ought to consent to it, is a precept built into English grammar, into the meanings of these terms. That a legitimate government is one which has the consent of (a majority of) the governed – is procedurally responsive to them or looks after their interests, or both – is one particular position about what kind of government is desirable for men. More accurately, it is a cluster of positions, depending on the relative weight given to procedural and substantive criteria. Though these positions are very widely shared today, and though they were shared by almost all traditional consent theorists, they are not the only conceivable positions on this subject. Someone might undertake to argue, for example, that a government is legitimate only to the extent that it fosters high culture, or to the extent that it promotes the evolution of a master race. That would be to reject majority consent as any sort of criterion for assessing a government. But the doctrine of hypothetical consent holds even for someone taking such an unorthodox position; even for him, a legitimate government would be the one that deserves consent, to which everyone ought to consent. Both the philosophical weakness and the historical persistence and strength of traditional consent theory rests in its failure to distinguish these very different arguments.

Finally, even if we succeed in evaluating a government, that does not seem fully to settle how we must behave toward it. One final, important consideration seems relevant: the action taken must be appropriate. To the diversity of ways in which one can obey or support, resist or overthrow a government, there correspond a diversity of conditions when

[12] For the former distinction, compare Benn and Peters, pp. 329–331.

the various actions may be appropriate or justified. The fact that some action is justified, that some abuse has taken place, does not mean that just any action will do. A man mistreated by his superior may kick his dog. We can understand, and perhaps even sympathize, but surely the action is not justified. Not just any violation of law will qualify as civil disobedience or attempted revolution. This observation is presumably related to the traditional assertion of consent theorists, that it is necessary to 'exhaust the remedies' available, to suffer 'a long train of abuses' before violent resistance is justified. Where other actions are appropriate, revolution may not be called for.

Thus it begins to seem that a decision about obedience and resistance ought to be measured not merely against the character of the government, but against all the relevant social circumstances – what alternatives one can envision, and what consequences resistance is likely to have. Revolution would not seem justified, for example, if one had no hope of its being followed by an improvement in conditions. If it would simply substitute one tyranny for another, or if it would annihilate the human race through the resulting violence, then it does not seem justified.[13]

But a doctrine that casts its net so wide, making all social circum-

[13] One difficulty of this discussion is that it seems to make human decisions look excessively rational. Are any abstract principles of this kind really relevant to what real people think about when they must decide? Is a man on the point of rebellion or revolution not much more likely to be moved by strong emotion – by an overwhelming anger or sense of outrage?

But I would like to suggest that the human capcity for outrage is, as it were, the emotional correlate to rational moral principles. It is our inner, helpless response to a violation of principles of right and wrong, as we sense them, perhaps quite inarticulately. Outrage (unlike mere anger), is an emotion of principle. I take it that this is what Albert Camus means when he insists that 'the act of rebellion is not, essentially, an egoistic act', even though it can, 'of course' have 'egoistic motives'. *The Rebel*, p. 16. The rebel, the man who acts from a sense of outrage, says not merely 'I don't want to put up with this', but 'No man ought to have to put up with this'. And by feeling 'no man ought . . .' he acts, in a sense on principle.

Of course a man's feeling that his situation is outrageous is one thing; whether the situation is in fact outrageous is another. A three-year-old may feel outraged at not being allowed to drink the detergent. We may sympathize with his feelings, but cannot condone the resulting violence. Not every feeling of outrage is a valid assessment of the world; but then, not every rational judgment that the limits of contractual obligation have been exceeded is valid either. No doubt rational judgments are more likely to be right; that is one advantage of rationality.

stances at least potentially relevant, that sees both an obligation to obey and an obligation to resist, and that stresses so much the individual burden of decision, seems very close to the social utilitarianism examined in the first part of this essay. It seems to say, with the social utilitarian, you are obligated to obey when that is best on the whole for society (all of mankind?), and obligated to resist when *that* is best on the whole. But that formula, and social utilitarianism, seem to neglect again the obligatory nature of law and authority in normal circumstances, the *prima facie* obligation to obey. Being subject to law, government, authority means precisely an obligation (normally) to do what *they* say is best, rather than judge the welfare of society for yourself and act on your private judgment. Yet there are times when you must resist in the name of something very like the welfare of society. Whether these two positions are compatible remains somehow problematic; but before we can make a final stab at the matter, we must finish applying our new doctrine to our four questions about political obligation.

VI *Justifying Political Obligation*

We come now to question four, the matter of justification: 'why are you ever obligated to obey even legitimate authority?' Here again our 'nature of the government' doctrine does not at first seem a very useful answer. For it can only say: because of the nature of the government, because the government is such that you ought to obey it and consent to it, because a rational man would do so. But that answer is not likely to still the question. For someone genuinely puzzled about obligation in this (philosophical) way is likely to persist: 'how does that "ought" bind me, *why* must I do what a rational man would do, what if I don't *want* to be rational?'

But the reader may have noticed by now that all of the theories and versions of theories we have considered are subject to this same difficulty to some extent. Some seem better designed to cope with it than others; yet we can always push the question further back: why must I do what God commands, why must I do what history teaches, why must I do what is best for me personally, why must I do what I have promised? Even traditional consent theory is liable to this difficulty; and it is remarkable that despite Hume's early criticism, we continue to believe in consent theory while ignoring this problem. For Hume had already told the consent theorist:

> You find yourself embarrassed when it is asked, *Why are we*

bound to keep our word? Nor can you give any answer but what would, immediately, without any circuit, have accounted for our obligation to allegiance.

The obligation to keep one's word is no more 'natural' and self-evident and indubitable than political obligation itself; though either may sometimes reinforce the other, neither can give the other absolute justification. The two obligations are essentially separate and equal in status.[14] Why, then, does the traditional consent theorist, so doubtful about the validity of political obligation, take the obligation of keeping contracts as obvious? Why, if he imagines a state of nature, is it always stripped of political authority but inevitably equipped with a natural law that dictates the keeping of one's word? Hume uses these questions as a rhetorical device to attack consent theory, but they can also be taken seriously as a way of learning something more about the consent theorist.

For a theorist does not choose his beliefs and his doubts. The traditional consent theorist simply finds himself in doubt about (the justification of, or limits of, or validity of) political obligation; it just seems obvious to him that there is a problem about it. And he simply is not in doubt about promises or contracts; it just seems obvious to him that they oblige.

At one level one can argue that both the consent theorist's doubt and his assumption spring from the peculiar picture of man and society he seems to hold. If your picture of man in the abstract is of a man fully grown, complete with his own private needs, interests, feelings, desires, beliefs and values, and if you therefore never think about how he grew up and became the particular person he became, then he may well seem to you an ineluctably *separate* unit, his ties to other individuals may seem mysterious or illusory and will require explanation. Given man as such a separate, self-contained unit, it does indeed seem strange that he might have obligations not of his own choosing, perhaps even without being aware of them, or even against his will. Furthermore, self-assumed

---

[14] This assertion is not about the relative claims that the two obligations – political obedience and promise-keeping – have on us, where they come into conflict. It seems obvious to me that no single, binding principle could be found to govern such a question. There are occasions when a vitally important promise is clearly a more important obligation than obedience to some minor law; on the other hand, the keeping of a minor promise is no excuse whatsoever for treason. But the assertion that the two obligations are separate and equal is not meant to bear on this question. It is meant only to say: there is no reason to suppose that promising is more 'natural' or basic than obeying authority, and hence no reason to derive the latter from the former.

obligations may then strike you as a way of overcoming this separateness. For it is easy to confuse the fact that promises and contracts are self-assumed, with the idea that the *obligation to keep* them is self-assumed as well. That is, the person who makes a promise seems to recognize and commit himself to the institution of promises; the person who makes a contract seems to acknowledge thereby the binding character of contracts, so that a later refusal to accept them as binding strikes one as a kind of self-contradiction. But of course this is a confusion. The making of particular promises or contracts presupposes the social institution of promising or contracts, and the obligation to keep promises cannot itself be founded on a promise.

In truth, there is something profoundly wrong with the consent theorist's picture of man. Every free, separate, adult, consenting individual was first shaped and moulded by his parents and (as we say) society. It is only as a result of their influence that he becomes the particular person he does become, with his particular interests, values, desires, language and obligations. The only thing truly separate about us is our bodies; our selves are manifestly social. But surely even the consent theorist knows this, so the problem becomes why he nevertheless holds, or is held captive by, a different and peculiar picture. Could that picture be not so much the cause as the by-product of his philosophical doubt?

After all, consent theorists are not the only ones troubled about political obligation. Political theorists of other persuasions have also been led, or have led themselves sometimes to ask 'why are you ever obligated to obey even legitimate authority?' But if none of the theories of political obligation is able to deal adequately with that question, it must be quite peculiar, not nearly as straightforward as it looks. Perhaps it is a question that cannot be fully answered in the ordinary way. But what sort of question is that; and if it cannot be answered, how should it be treated? Tussman rejects it as a sympton of 'moral disorder'; I would suggest instead that it is a symptom of philosophical disorder, the product of a philosophical paradox. If so, it will not disappear – the theorist will not stop being bothered by it – unless we can show how and why it arises, why anyone should so much as suppose that political obligation in general needs (or can have) a general justification. But that would require a discussion of the nature of philosophical puzzlement far beyond the scope of this essay.

What can be done here is something much more limited and less effective. Having suggested that the status of political obligation and of the obligation to keep promises is essentially the same – that neither is more 'natural' than or can serve as an absolute justification for the other –

we can approach our question four about political obligation by first pursuing a parallel question about promises. For in the area of promises some extremely useful work has been done in philosophy in recent years – work which can be applied to the problem of political obligation.[15]

Philosophers have sometimes asked a question like our question four about promises: 'why are you (ever) obligated to keep (any of) your promises (whatsoever): why do promises oblige?' This question, too, can be answered in terms of divine commandment or utilitarian consequences, social or individual; and here, too, the answers are less than satisfactory. 'God commands you to keep your word' is no answer to the non-believer, nor to someone heretical enough to demand proof of God's will. The utilitarian response tends to dissolve the obligation altogether, so that your duty is always to do what produces the best results, quite apart from whether you have made any promises on the subject. And, of course, a consent argument is out of the question here ('you have promised to keep your promises'?).

What has been suggested by philosophers is this: 'promise' is not just a word. Promising is a social practice, something we *do*, something children have to learn *how* to do. It has rules, penalties, roles and moves almost in the way that games have them. Children do not learn what a promise is by having one pointed out to them; they learn gradually about what it means to 'make a promise', 'keep (or break) a promise', 'be unable to promise but certainly intend to try', 'have said something which, in the circumstances, amounted to a promise', and so on. Promising is not just producing certain sounds ('I promise'), for a phonograph might make those sounds, or a man rehearsing a play, or a philosopher explaining the practice, yet none of these would actually be promising. Promising, rather, is taking on an obligation. That is, 'to promise' does not mean 'to make certain sounds', but rather 'to take on an obligation'.

Now, of course, we do not always do what we have promised. Sometimes we act contrary to our obligations, and sometimes we are wholly or partly excused from performing what we had promised. If for example, keeping a promise would frustrate the purpose for which it was made, or would lead to great evil, or has become impossible, we

---

[15] See particularly J. L. Austin, *Philosophical Papers* (Oxford: Clarendon, 1961), chs. 3, 6 and 10; John Rawls, 'Two Concepts of Rules', *Philosophical Review*, LXIV (January, 1955), 3–32; and S. L. Cavell, 'Must We Mean What We Say?' in V. C. Chappell, *Ordinary Language* (Englewood Cliffs, N.J.: Prentice-Hall, 1964), esp. pp. 94–101.

may be excused from performing. So about any particular promise we have made it may sometimes be relevant to ask: am I still obligated to perform or not? That is, normally, in principle promises oblige; a promise is a certain kind of obligation. But sometimes, under certain circumstances, there is reason to question or withdraw or cancel that obligation in a particular case. In such circumstances we weigh the alternatives, the possible consequences of performance and failure to perform. But our obligations, including that of the promise, continue to be among the factors that must be weighed in the decision. The obligation of a promise does not simply disappear when there is occasion to question it; it only is sometimes outweighed.

But philosophers are sometimes led to wonder *categorically*, about *all* promises: do they oblige; what are the reasons pro and con; why am I ever obligated to keep any promise? And here, of course, there are no *particular* circumstances to weigh in the balance; the question is abstract and hypothetical. What sort of answer is possible to this question? First, that this is what a promise *is*, what 'promise' means. A promise is a self-assumed obligation. If you *assume* an obligation and have not yet performed it, nor been excused from it, then you *have* an obligation; in much the same way as someone who puts on a coat, has a coat on.[16] To ask why promises oblige is to ask why (self-assumed) obligations oblige. And to the question why obligations oblige the only possible answer would seem to be that this is what the words mean.

Beyond this one can only paraphrase Wittgenstein: there are a hundred reasons; there is no reason. There is no absolute, deductive answer to the question 'why does any promise ever oblige?' beyond calling attention to the meaning of the words. There is no absolute, indubitable principle from which the obligation can be deduced. It is, to be sure related to any number of other principles, obligations and values; but the relationship is more like a network (or patchwork) than like a hierarchical pyramid. It is simply a mistake to suppose that there might be such an absolute principle, such a deductive proof. We have no right to expect one. (Why, then, does the philosopher expect one; why can we ourselves be led to share his expectation when we are in a 'philosophical mood'?)

John Rawls has pointed out that utilitarianism will not do as a criterion for the keeping of particular promises – as a standard for *when* promises oblige. To say 'keep your promises only when that maximizes pleasure and minimizes pain' is to miss precisely the *obligatory* nature of a promise; having once promised you are not free to decide what to do

[16] Compare Cavell, 'Must we mean what we say?' *op. cit.*, pp. 96, 99.

merely on utilitarian grounds. But, Rawls says, utilitarian considerations *are* relevant at a different level of argument, for assessing the social practice of promising. For we can ask 'must be (should we) have an institution like promising and promise-keeping at all?' And here utilitarian reasons seem relevant; we may try to justify the social practice by its useful consequences.

Stanley Cavell has argued that this implies a degree of freedom of choice on our parts which we do not in fact have.[17] To evaluate the practice of promising pro and con, we would have to envision alternatives. And how shall we envision a society which knows no obligation to keep one's word? (For it is not, of course, the particular English locution 'I promise' that is being assessed, but the practice of assuming obligations and holding people to their word.) We seem to have no choice about the pros and cons of such an institution. It is not socially useful; it is indispensable to the very concept of society and human life.

But even if we could and did evaluate as Rawls suggests, and 'decide' that the institution of promising is on balance socially useful, even this would not provide an absolute justification for the keeping of particular promises. For what are we to answer the man who says: 'granted that we must have the practice of promising, and granted promising means taking on an obligation; still, why am *I* obliged to keep my promise? Why can't *I* be an exception?' To him we can only say, that is how obligation and promises work. Of course you *can* refuse to keep your promise, but then you are failing to perform an obligation.

Now the same line of reasoning can be applied to the question 'why does even a legitimate government, a valid law, a genuine authority ever obligate me to obey?' As with promises, and as our new doctrine about political obligation suggests, we may say that this is what 'legitimate government', 'valid law', 'genuine authority' *mean*. It is part of the concept, the meaning of 'authority' that those subject to it are required to obey, that it has a right to command. It is part of the concept, the meaning of 'law', that those to whom it is applicable are obligated to obey it. As with promises, so with authority, government and law: there is a *prima facie* obligation involved in each, and normally you must perform it. Normally a man is not free to decide on utilitarian grounds whether or not he will do a certain thing, if that thing happens to be against the law or required by law; he is not free to make a decision on his own the way he would be free where the law is silent. The existence of the law on this subject normally constitutes an obligation, just as having promised normally constitutes an obligation, so that one is not

[17] 'The Claim to Rationality', Chapter VIII.

free to decide what to do just as if no promise had been made. (This is not, of course, to say that everything claiming to be law is law, that everyone claiming to have authority has it, that every statement alleged to be a promise is in fact one. It says only: *if* something is a promise, law, obligation, *then* normally it obliges.) This kind of response to question four is obviously almost the same as the one our doctrine of hypothetical consent yielded to question three: government and authority are concepts grammatically related to obligation and obedience. A legitimate government is one that you ought to obey and ought to consent to because that is what the words mean. But as before, this answer is likely to seem purely formal, and empty. It will not satisfy someone genuinely puzzled about the justification of political obligation.

But as with promises, all that one can say beyond calling attention to the meanings of the words, is that no absolute, deductive justification exists or is necessary. There are no absolute first principles from which this obligation could be derived. It is related to all kinds of other obligations in all kinds of ways, to be sure, but the relationship is not hierarchical and deductive. In particular, as we have seen, the obligatory nature of promises is no more or no less absolute and indubitable than the obligation to obey laws. Again, following Rawls' suggestion, one might attempt a utilitarian assessment of such institutions or practices as law, government and authority. And here, I suppose, there may be somewhat more room for discussion than with promises. For it is not at all obvious that government and law are indispensable to human social life. But can we conceive society without any such thing as authority? One function of the idea of the state of nature in classical consent theories does seem to be a kind of indirect demonstration of the utilitarian advantages of having governments and laws. If such things did not exist, Locke seems to argue, we would have to invent them. It is significant, in this respect, that consent theorists so often speak of contracts or covenants, rather than simple promises or oaths. For of course the idea of a contract or covenant implies that you get something in return for the obligation you take on, and in a way at least suggest the informal additional ties of gratitude. But there are other differences as well, a contract being more formal and usually more explicit than a promise.

But as with promises, even a recognition of the necessity or utilitarian advantages of such things as authority, law and government is no absolute answer to the man who is questioning his particular obligation to obey, who wants to be an exception. There is no such absolute answer, and can be none. Nothing we say is absolutely beyond question. Again, you *can* disobey but in the absence of excuses or justifications you violate an obligation when you do so.

The parallel between promises and authority as obligations is not perfect. For one thing, promises are explicitly taken on oneself; political obligation (I have argued) need not be. Furthermore, promises are normally made to particular persons, whereas political obligation is sometimes confounded by our question two, by the problem of rival authorities. We have noted the difficulty of determining to whom or what consent is given: particular officials, their position, the laws, the Constitution, the people of the society. This means, among other things, that political obligation is open to a kind of challenge not normally relevant to promises. We saw that, following Rawls, both promises and political obligation can be challenged at two very different levels: sometimes we may claim to be excused from performing in a particular case (for instance because of conflicting obligations or overwhelming difficulties). And sometimes we may want to challenge and assess the whole institution with the obligations it defines. But in addition, political obligation can be challenged also on a third level. Sometimes we may refuse to obey neither because our particular case is exceptional, nor because we question such obligation categorically, but because the one who is claiming authority over us does not in fact have it. We may resist a government that has become tyrannical not as a special, personal exception, and not because we are against government, but because *this* government no longer deserves obedience. Such a challenge is made on principle, *in accord* (as it were) with the 'rules' of political obligation.

But the differences between promises and political obligation do not affect the point to be made here. That point concerns our question four, the search for a justification for having to obey (or having to keep a promise); and it is essentially twofold. First, we have said, 'authority', 'law', and 'government' are grammatically, conceptually related to obligation, as is 'promise'. And beyond this, the quest for some 'higher', absolute, deductive justification is misguided. Insofar, then, as the grammatical point does not seem to still the question, does not get at what someone philosophically puzzled wants to ask, what is needed is not a better justification, but an account of why the philosopher is driven to ask the question in the first place.

VII *The Duality of Obligation*

As Locke suggests in his preface, the consent theorist's purpose is a dual one. He wants both to show that men are sometimes justified in making revolutions, and to show that men are normally bound to obey governments and laws. And this is, indeed, what must be shown, since both these things are in fact true. The fact is that on one hand men are in some sense above or outside the institutions of their society, its laws, its government. They can measure and judge these institutions. Though they have not themselves made them they can change them; and sometimes even violent change may be justified. On the other hand, men are also part of and subject to their society, bound by its norms and authorities. Not every attempt at revolution is justified.

To say that men are both superior to their government and subject to it is to express a paradox. Because it seems so paradoxical, the traditional social contract theorists saw it instead as a temporal sequence: *first* men were free and could make a commonwealth, *then* they became bound by it (within the limits of a contract). We have seen some of the difficulties that result. Finding an accurate and unparadoxical way to express this paradoxical truth seems to me the most interesting problem connected with political obligation, but it is important to notice that this problem is not confined to political obligation. We are both superior to and subject to *all* our obligations, and *that* is what requires an accounting. Discussing it will reveal one final, rather subtle way in which obligation both is and is not a matter of consent – but all obligation, not just the obligation to obey.

We are familiar enough from ethics with the view of a number of philosophers (notably Kant) that an action is not fully moral unless the actor knows what he is doing and does it for the right reasons. An action done for selfish motives but accidentally producing some charitable result is not (really, fully) a charitable action. A moral action is one taken *because* it is right, on principle. On analogy we might want to say that a man cannot (really, fully) obey an order unless he recognizes that it is an order, that the man issuing it has authority over him. He cannot (really, fully) obey a law or a government unless he recognizes it as valid law or legitimate government; only then will what he does (really, fully) *be* obeying. If I 'order' a leaf to fall from a tree, and the leaf immediately does so, it is not obeying my order; if I silently and secretly 'order' my neighbour to mow his lawn and he does so, he is not (really, fully) obeying my order. Even if he hears and understands what I am saying, he is not (really, fully) obeying me unless he recognizes what I say as an order, considers me as having authority to order him about, and mows his lawn *because* of my order.

Consequently, the capacity for this kind of awareness and intention is a precondition for being fully obligated. This is why leaves cannot be obligated (except in storybooks, where they are anthropomorphized), and children cannot fully do so. It may be right to punish or reward a child, but the child is not yet fully a moral agent capable of recognizing and therefore of having obligations.

It is not difficult to regard this kind of awareness and intention as a form of consenting to one's obligation. If (really, fully) obeying an order presupposes the recognition of it as an order and of the man who issues it as having authority, then surely that recognition resembles a kind of (perhaps tacit) consent to his authority. And then it becomes easy to take a final further step, and say you are not (really, fully) obligated unless you recognize, acknowledge, accept, acquiesce in, consent to that obligation. Such a line of reasoning undoubtedly has heightened the appeal of consent theory for a number of writers, and it clearly is the main basis for Tussman's stress on consent. He chooses agreement rather than force or habit as the nature of political association precisely because,

> 'I have a duty to . . .' seems to follow from 'I have agreed to' in a way that it does not follow from 'I am forced to' or 'I am in the habit of.' This is sometimes expressed as the view that obligations are, or even must be voluntarily assumed.[18]

But even if one accepts these transitions and concludes that obligation in the full moral sense always requires consent, it by no means follows that obligation consists *only* of this inner awareness and intent. For that would imply that anyone failing or refusing to consent for any reason whatsoever is thereby excused from the obligation in question, does not have that obligation, cannot meaningfully be blamed or criticized for failing to perform it.[19] But no major ethical theorist, least of all Kant, would be willing to accept that consequences, any more than Tussman is willing to let the morally unaware clods in society disobey laws whenever they please.

It is necessary to recognize that obligation has not one, but two fundamental aspects – the inner, 'awareness' aspect stressed by Tussman, and an outer aspect having to do with the way others see what we do, how it looks objectively. These two aspects of obligation may be seen as corresponding to two familiar strains in ethical theory: the teleogical, concerned with the consequences of action, and the deontological, concerned with its motives.[20] The former deals primarily in the outer, shared world of facts and events, and takes as fundamental the concept of the *good*; the latter deals primarily in the inner, personal world of thoughts and feelings, and takes as fundamental the concept of *right*. I would suggest,

---
[18] *Op. cit.*, p. 8.
[19] Benn and Peters, p. 322.
[20] This and the next three paragraphs lean heavily on Cavell, 'The Claim to Rationality', p. 323 and all of Part II.

following Cavell, that both are a necessary part of any valid account of morality and obligation, that neither can be ignored outright in assessing action.

Those moral philosophers who have stressed the deontological side of moral appraisal have been concerned particularly with the matter of giving praise: a person does not deserve full credit for an act of charity, of courage, of obedience, unless his intentions were charitable, courageous, obedient. He should not get full credit for an action that merely looks charitable 'from the outside', if his own perception of what he was doing was quite otherwise. To a lesser extent this is also true of blame: you are responsible for the damage you do, no matter how good your intentions were, but good intentions may be a *partial* excuse. Those philosophers who have stressed the teleological orientation of moral appraisal have been more concerned with blame or responsibility, but most particularly with duty. Your duty is not merely to intend good behaviour, but to behave well; the performance and its results are what define your duty.

But in a way this dichotomization – deontology for praise, teleology for duty – misses the point. For the real difficulty is in determining *what* action has been performed, what actually was done. It is naming the action (correctly) that is the problem: was it, should we call it, an act of charity, an act of obedience, considering what took place, considering his intentions? Having put it that way, one wants to say that the two modes of assessment are always both relevant, but not equally relevant to all actions. To the assessment of certain actions, inner intention is much more relevant; to the assessment of others, outer events will seem decisive. Lying is more a matter of inner intent, deceiving more a matter of outward results. Moreover it may be that, in a broader sense, whole categories of action vary in this respect. It may be, for example, that inner awareness is categorically more relevant in face-to-face, personal relationships than in public, political conduct. We do care more about motive and intention in assessing personal relationships and actions – love, anger and forgiveness – than in assessing political actions in the public realm.

If this is so, it deserves more attention than it has received from political theorists. No doubt it has something to do with the fact that in personal morality there is no umpire, no arbiter or judge; it is of the essence of morality that we confront each other directly. In the political, public realm, on the other hand, the normal situation is one where official 'interpreters' are supplied by the society to tell the individual what the law or Constitution says, whether he has or has not committed grand larceny. But what happens at times of resistance or revolution is precisely that these normal official interpreters are themselves called into question. We are both bound by, and yet sometimes free to challenge or change all our obligations; but political obligation has an additional complexity, in that its *content* seems to be a subordination to the judgment of others.

But if normally law and authority oblige and resistance requires justification, and if normally judgment is to some extent subordinated to that of the authorities, and if revolutionary situations are precisely the ones that are not normal in these respects, then the crucial question seems to be: *who is to say?* Who is to say what times are normal and what times are not, when resistance is justified or even obligatory? If we say 'each individual must decide for himself', we seem to deny the normally binding character of law and authority. If we say 'society' or 'the majority' or 'the duly constituted authorities decide', then we seem to deny the right to resist, since it may be the majority or the authorities themselves that need to be challenged. Yet these seem to be the only two alternatives.

The matter is very difficult, though the question seems so simple. This essay will only briefly indicate a direction in which a solution might be sought. What needs to be said seems to be this: the decision both is and is not up to each individual. Each individual does and must ultimately decide for himself and is responsible for his decision; but he may make a wrong decision and thereby fail to perform his obligations. But then who is to say someone has made a wrong decision? Anyone can say, but not everyone who cares to say will judge correctly; he may be right or wrong. And who decides that?

Each person decides for himself what to say and do; yet people sometimes speak and act in ways that are cowardly or cruel, thoughtless or irresponsible. And it is not merely up to the actor to assess his own action in this respect. Other people who want or need to assess the action may also do so; each of them will make a decision for which he bears responsibility, yet none of these decisions is absolutely definitive. The judge trying a would-be rebel makes a decision; the foreign onlooker asked to give money for a revolutionary cause makes a decision; the historian examining the record in a later generation makes a decision. Each of us who talks or thinks or acts with regard to the situation assesses it, and no theory or God or Party can get us off that hook. Thus not only citizens, but also bystanders and commentators may need to decide about a government. Their problems are not the same, to be sure. The citizen must decide whether to obey or resist; the bystander never had an obligation to obey, so he at most must decide whether or whom to assist; the commentator only makes a judgment. Therefore the evaluation of governments as to their legitimacy, their entitlement to be obeyed by their subjects, is a topic that ranges beyond problems of political obligation.

But the argument I am pursuing does not mean that all judgments are arbitrary or merely a matter of personal preference or whim. Some decisions are made arbitrarily or whimsically or selfishly or foolishly; others are made on principle, rationally, responsibly. These are ways or modes of deciding; none of them characterizes decision as such. And an individual's decision does not become rational, responsible or right merely because he thinks it is, merely because he urgently wants it to be. What is ultimately needed here is a better understanding of the role played in our language and our lives by assessments like 'he was right', 'he made a bad decision', 'he betrayed the cause', and the like.

Who is to say? I want to answer, each person who cares to, will say – not merely the one who acts, not merely his associates, not merely those in authority over him, not merely the detached historian or observer. No one has the last word because there is no last word. But in order to make that clear, one would have to say a great deal more about how language functions, and why we are so persistently inclined to suppose that there must be a last word.

4 'Normal' Science or Political Ideology?

Alan Ryan

Among the many motives which impelled the so-called 'behavioural revolution' in political science, two major and potent anxieties have played an important part. Both have persuaded political scientists to turn away from the traditional political science curriculum, and both have persuaded the practitioners of the new political science that their new science was to be one natural science among others. 'Real' political science would be the natural science of political life. The first anxiety was the fear of what David Easton's *The Political System* labelled as 'hyperfactualism'. Political scientists had all too often become mere compilers of facts about political systems, especially facts about the minutiae of constitutions. No one denied the importance of facts; indeed, it was freely admitted that a developed political science would demand far more factual evidence than we presently possess. But it was recognized that the developed and prestigious physical sciences were very far from being compilations of facts; and it was seen that, by itself, sticking to the facts was quite inadequate to generate anything that aspired to the name of political *science*. The cure for 'hyperfactualism' was to be the creation of an organized body of theory, for theory alone enables us to classify and assess the significance of, the factual data acquired by experiment and observation. But such theory would also assuage the second anxiety – the fear that political scientists might be taken for political ideologists. For such theory was to be quite different from 'traditional' political theory; it was to be empirical and descriptive, not moral and prescriptive theory. The goal was the creation of a properly validated body of scientific theory, not the production of ideology. If the outlook of physical scientists could be emulated, and their techniques borrowed, the taint of ideology would be purged, and scientific advance would take place in a professional atmosphere unruffled by the clash of rival and subjective evaluations of political practice.

Why these anxieties should have taken such hold on American political scientists in particular is a question in the history of ideas which has already received some attention. But here we can evade that issue and concentrate on the avowals of social and political scientists about their aims and methods. And at this level, it is easy enough to see the attraction of one famous solution to their anxieties. This solution is a highly persuasive account of the nature of science, and one reason for its persuasiveness is its apparent implications for the institutional framework within which science can be practised. The account is that of Professor Popper – to choose its most lucid and influential exponent – but many of its elements are to be found in J. S. Mill's *System of Logic* and in *The International Encyclopedia of Unified Science* in the nineteen thirties. According to such an account the line between science and ideology is simply drawn. The aim of the scientist is to establish well-confirmed empirical hypotheses, preferably in the form of universal generalizations which will deductively validate the explanation both of particular events and sequences of events. The relative importance of theory compared with fact follows from our concern for the *scope* of explanation; a theoretical law may 'cover' or provide the logical backing for, the explanation of a great many facts. A law which is embedded in a theory which involves our redescribing the facts in very non-everyday terms is especially important in its ability to cover the explanation of what look – at first sight – like very dissimilar phenomena. This is a feature of science which many discussions of the differences between 'high-level', theoretical laws and 'low-level', 'merely empirical' laws have dwelt upon, so we may leave the matter there for the moment. For what it is vital to emphasize here is that all scientific laws, no matter how 'high-level', must be testable, refutable by the results of experiment and observation.

This insistence serves as a demarcation criterion between science and ideology. To analyse what is merely ideological we enquire into the origins of the ideologist, or ask whose interests are served by putting forward the doctrine in question. To science such questions are irrelevant. It does not matter who puts forward a hypothesis, nor does it matter what his motives are. Certainly, we may be curious *qua* sociologist or psychologist about the social or temperamental factors tending to promote or to diminish mental fertility; but this has nothing to do with assessing hypotheses in a scientific way. To do this we must deduce empirical consequences from the hypothesis in question (together with such 'initial conditions' as are necessary) and then set these against the facts. If a hypothesis has no empirical consequences, we may have to decide that what we are offered is a disguised moral imperative – which, being an imperative, can be followed or disregarded, but cannot be true or false – or else a claim which is 'metaphysical' rather than scientific.

These elementary, but powerful truisms about scientific explanation have certain apparent consequences for the practise of science. If this is what science *is*, then some obvious consequences follow about the best way to practise it. These can be summed up in a Popperian slogan: 'the scientific community must be an open society'. Since progress demands an evolutionary struggle for survival among competing hypotheses, we must provide an abundance of competitors and be totally callous about the demise of almost all of them. Refuted hypotheses must be dispatched without mercy; affection for our brainchildren must be stifled and the unnatural vice of infanticide must be encouraged. However, another Darwinian platitude is also much to the point here, namely the need for a certain tenacity in the holding of hypotheses, in case an apparent, but only apparent, falsification should make us renounce a good hypothesis too soon. Abundance requires that anyone should be able to put forward hypotheses, and competition requires that no one should be in a position to say which hypotheses may be put forward nor to protect hypotheses which have been refuted. These look like the only conditions under which science, understood as 'conjecture and refutation' can be successfully practised. The attractions of the scientific community hardly need spelling out; what political scientist would turn his back on a community of non-authoritarian, tolerant, energetic, open-minded and encouraging colleagues who provided such an intellectually bracing environment? Recent horror stories only serve to drive home the moral. The most famous of these makes the issue almost more clear than we could make it by invention. The effects of Lysenko on Soviet biology and Soviet agriculture alike were disastrous. Attached for ideological reasons to non-Mendelian genetics, he assumed that since Gregor Mendel had been a monk he could not possibly have stumbled on the truth about genetics. Once Lysenko had attained a position of power he did his best to ensure that no one could perform the experiments or publish the results which would show him up as the charlatan he was. This, of course, was breaking all the rules of the open society; scientific hypotheses just aren't the sort of thing to which one should feel a political attachment. By making adherence to exploded hypotheses a touchstone of political rectitude, he did his level best to render the practise of science impossible.

That this view has for years been a near-orthodoxy among political scientists is not surprising. But social scientists have also been heard to describe the plight of their discipline in terms of the absence of a 'paradigm' for research and speculation. This talk of 'paradigms' brings us to the man who has slipped a serpent into the scientific Garden of Eden – Professor T. S. Kuhn. Kuhn's best-known book: *The Structure of Scientific Revolutions* is most readily described as an essay in the sociology of knowledge, though it is an essay with obvious philosophical implications. This claim may seem a dubious one, since many philosophers of science would suppose that an adequate philosophy of science is compatible with any history – just as an adequate formal logic has nothing to fear from the empirical investigation of what arguments people have in fact accepted. But Kuhn's account, of 'normal science' and of science in a state of revolution, was written against the background of Popperian orthodoxy, for Kuhn both recognizes that the interest of what he says depends upon describing science in profoundly non-Popperian terms and claims that his picture of scientific practice discredits Popper's. The impact seems to occur thus: if scientists have never behaved as we should expect them to do on a Popperian account of the matter, what can we say? Are we to say that the men who have set our standards for the rational study of the world have themselves been systematically irrational in the way they have carried out that activity? It would be alarming to have to do so, and yet it is hard to see what else we can say if we both wish to accept Kuhn's history and Popper's philosophy. The alternative must be to side with Kuhn and say that science is in principle something other than Popper supposes, and that the activities of scientists cannot be understood and assessed by reference to Popper's image of science. Kuhn's second thoughts on the matter (contained in the second edition of *Scientific Revolutions* and in *Criticism and the Growth of Knowledge*) are more conciliatory. For Kuhn suggests that his own account applies to 'normal science' as described below, while Popper's story of conjecture and refutation applies to periods of revolution. Popper himself shows no sign of accepting any such compromise, and it is not hard to see why.

For, a second consequence of Kuhn is that the scientific community now looks an infinitely less attractive place than did the open society. What we represented as impersonal arguments about the impact of the factual evidence upon suggested hypotheses now reappear as something much more closely resembling ideological conflicts after all. The escape route from political conflict into political science is barred because science itself turns out to be a form of political conflict, or perhaps more accurately a form of activity in which overt conflict is suppressed by massive indoctrination. If the attraction of the scientific study of politics has, as we have so far suggested, stemmed from the belief that science is a tolerant, impersonal activity where disputes are settled always and only by reference to the facts, then the discovery that scientific disputes are not and cannot be, settled in this way much diminishes the attractions of the life of science.

That any account of the history of science can create such doubts may look quite extravagant. But a short account of Kuhn's case will serve to dispel the air of paradox. Kuhn's case resists summary, if only because it is hard to produce a summary which does not beg the analysis of the numerous ambiguities in his own statement of that case; but it runs somewhat as follows. The 'normal' condition of science involves the acceptance by scientists of what Kuhn calls a 'paradigm', the function of which is both to define the scope of the science in question, to define what counts as a 'puzzle' for the scientist, and to set standards for the solution of those puzzles. A paradigm is not quite on a par with common or garden theories, though it is none too clear just what Kuhn takes to be the crucial differences. Though Kuhn does not say so, a paradigm functions in the same fashion as a Kantian Idea of Reason; it provides a framework of assumptions about the nature of the phenomena and about the sort of lower-level theories we can put forward to explain the phenomena, but it itself is not empirically testable. But true to his sociological interests, Kuhn argues that the way in which the paradigm as an intellectual framework is transmitted is via examples of 'good research' – that is, by way of paradigms in the sense of examples shown to the fledgling scientist as something to be emulated. One thing that is clear is that paradigms are not much like Popperian hypotheses; we do not set out to refute them, but wear them as we might wear conceptual spectacles, yielding an order which we set out thereafter to analyse.

But they are yet more different. Most importantly, they have such an entrenched status within the scientific community that their acceptance and rejection is truly a matter of revolution. On the face of it, Popper's account of conjecture and refutation suggests a piecemeal and reformist process quite at odds with Kuhn's account, even if Kuhn seems to regard Popper as the revolutionary and himself as the defender of 'normal science'. At least we can say that Popper's account suggests that what goes on is a continuous process of more or less drastic revision, where Kuhn claims that unrevisable paradigms dominate the scientific community until such time as intolerable strains are created and revolution occurs. For what is striking in Kuhn's account is the argument that the view of the world which the paradigm embodies is enforced with a positively totalitarian severity. A man who does not practise science in the approved manner will simply not count as a scientist at all. In a graphic phrase, he will be 'read out' of the profession. And in the twentieth century this is a heavily sanctioned matter, for it means that he will get no grants, have no research workers to help him and find it impossible to get his ideas published. As in Orwell's *1984* he will become for scientific purposes an 'unperson'. And this is not because scientists are unduly unkind or unduly fanatical. Rather it is to argue two theses fundamental to Kuhn's case. These are that the 'facts' to which the scientist appeals are not so to speak givens of an unmistakable and immediately recognizable kind; rather, they are psychologically and conceptually dependent on the paradigm with which the scientist works;

and secondly, that changes of paradigm cannot be reformist improvements whereby the same old facts are accounted for rather better than before, but must be conceptual shifts whereby scientists come to live in a new world. Hence the appropriateness of the term 'revolution', for what the course of scientific revolution shares with its political counterpart is that it ushers in a new regime under which the facts of life under the old regime retrospectively lose their former character. What was previously legitimate now appears as at best mistaken and at worst positively a crime against reason. We have not simply altered direction under the old rules; we have so changed the rules that we have acquired a new sense of direction altogether.

Scientific Revolutions employs a mixture of psychological and conceptual arguments to support the above account, and it is to be hoped that the account so far given reproduces only those ambiguities inherent in such a mixture. The point of Kuhn's account is to question the minimal empiricist assumption that there is, or can be, some description of the facts, neutral between competing explanatory theories. Kuhn's case is that facts are essentially facts-as-interpreted. Thus he employs the evidence of Gestalt psychology to show how heavily our basic perceptual experiences are determined by our expectations and preconceptions about how things must be. This *a posteriori* argument runs in harness with a familiar quasi-Kantian argument to the effect that all descriptions of 'reality' embody various assumptions about what reality is and how it works. There is no bare account of bare reality, unclouded by assumptions. Thus it is not the opposition of fact and theory which is decisive, but the clash of opposing conceptualizations. And since this is discussed in terms which imply that the tailoring of theory to fact is a screen for the successful conversion of true believers, we should expect scientific controversy to include a large element of ideological warfare. Since the publication of *Scientific Revolutions*, Kuhn has taken some pains to play down this aspect of his position; it cannot be said that he has much appeased such critics as Imre Lakatos (in *Criticism and the Growth of Knowledge*), and it cannot be said that it is wholly clear how much of his original views survives the qualifications.

If Kuhn's picture of science were correct, its implications for any attempt to turn the social and political sciences into 'normal' sciences would be extremely alarming. So far from the new science being a way out of ideological conflict, it seems that it enmeshes us more deeply than ever. Indeed, the situation is worse than ever, with the added anxiety that our ideological preconceptions may become invisible to us, since we cannot see our conceptual spectacles except on those rare occasions when we try on different ones. Now, it might be said that this is so out of touch with what we observe of the practice of social and political science that we ought to reject it out of hand. There will, indeed, be grounds for complaint in due course; but just as it would be hard to account for the popularity of Kuhn's image of the natural sciences unless we admit that it contains genuine insights, so it would be foolish not to explore his attractions for the social scientist. It must, however, be said that Kuhn himself has resolutely steered clear of the social sciences, and that nothing of what follows can be laid at his door. It is, in any event, clear that on a Kuhnian analysis, the social sciences are in a 'pre-paradigm' condition, so that anything said about the nature of 'normal' sociology or 'normal' political science is inevitably speculative.

It has been argued by Sheldon Wolin that the concept of the paradigm is very much at home in the realm of political theory. It is this suggestion which we must now take up, but in order to stress how different is the role of the paradigm in the human sciences. The different role played by the paradigm stems from the elementary observation that whereas the inanimate subject matter of the natural sciences does not have its own point of view, human beings do, and often a complex and articulate point of view at that. What people do, and thus what we need to explain, depends on what they believe and intend – i.e. on their point of view. The electron is not uncertain whether to observe the uncertainty principle, but the speculator may well feel uncertain what to do when faced with a series of unintelligible fluctuations in the market – and it is *his* uncertainty that explains why the economist finds his behaviour unpredictable. When, in the social sciences, we set out to construct our picture of the world, we find ourselves confronted by a world which is already permeated by the stories which people are telling about the world. Indeed, for the purposes of the social sciences, the stories and the world are inseparable, for what is usually investigated are the causes and effects of people telling the stories they do.

A situation where this is particularly obvious arises when we study voting behaviour and try, let us say, to link allegiances to feelings about social class. When the authors of *The Affluent Worker* enquired into the extent to which their respondents voted for class reasons, they placed a good deal of emphasis on whether the responses they obtained indicated that the voters saw the world in terms of 'them and us'. (In fact, of course, they discovered that their respondents did not have *that* image of the social world at all, but something much looser, structured by recognition of money hierarchies and little else.) Political sociologists have often emphasized the affective and emotive nature of such responses, and have pointed out that they are not based on a detached investigation of the facts of social life. But even if we accept that such responses are affective rather intellectual, the fact remains that human affective responses are only elicited because we identify certain objects, persons, or events as *proper* or *appropriate* objects of our emotions. This in turn requires that we possess criteria for making such identification; and we may equally well express this by saying that it requires that we have some kind of *Weltanschauung* or to use the Kuhnian term, a paradigm. The importance of social paradigms is every bit as great as that of their scientific counterparts. Indeed, it is greater. For it is only in the context of shared paradigms that a person's behaviour can be made intelligible, not just to the spectator but even to the agent himself. Only in terms of some paradigm can he represent what he is doing as a rational activity. At once, this seems to create difficulties for the ideological neutrality of social and political science. For social paradigms are also moral paradigms. It is important not to be confused over this; they do not commit us to any particular moral or political evaluation. but, again in the manner in the natural science paradigm, they do define the range of *possible* moral arguments, and define what *sort* of puzzle a particular moral puzzle is. The value which an actor places on his actions is only intelligible or defensible within the framework provided by the appropriate social paradigm, the paradigm which renders his behaviour expected or unexpected, defensible or inexplicable. It is no wonder that many writers – of whom Professor Winch is the best known – have been so impressed by these truisms that they have seemed to suggest that the task of the social scientist is to understand the ongoing activities of the society they study solely in terms of that society's own paradigms.

But this doctrine of acquiescence in the validity of the paradigms being studied raises the possibility of a subversive attitude towards them. Indeed, the dilemma is that it is hard to see what alternatives exist other than acceptance and subversion. For what non-acceptance involves is the belief that the paradigm presents something worse than puzzles, that it has some internal incoherence or has intolerable consequences. But in a fashion which is not to be found in the natural sciences, where all the scientist need say about anomalous phenomena is that that is what they are, we are likely in the social sciences to find ourselves saying that the paradigm validates behaviour which it ought not, or else that it fails to validate behaviour which it ought. And it seems that however abstemious we are about offering our moral views for general inspection, we will find it hard to escape such commitments. The debate about 'cultural relativism' which has so preoccupied anthropologists is plainly centred on such anxieties. The assumption that in so-called 'primitive' societies there is no conflict between role and personality is one which has been subjected to some devastating criticism in the light of just these considerations, to take a familiar example. Another is the suggestion to be found in the works of Dr R. D. Laing that what we all (in the light of the majority paradigm) see as the unintelligible behaviour of the schizophrenic is in reality intelligible as a well-founded protest against the intolerable relationships into which the sufferer has been thrust. Laing, of course, regards such protests as political on the grounds that the family could not secure the paradigmatic consensus it does without outside assistance, but there are some more conventional political arguments which rest on a similar concern to subvert the current paradigms. In his *Essay on Liberation*, Herbert Marcuse argues that the politics of the establishment are carried on in terms of a vocabulary and a set of expectations which are mutually supportive. If, for example, we see the law courts where protesters are tried *as* law courts, we involve ourselves in playing roles to which the regime's officials know how to respond; our roles are, in this sense though in no other, supportive of each other. But if we were to decide that what we are witnessing is some sort of elaborate charade, a costume drama of a none too serious kind, then this would be a very radical kind of debunking of existing authority. Marcuse traces the enthusiasm which the American New Left brought to the politics of extreme obscenity to their recognition of just this fact. In this he has for once some intellectual support from Miss Arendt who has recently argued that authority is more vulnerable to ridicule than to any other form of attack. If we concede enough to the establishment to employ its vocabulary, then we are conceding the legitimacy-in-principle, the possibility-of-justification in what they say and do; but to re-enact in metaphor the childish urge to cover our enemies in excrement is to render the legal game simply unplayable, by taking away the epistemological conventions on which it is based.

More conventional political science offers the same message. There is now a near consensus on the ethnocentricity of the functional analysis of politics which is presented in Almond and Coleman's *Politics of the Developing Areas*. The simplest and most obvious aspect of the claim is that if we accept these analytical categories and the additional hypothesis that development consists in a process of increasing functional specificity, it is impossible to escape the conclusion that the goal of progress is the politics of the United States. Interest group politics, with passive, ideologically bland political parties form obvious solutions to the problems of interest articulation and interest aggregation; but this is largely because the paradigm within which these 'needs' are understood is itself a fairly low-level generalization from American experience.

Suppose we go on to raise the question of how readily the terms in which politicians understand themselves translate into those in which the political scientist understands them. Now the situation is a good deal less tidy. It seems that many American politicians do see themselves as playing the role of honest broker to competing interest – in other words that their normative paradigm matches Almond's descriptive paradigm quite closely. But it seems equally clear that it is an image of themselves which British politicians would for the most part repudiate. Indeed, it is just this trait of British politicians to which Richard Rose's *People in Politics* takes exception, a fact which is no surprise in view of that work's debt to Almond's framework. Yet Rose's complaint against British politicians is interestingly ambiguous, for it is not at all clear what sort of error Professor Rose thinks British politicians are making – whether they are simply making a factual error or whether they are to be censured for their unwillingness to play the game the American way. But if we have been right so far to stress the mingled descriptive and normative nature of the social paradigm, then this ambiguity is at once intelligible.

Having thus far accepted without demur the mode of analysis suggested by Kuhn's work, we must now turn and bite the hand that has fed us. Once again we may begin with Kuhn's claims about the natural sciences. Here, it is clear, Kuhn's analysis has to be stripped of so many of its distinctive features that what we are left with can without difficulty be smuggled back into the fold of Popperian orthodoxy. The striking feature of Kuhn's initial statement of his case was the apparent eagerness to claim that sociological rather than epistemological considerations are responsible for the acceptance and rejection of paradigms. This appears most clearly in his much criticized slide from arguing that we might 'almost say' that the scientist lives and works in a different world after the shift of paradigm into *saying* just that. But the extremer statement of his case is at odds with his own detailed exposition of what happens during the shift of paradigm. The process whereby the facts as represented by one paradigm are newly interpreted in terms of the new paradigm would be simply indescribable if it were not the world rather than the scientific community which circumscribed what can be said about the world. If the scientist *literally* worked in a new world when he worked with a new paradigm, it would be hard to make sense of the idea that new paradigms set new puzzles for the scientific community, and it would be hard to know what scientific work could consist in beyond an elaboration of the internal requirements of the paradigm. Unless the world impinged on us in a fashion not wholly determined by our frame of mind, there could be no puzzles at all, let alone anomalies. Kuhn, responding to his critics, now insists that he has never denied any of this and ascribes the extremer conclusions to his critics rather than himself. He therefore calls attention to the claim he has always made to the effect that we employ the paradigm to ask questions of *nature*, and that it is nature which leads us to accept or reject the paradigm. But this clarification robs Kuhn's case of its distinctiveness; for now all we have left is a claim to which Popper certainly assents, namely that whatever we say about the world involves assumptions which we *make* even when we do not state them. Thus, during the life of the paradigm we shall no doubt assume that the world really is the way we accept it must be in the light of the paradigm, without on every occasion bringing up a defence of the paradigm's adequacy. But this is not to say that no attack or defence is possible, only that they are not likely to occur unless something happens to provoke them. This, however, is the most harmless of observations, for a similar principle of linguistic economy operates throughout every aspect of life – we do not insist on pointing out the fact that we are wearing our clothes, for most of the time we take that for granted, but this is not to say that we cannot say that we are clothed if the question arises. Equally, Kuhn is plainly correct in saying that we often employ theories even after they have received what ought formally to count as falsification; but here too we may readily agree that some guide is better than none, even if we are not convinced that our guide is wholly reliable.

But the fact that Kuhn's case hardly stands up to assault is not the same as reassurance that all is saved for Popperian orthodoxy in political science. For once again the distinctive features of what we earlier called a social paradigm suggest that aspirations to join the ranks of the natural scientists could well be a mistaken ambition for the social scientist. But these features present problems for what are substantially non-Kuhnian reasons. Kuhn, as we have said, agrees with his critics that in the last resort it is the confrontation of nature and paradigm which decides the paradigm's acceptability. But this raises the old and unlucid question of whether human culture can be scrutinized as if it were part of nature. Let us return to the issue of honest broker politics. In a political community where the paradigm is that of brokerage – that is, a society whose politics are largely intelligible in economic terms as a process of group competition for benefits – there are consequences for all the actors in the system. Since the model underpinning the actors' behaviour is an economic model, the activities of those who take part in politics are to be seen as a kind of higgling in the market. Now it is not required that all those who take part in the political process should have a very articulate grasp of its underlying logic. What is required is that for the model to have *de facto* applicability the actors should accept *de jure* standards of what is rational and acceptable behaviour. The entrepreneurs and labourers whose behaviour was described by classical economics did not do so because they had a clear grasp of classical economic theory; what they did do was act on promptings of a cost-benefit kind, uninhibited by principles which their own forefathers or their contemporaries in other societies would have thought sacred. Classical economics explains the behaviour of people who are utilitarians so far as their economic activities are concerned. So the analogous model in politics explains the activities of those who are utilitarians in their political behaviour. Where those who take part in politics do act according to some sort of cost-benefit calculation, their behaviour is prescribed by the normative side of the paradigm which supplies the descriptive premises for a theory of their behaviour.

This has an important consequence. It is an overworked truism of recent social science that the social 'game' is only playable so long as we all play roles which are congruent with the expectations we entertain about each other. The sociological literature is full of variously coherent accounts of the way we maintain social order by rewarding conformity and sanctioning deviance, that is, by way of securing that people do fill the roles they are assigned. In terms of our discussion so far, what this means is that these are accounts of the way in which society offers – and indeed imposes – paradigms for the prescription and description of behaviour. Society compels us to accept a range of answers to the questions of who we are, what we are meant to be doing and why we are meant to be doing it. If Goffman is to be believed, even those unlikely role-players, the inhabitants of back wards of mental hospitals, have been allotted roles to play and are coerced where necessary into playing them – though those roles are the somewhat back-handed roles of deviant activity which will be forgiven upon adequate evidence of repentance. We the sane assure them they are mad; if they take our word for it, we may forgive them the trouble they cause us and eventually call them 'cured'; if they resist us, we shall decide they are madder than ever. The importance of the work of Goffman and a small host of other writers in the same vein, is that it goes at least some way towards explaining what underpins the constant complaint by radical activists that political scientists have been engaged in an underhand attempt to 'read them out' of political life altogether; and, of course, it must equally help to explain the counter-strategy of trying to read everything back into politics in the manner of Dr Laing. Even without trying to pronounce on the rights and wrongs of particular cases, two things emerge very clearly. The first is that political scientists have neglected the (obvious) truth that an agreed definition of what *counts* as activity of a given kind is politically significant. Those who have recognized the fact – whether on behalf of autocracy as in Hobbes's *Leviathan* or on behalf of anarchy as in Godard's film of *Alphaville* – have recognized something important. Secondly, it casts doubt on the desire to create a 'normal' political science. If we have been right to argue that the applicability of a descriptive paradigm depends on the establishment of a related normative paradigm, then it seems that a 'normal' social or political science is the science of a social order whose monolithic ideological rigidity would be quite at odds with anything that a generally liberal profession would really enjoy contemplating.

To the extent that there is an agreed (or enforced) normative paradigm operative in a given social order, it creates one further problem for Popperian and Kuhnian alike. It makes the concept of falsification, of testing against the facts, a good deal harder to apply. For we may find ourselves faced by a kind of spurious corroboration of our assumptions wherever these are in agreement with those of the actors under observation. Thus, Marx noticed the misleading appearance of truth which attached to classical economics in bourgeois society. Within that society, the so-called 'laws' of classical economics were allowed full sway, in large part because it was thought that they were natural laws – and that belief tended to be self-confirming. But this was not because the laws of economics really were laws of nature in the same sense as the laws of physics. Had society been differently organized, then the 'laws' of classical economics would not have applied – insofar as people had the beliefs, wishes and skills which the theory supposed, this was a consequence of how society had made them, not of how they naturally were. Once embarked on this analysis, the thought soon occurs to us that if societies can *make* theories true in this fashion, it poses the problem whether whole societies can be usefully said to be making mistakes about the nature of their own activities. Not surprisingly, some writers have thought they cannot. As outsiders, we might say a society was, by its own standards, coherent or incoherent in the way it described the activities of its members, but we could not say it was right or wrong in any very solid sense. If the 'facts' were themselves constructs of the going paradigm, they would hardly provide an impressive foundation for the testing of that paradigm.

The way out of this corner seems to be to drop the assumption inherent in the use of 'paradigm' terminology, that there is always – or even usually, or perhaps even ever – the kind of coherence and unanimity about what we are up to in social life that we achieve in deciding what inanimate matter is up to. Many of Kuhn's critics dispute the belief that even in the natural sciences there is the kind of agreement which would justify the use of 'paradigm' terminology. But whatever the situation of the natural scientist, the situation of the social actor seems clear enough. If we return to our earlier acceptance of the fact that whatever we say about the world, we make assumptions which we do not state, we may make exactly the same point about social life. Although it is worth pointing out such sociological phenomena as the mechanisms which induce compliance with role-definitions and so on, it is also worth pointing out that such definitions rest upon much more than themselves. They rest upon beliefs about the world and about the consequences of our activities as social beings which are themselves assessable for truth and falsity. It is true that the behaviour of judge and jury, lawyer and client rests in the first place upon their identifying themselves and each other as occupants of established roles in a legal activity. But this is scarcely a good excuse for ignoring the fact that the whole practice of law as a system of social control rests upon a variety of beliefs about the reasons for which people commit crimes, about the effectiveness of methods of detection, about the usefulness of procedures for ascertaining guilt and so on. These beliefs, once identified, can be handed over to sociologists, psychologists and so on, to be assessed for their truth and falsehood. Of course, it is hardly possible for a judge to go on doing *his* job, if he disbelieves in the psychological and sociological underpinnings for it; but the sociologist and the psychologist need not be in the least committed to seeing the judicial process continued in its present form. The psychologist in his turn will doubtless have to accept certain assumptions about the underpinnings of *his* science – about the biological, chemical, genetic or whatever basis of human character – and he, too, cannot practise psychology while disbelieving in its current basis. But it should be noticed that *what* he takes for granted is very different from what the judge and the lawyer take for granted, and should he feel doubts about the foundations of his own discipline he can, of course, expect the physicist, geneticist or whoever to cast some light on those doubts.

In general, then, it is only in a Pickwickian sense that we are the prisoners of our own concepts, for we may always step back and enquire about the assumptions on which we have hitherto relied. Such an activity – taking fallibility seriously – runs into a number of sceptical puzzles which a Popperian account of science will find hard to avoid. But for the limited purpose of this essay, it is sufficient to have shown that the social scientist is not in principle worse off than the natural scientist so far as bringing his theories to the test of factual evidence is concerned. Indeed, the fact that we cannot say anything at all without making *some* assumptions seems to have created the anxieties it has done for two very feeble reasons. The first is the belief associated with Karl Mannheim that objective accounts of social life require a God-like presuppositionless stance which it is hard to make sense of, let alone to claim to occupy. The second is the illicit slide from the truism that we always make some assumptions to the falsehood that there are some assumptions which we always make. But neither of these reasons touches the claim that we can with an effort, distinguish social science from political ideology precisely by being willing to uncover our assumptions when challenged and give them up if they are false.

5 Coercion[1]

Robert Nozick

This study of coercion is intended as a preliminary to a longer study of liberty, whose major concerns will be the reasons which justify making someone unfree to perform an action, and the reason why making someone unfree to perform an action needs justifying. Though coercion is intimately connected with liberty (some writers capsulize freedom as absence of coercion), it does not exhaust the range of nonliberty or unfreedom. In particular, being coerced into not doing an act, is neither a necessary nor a sufficient condition for being unfree to do it. That it is not necessary is shown by the following examples:

> (a) A person robs a bank and is caught and punished. If he knew for sure he would be caught and punished for robbing the bank, he would not do so, but he does not know this and so robs the bank. He was unfree to rob the bank, though he was not coerced into not doing so.
>
> (b) I was not coerced into not murdering a member of the audience at Columbia when I read this paper, though I was unfree to do so.
>
> (c) If I lure you into an escape-proof room in New York and leave you imprisoned there, I do not coerce you into not going to Chicago though I make you unfree to do so.

That being coerced into not doing act A is not a sufficient condition for being unfree to do A is shown by the following example: You threaten to get me fired from my job if I do A, and I refrain from doing A because of this threat and am coerced into not doing A. However unbeknownst to me you are bluffing; you know you have absolutely no way to carry out this threat, and would not carry it out if you could. I was not unfree to do A (no doubt I thought I was), though I was coerced into not doing A. But though coercion does not exhaust the notion of unfreedom, it is obviously closely connected to it.

This paper attempts to clarify the concept of coercion, and some related concepts. Though this is an interesting and intriguing task, I do not pursue it for its own sake. I am primarily interested in the uses to which such a clarification can be put; the questions one will be in a better position to answer given this clarification (*other* than questions like: what

---

[1] This paper was first published in S. Morgenbesser *et al.*, eds., *Philosophy, Science and Method: Essays in Honor of Ernest Nagel* (New York, 1969). Some footnotes which provide more detail have been omitted.

are the necessary and sufficient conditions for P's coercing Q into not doing A, or for P's threatening Q). I shall not be able here to get to these further questions, and shall be engaged largely in tool-sharpening rather than in tool use.

One final preliminary remark, or warning, or apology. This study of coercion is an *exploratory* study, and is meant to raise questions and suggest problems. To many of these questions and problems I propose tentative answers and solutions, but some are left open. I would be happier if I could answer or solve them all. But in philosophy questions and problems often outlive specific proposed answers and solutions. Unfortunately, so it was in the course of writing this paper.

Conditions for Coercion

I shall begin by considering an account of coercion obtained from combining some things said on this subject in Hart and Honoré's *Causation in the Law* (Oxford, 1961) with some remarks of Hart in his *The Concept of Law* (Oxford, 1959). According to this account, person P coerces person Q into not doing act A if and only if

(1) P threatens to do something if Q does A (and P knows he's making this threat).
(2) This threat renders Q's doing A substantially less eligible as a course of conduct than not doing A.
(3) P makes this threat in order to get Q not to do A, intending that Q realize he's been threatened by P.
(4) Q does not do A.
(5) P's words or deeds are part of Q's reason for not doing A.[2]

---

[2] Hart and Honoré list one further condition: Q forms the intention of not doing A only after learning of P's threat. That Q formed the intention of not doing A after learning of P's threat may be reason for thinking that he did A because of the threat. But Q may have refrained from doing A because of the threat even though he formed the intention of not doing it before learning of the threat. For example, Q intends to visit a friend tomorrow. P threatens him with death if he doesn't go. Q then learns that this friend has a communicable disease such that were it not for the threat, Q wouldn't visit him. But Q goes because of P's threat, though he'd formed the intention of going before learning of the threat, and never lost this intention. Though Hart and Honoré's further condition is not satisfied, P coerced Q into going.

Conditions 1–5 do not appear to be sufficient for coercion. For example, P threatens Q, saying that if Q performs a particular action, a rock will fall and kill him. P thinks Q knows of his (P's) infamous procedure of murdering people, but Q thinks that P is telling him about some strange natural law that holds independently of human action, namely whenever someone performs this action, he gets killed by a falling rock. That is, Q understands what P says, not as a *threat* but as a *warning*. If Q refrains from performing the action, P has not coerced him into not doing it, even though the five conditions are satisfied. This suggests that we add as a further condition:

> (6) Q knows that P has threatened to do the something mentioned in 1, if he, Q, does A (or, to handle cases of anonymous threats, Q knows that someone has threatened to do something mentioned in (1) if he, Q, does A).

It is not clear that the conditions thus far listed are sufficient. You threaten to do something if I do A, thinking that I don't want this something done. But in fact, I don't mind it or even slightly want it. However I realize that you must feel very strongly about my doing A, since you've threatened me, and that you will be very upset if I do A (*not* that you will *choose* to be upset to punish me for doing A). Since I don't want you to be upset, I refrain from doing A. You did not coerce me into not doing A, though it seems that the conditions listed are satisfied; in particular it seems that the relevant conditions 5 and 2 are satisfied. Or, if they can be so interpreted so that they're not satisfied, it would be well to make this interpretation explicit, replacing 5, 1 and 2 by:

> (5′) Part of Q's reason for not doing A is to avoid (or lessen the likelihood of) the thing which P has threatened to bring about or have brought about.[3]
> (1′) P threatens to bring about or have brought about some consequence if Q does A (and knows he's threatening to do this).
> (2′) A with this threatened consequence is rendered substantially less eligible as a course of conduct for Q than A was without the threatened consequence.

---

[3] This condition requires further refinements to handle cases in which unbeknownst to P, Q wants to avoid P's inflicting the threatened consequence only because this will lead to some further consequence detrimental to P, which Q (only out of concern for P's interest) wants to avoid. For example, Q refrains from A because he knows that P will feel enormously guilty after he's inflicted the consequence, and Q doesn't want this to happen. Or, Q refrains from A in the face of P's threat to fire him only because without Q working for him, P will go

Must P make the threat *in order* to get Q not to do A? Must condition 3 be satisfied? In normal situations it will be satisfied; e.g., a highwayman says 'If you don't give me your money, I'll kill you,' making this threat in order to get me to give him my money. But suppose that we are conducting an experiment for the Social Science Research Council, to study people's reactions in the highwayman situation. We don't care how he reacts to our threat (if he gives over the money we must turn it over to the SSRC; if he resists we are empowered to kill him and, let us suppose, have no moral scruples about doing so). We do not say 'your money or your life' in order to get him to give us his money, but in order to gather data. We might even suppose that I think him very brave and have bet with you that he'll resist and be killed. After making the bet, I want him *not* to hand over the money, and I don't make the threat in order to get him to hand it over. In the grip of fear and trembling, he hands over the money. Surely we coerced him into doing so. This suggests replacing 3 by a more complicated condition:

> (Part of) P's reason for deciding to bring about the consequence or have it brought about, if Q does A, is that P believes this consequence worsens Q's alternative of doing A (i.e. that P believes that this consequence worsens Q's alternative of doing A, or that Q would believe it does[4]).

bankrupt, and Q doesn't want this to happen. I shall not pursue here the details of a principle which would exclude these as cases of coercion.

[4] I included the latter disjnct since I can threaten you with a consequence which I don't believe would actually worsen your alternative of doing A, but which I know that you believe would do so. Subtle questions arise about cases where it is the making of the threat itself that causes the person to believe that one consequqence is worse than another. For example, a Gestapo agent questioning a prisoner believes that two concentration camps are equally bad, and the prisoner too initially believes this. The Gestapo agent tells the prisoner, in a threatening voice, that he will be sent to a concentration camp in any case, but if he cooperates during the questioning he will be sent to the first camp, whereas if he does not, he will be sent to the second camp. Here it is the very making of the threat which causes the prisoner to think that the second camp is worse than the first.

I might note one refinement of this condition, to handle cases where (part of) P's reason for so deciding is as described in the condition, but this part drops away and P sticks with his decision for another reason entirely and thereafter announces the decision. It might be more appropriate to say something like: (Part of) P's reason, at the time he informs Q he will bring

The SSRC example satisfies this condition, since (part of) the researchers' reason for deciding to kill Q if he doesn't turn over the money is that they believe this consequence worsens Q's alternative of not giving them the money.

But the condition formulated is not broad enough, for we want to cover cases where P has not decided to bring about the consequence if Q does A, but is bluffing instead, or neither intends nor intends not to bring it about if Q does A. This suggests disjoining another condition with the one above:

> If P has not decided to bring about the consequence, or have it brought about, if Q does A, then (part of) P's reason for saying he will bring about the consequence, or have it brought about, if Q does A is that (P believes) Q will believe this consequence worsens Q's alternative of doing A.[5]

One is tempted to say that this disjunctive condition is superfluous, because it is built into the notion of threatening, and hence follows from condition 1'. That is, one is tempted to say that if this condition is not

---

about the consequence or have it brought about if Q does A, for planning to bring about the consequence or have it brought about if Q does A, is that P believes. . . .

The condition in the text should also be interpreted or extended so as to cover cases in which the worsening of Q's alternative of doing A is not part of P's reason for deciding to bring about the consequences if Q does A, but rather
(a) P decides to bring about the consequences if Q does A because he believes he has a duty or obligation to do so.
(b) P knows this consequence would worsen Q's alternative of doing A.
(c) Part of the reason for P's bringing about of such a consequence if Q does A originally being thought to be his duty or obligation, or being continued to be so thought, is that such a consequence worsens Q's alternative of doing A.

[5] This disjunction is condition 3'. Thus the full condition 3' is: (Part of) P's reason for deciding is . . . , *or*, if P hasn't decided, (part of) P's reason for saying is. . . . An alternative condition would be just: (Part of) P's reason for saying is to get Q not to do A, or to worsen. . . . This alternative condition differs from the one under consideration for cases where P has decided to bring about the consequence if Q does A, and no part of his reason or motive is as described, but part of his reason for *telling* Q that he will bring about the consequence if Q does A, *is* to get Q not to do A. I find it difficult to decide between these conditions, though I lean towards the one presented in the text. A specific example for which the condition in the text and the alternative condition diverge is discussed (as case 3) in the section on Threats and Warnings.

satisfied, if P's reasons or motives are not as described, then P has not *threatened* Q. I shall have more to say about this later.

The conditions listed still do not appear to be sufficient. Consider cases where Q wants to do A in order to bring about x, and P says that if Q does A, he (P) will do something which just prevents A from bringing about x. This makes A substantially less eligible as an alternative for Q (Q now, we may suppose, has no reason to do A), and the other conditions may well be satisfied. Yet, at least some cases of this sort ('If you say another word, I shall turn off my hearing aid') are not cases of coercion.[6]

Cases of this sort suggest the following condition:

> (7) Q believes that, and P believes that Q believes that, P's threatened consequence would leave Q worse off, having done A, than if Q didn't do A and P didn't bring about the consequence.

In the application of this condition, in deciding how well or poorly off Q is having done A and having had his purpose x thwarted, one must ignore Q's wasted effort, humiliation at having failed to bring about x, and (in some cases) Q's foregoing opportunities. Similarly in deciding how well or poorly off Q would be not doing A and not having P bring about the consequence, one must ignore any regret Q might feel at not doing A.[7]

---

[6] Note the difference, with respect to coercion, between saying to a man who intends to do A in order to bring about x:
(1) If you do A, I'll do something which (just) prevents your A from bringing about x.
(2) If you do B, I'll do something which would, were you to do A, (just) prevent your A from bringing about x.

[7] I should note that I do not discuss in this paper, and wish here to leave open, two further conditions. (Hart mentions something in the area of the first.)

> (1) The consequences which P has threatened *is* so weighted by Q as to override the weight which Q (morally) *ought* to give to not doing A.

For example, Q who is not in dire financial condition, and would just slightly rather not kill people (he feels about killing people as most people do about killing flies), kills R because P has threatened not to return the $100 he's borrowed from Q unless Q kills R. Did P coerce Q into killing R?

> (2) The weight which Q *does* give to not doing A does not fall far short of the weight he (morally) *ought* to give to not doing A.

For example, Q destroys R's home because P has threatened a consequence, if Q does not destroy the home which R has laboriously built, which Q weights *and* anyone (morally) ought to weight as worse than destroying R's home. However, Q just *slightly* would rather not destroy R's home. Did P coerce Q into destroying R's home?

According to our account of 'P coerces Q into doing A,' the following cases are *not* cases in which P coerces Q into doing A.

(1) Q mishears P as having said 'Your money or your life' and hands over his money, but P said something else, or said this as a question about something he thought Q said, etc.
(2) P doesn't speak English, but has picked up the sentence 'Your money or your life' from a movie, though he does not know what it means. To be friendly, P utters this one sentence to Q who is sitting next to him in a bar (perhaps while showing Q his unusual knife for Q to admire). Q hands over his money.
(3) Q walks into a room, and unbeknownst to him there is a tape recorder in the next room playing part of the soundtrack of a movie. Q hears 'Put all of your money on the table and then leave, or I'll kill you.' Q puts his money on the table, and leaves.

I suggest that in these cases, though Q feels coerced and thinks he is coerced, P does not coerce Q into giving over the money. (In the third case there is no plausible person P to consider.) Those who refuse to accept this might hold the view that though P does not coerce Q into giving over the money, nonetheless Q is coerced into giving over the money. Such a person would reject the view that 'Q is coerced into doing A' is equivalent to 'there is a P who coerces Q into doing A,' and perhaps suggest that Q is coerced into doing A if and only if

(1) There is a P who coerces Q into doing A.
or (2) Q is justified in believing that there is a P who has threatened to bring about a consequence which significantly worsens his alternative of not doing A (and that P has the appropriate reasons and intentions), and (part of) Q's reason for doing A is to avoid or lessen the likelihood of this consequence he believes was threatened.

I should mention that a threat need not be verbally expressed; it may be perfectly clear from actions performed what the threat is, or at least that something undesirable will occur if one doesn't perform some appropriate action. For example, members of a street gang capture a member of a rival gang and ask him where that gang's weapons are hidden. He refuses to tell, and they beat him up. They ask again, he refuses again, they beat him again. And so on until he tells. He was coerced into telling. His captors didn't have to *say*, 'if you don't tell us we will continue to beat you up or perhaps eventually do something worse.' This is perfectly clear to all involved in the situation. In many situations the infliction of violence is well understood by all parties to be a threat of further infliction of violence if there is noncompliance. Nothing need be *said*. It may be for reasons such as this that some writers (e.g. Bay) say that all infliction of violence constitutes coercion. But this is, I think, a mistake. If a drunken group comes upon a stranger and beats him up or even kills him, this need not be coercion. For there need have been no implicit threat of further violence if the person didn't comply with their wishes, and it would indeed be difficult for this to be the case if they just come upon him and kill him.[8]

There is another type of situation very similar to the one we have thus far been concerned with, for which similar conditions can be offered. I have in mind cases where no one threatens to inflict some damage on Q if he does A, but someone sets things up so that damage is automatically inflicted if Q does A. It's not that if you do A, I will bring about a consequence which you consider to be bad, but rather that I now do something (the doing of which is not conditional upon your doing A) which is such that if you do A after I have done this thing, there will be a consequence which you consider to be bad. Though in such situations a person is deterred from doing something, it is not obvious to me that he is coerced into not doing it. If it is coercion then the account of coercion would say that P coerces Q into not doing A if and only if either of the two sets of conditions is satisfied.

I suggest that it is as a case of this sort of situation, rather than the one discussed earlier, that we are to understand the following: some adult's mother says to him, 'If you do A I'll have a heart attack, or the probability=p that I'll have a heart attack.' I have in mind a case where the mother does not *choose* to have a heart attack if her son does A or to do something which will bring on or raise the probability of a heart attack. She just knows she will (or that the probability =p). It seems to me that the mother's statement is not plausibly construed as a threat to (choose to) do something or bring about a consequence if her son does A. To use a distinction which will be discussed later, what the mother issues is not a threat but rather a nonthreatening warning. If we look just at the first sort of situation, we will conclude that the mother did not coerce the son into not doing A. But this example can plausibly be viewed as a case of the second sort of situation, in which before Q does A, P does something, making this known to Q, which worsens Q's alternative of doing A. And if this counts as coercion, then the mother may coerce the son. We should look, in this case, at the mother's act, prior to her son's doing A, of telling him that she will or probably will have a heart attack if he

---

[8] Complication: Suppose that as the stranger is being beaten, he says that if they stop and promise to release him, he'll sign over a traveller's cheque to them for $1,000. They stop, he signs it over, they release him. Was he coerced into signing it over?

does A. We may suppose that without her announcement the consequence of her son's doing A is some probability of her having a heart attack and some probability of his feeling guilty (a function of the probability of his realizing why she died and the probability that he will feel guilty anyway because he did something she didn't like and then she died) and some probability of A's having quite nice consequences. And we may suppose that after the mother's announcement the consequences of his doing A are changed significantly. For now there is some probability of her dying and his feeling *enormously* guilty (because he ignored her warning), and even if she won't die because of his doing A, if he does A he will worry over this possibility, feel guilty about doing something he knows upsets her, etc. Her act of making her announcement before he did A worsened the consequence of his doing A. If we suppose, furthermore, that one of her reasons for making the announcement was to worsen the consequences, and that one of his reasons for not doing A was *this* worsening of consequences, then we have a situation of the second sort. And if this sort of situation counts as coercion, the son was coerced into not doing A.[9]

Noncentral Cases of Coercion

I have thus far concentrated upon the central part or core of the notion of coercion, and, in order to avoid too many complications all at once, have spoken of necessary and sufficient conditions for coercion (period). However, I believe that there are further cases of coercion which do not themselves satisfy the conditions thus far discussed, but which are cases of coercion by virtue of standing in certain specifiable relations to central

---

[9] It should be mentioned, in fairness to my mother, that this example was suggested by someone else, whose name I shall not mention, in fairness to his mother.

It is as a special example of this sort of situation that one might understand the activities of some charitable organizations which, along with an appeal for funds, send a 'gift', attempting perhaps to present one with the alternatives of
(a) returning the gift, making no contribution, and feeling slightly embarrassed,
(b) keeping the gift while making no contribution, and feeling somewhat guilty and uneasy,
(c) making a contribution.

cases of coercion.[10] It is a task of some intricacy to get these relations just right. The statements which follow are meant to *indicate* areas in which principles must be formulated. It is *not* claimed that these statements are the formulations which one would eventually arrive at, nor is it claimed that the statements which follow exhaust the areas for which principles must be formulated. Let me repeat: the statements below are meant to indicate areas for which principles must be formulated and are *not* put forward as the correct formulation of principles in these areas. I would expect that, after such principles are adequately formulated, a recursive definition of 'P coerces Q into doing A' would be offered, which would begin with the conditions for the central cases discussed earlier.

(1) If P coerces Q into doing A, and 'A' contains as a proper part the referring expression 'r_1,' and 'B' is obtainable by substituting the referring expression 'r_2' for 'r_1' in 'A', and 'r_2' and 'r_1' have the same reference, and 'r_1' occurs transparently in 'Q does A,' then P coerces Q into doing B.[11]

(2) If P coerces Q into doing A, and it is a necessary truth that if anyone does A he does B, and it is not a necessary truth that if anyone does anything he does B, then P coerces Q into doing B.

(3) If P coerces Q into doing A, and it is a nomological truth that if anyone does A he does B, and it is not a nomological truth that if anyone does anything he does B, then P coerces Q into doing B.

---

[10] An interesting question arises for accounts of a notion, such as mine, which (attempt to) provide necessary and sufficient conditions for the central part or core of the notion, and then handle further cases by specifying the relations in which they stand to the core cases. Given a set of conditions, which are purported to be necessary and sufficient for the core cases of a notion, and given an example to which the notion applies but which does not satisfy the conditions, how is it to be decided whether the example is a counter-example requiring the modification of the conditions, or whether the conditions are to be retained and the example handled as a non-core case by specifying its relation to cases satisfying the conditions?

An alternative procedure to the one followed in the first part of this section is to accept the previous account as the full account of coercion, and to widen the notion of what actions a threat is about.

[11] Readers who notice my sloppiness in the use of quotation marks here will know how to remedy it. One may wish to limit the final formulation of such a principle so that some cases in which P does not know that r_1 and r_2 have the same reference, do not count as P coercing Q into doing B.

(4) If P coerces Q into doing A, and if the only way anyone can do A is by doing either B_1 or B_2 or, ..., or B_n, then P coerces Q into doing B_1 or B_2 or, ..., B_n.[12]

(5) If P coerces Q into doing A, and the only way in which Q can do A is by doing either B_1 or B_2 or, ..., or B_n, then P coerces Q into doing B_1 or B_2 or, ..., or B_n.[13]

(6) If Q can do A only by doing B_1 or B_2 or, ..., or B_n, and Q sets out to do A (intending to do it) because of P's threat of a harmful consequence if Q doesn't do A, and Q does one of the B_1 in order to do A, then Q is coerced into doing B_1 or B_2 or, ..., or B_n, even if Q does not do A (whether because he's prevented from doing A or because he's changed his mind about doing it).

(7) If P coerces Q into doing B_1 or B_2 or, ..., or B_n, and B_1 is the best of the B_1's, the only one of the B_1's it would be reasonable to do, etc., and Q does B_1 for this reason, then P coerces Q into doing B_1.

(8) If P coerces Q into doing A, and x is a consequence of Q's A, and ———————, then P coerces Q into bringing about x. (What further conditions are needed in the blank?)

In order to avoid concluding that Q was coerced into doing B when Q does A (partly) because of the threat, and does B (which stands in one of the stated relations to A) for some *other* reason, we must add to the antecedent of each of these statements the qualification that (part of) the reason Q does B (or, B_1, or B_2, or ..., or B_n) is to avoid or lessen the likelihood of P's threatened consequence (if Q does A).

---

[12] Note that the consequent of 4 is not equivalent to: P coerces Q into doing B_1 or P coerces Q into doing B_2 or ..., or P coerces Q into doing B_n.

[13] One may be reluctant to apply this principle, as it stands, to situations where unbeknownst to P, Q is specially handicapped so that he can do A only by doing some horrendous B_1. One must also be careful not to misinterpret conclusions reached by applying this condition, as in the case (where n = 1) where R advises Q to go to the movies and P threatens Q with death if he does not go to the movies. Since Q, whom P coerces into going to the movies, can go to the movies only by doing what R advised, by applying the condition we reach the conclusion that P coerces Q into doing the action advised by R, which is easily misinterpreted.

Threats and Offers

The notion of a threat has played a central role in what has been said thus far. In this section we shall consider the differences between threats and offers, and in the next section we shall consider the differences between threats and warnings.

If P offers Q substantially more money than Q is earning at his current job to come to work for P, and Q accepts because he wants to increase his income, has P coerced Q into working for him? Some writers (Hale, Bay) would say that P has; the threat being 'come to work for me or I won't give you the money.' On this view, every employer coerces his employees, every employee his employer ('give me the money or I won't work for you'), every seller of an object coerces his customers ('give me the money or I won't give you the object'), and every customer the person from whom he buys. It seems clear that normally these aren't cases of coercion. Offers of inducements, incentives, rewards, bribes, consideration, remuneration, recompense, payment do not normally constitute threats, and the person who accepts them is not normally coerced.

As a first formulation, let us say that whether someone makes a threat against Q's doing an action or an offer to Q to do the action depends upon how the consequence he says he will bring about changes the consequences of Q's action from what they would have been in the normal or natural or expected course of events. If it makes the consequences of Q's action worse than they would have been in the normal and expected course of events, it is a threat; if it makes the consequences better, it is an offer.[14] The term 'expected' is meant to shift between or straddle *predicted* and *morally required*. This handles pretty well the clear cases of threats and offers. Let us see how it fares with more difficult examples.

> (a) P is Q's usual supplier of drugs, and today when he comes to Q he says that he will not sell them to Q, as he normally does, for $20, but rather will give them to Q if and only if Q beats up a certain person.
>
> (b) P is a stranger who has been observing Q, and knows that Q is a drug addict. Both know that Q's usual supplier of drugs was arrested this morning and that P had nothing to do with his arrest. P approaches Q and says that he will give Q drugs if and only if Q beats up a certain person.

---

[14] A more complicated statement would be required to take into account condition 7 in the section on Conditions for Coercion.

In the first case, where P is Q's usual supplier of drugs, P is *threatening* not to give Q the drugs. The normal course of events is one in which P supplies Q with drugs for money. P is threatening to *withhold* the supply, to *deprive* Q of his drugs, if Q does not beat up the person. In the second case, where P is a stranger to Q, P is not *threatening* not to supply Q with drugs; in the normal course of events P does not do so, nor is P expected to do so. If P does not give Q the drugs he is not *withholding* drugs from Q nor is he *depriving* Q of drugs. P is *offering* Q drugs as an inducement to beat up the person. Thus in the second case, P does not *coerce* Q into beating up the person, since P does not threaten Q. (But the fact that P did not coerce Q into beating up the person does not mean that it would not be true for Q to say, in some legitimate sense of the phrase: 'I had no choice.')

There is a further point to be considered about the first case in which P is Q's usual supplier of drugs. In addition to threatening to withhold the drugs if Q doesn't beat up a certain person, hasn't P made Q an offer? Since in the normal and expected course of events Q does not get drugs for beating up the person, isn't this a case in which P then offers Q drugs as an incentive to beat up the person? And if P *has* made this offer, why do we view the overall situation as one in which P threatens Q, rather than as one in which P makes Q an offer? We have here a situation in which P takes a consequence viewed as desirable by Q (receiving drugs) off one action (paying $20) and puts it onto another action (beating up the person). Since Q prefers and P believes that Q prefers paying the money and receiving the drugs to beating up the person and receiving the drugs, and since Q would rather not beat up the person, P's statement is a threat to withhold the drugs if Q doesn't beat up the person, and this threat predominates over any subsidiary offer P makes for Q to beat up the person, making the whole situation a threat situation.

But instead of subtracting a desirable consequence from one of Q's actions and tagging the *same* consequence onto another of Q's actions, P may subtract a desirable consequence C from one of Q's actions A_1 and add a *more* desirable consequence C' onto another action A_2 available to Q. For example, the dope peddler might say to Q, 'I will not give you drugs if you just pay me money, but I will give you a better grade of drugs, without monetary payment, if you beat up this person.' It seems plausible to think that as one increases the desirability of C' to Q, at some point the situation changes from one predominantly involving a threat to deprive Q of C if he does A_1 (doesn't do A_2) to one which predominantly involves an offer to Q of C' if he does A_2. And it seems plausible to claim that this turning point from threat to offer, as one increases the value of C′ for Q, comes at the point where Q begins preferring A_2 and C′ to A_1 and C (stops preferring the latter to the former?).

The following principle embodies this claim, and also covers the case where it is the same consequence which is switched from one action to another as in the earlier example. It also is meant to apply to obvious mixtures of threats and offers, e.g., 'If you go to the movies I'll give you $10,000. If you don't go, I'll kill you.'

> If P intentionally changes the consequences of two actions A_1 and A_2 available to Q so as to lessen the desirability of the consequences of A_1, and so as to increase the desirability of the consequences of A_2, and part of P's reason for acting as he does is to so lessen and increase the desirabilities of the respective consequences then
> (a) This resultant change predominantly involves a threat to Q if he does A_1 if Q prefers doing the old A_1 (without the worsened consequences) to doing the new A_2 (with the improved consequences).
> (b) This resultant change predominantly involves an offer to Q to do A_2 if Q prefers doing the new A_2 (with the improved consequences) to the old A_1 (without the worsened consequences).

This principle ties in nicely with something we shall say later. For when the change predominantly involves a threat, Q would normally not be willing to have this change made (since he'd rather do the old A_1 than either of the two alternatives after the change), whereas when the change predominantly involves an offer, Q would normally be willing to have the change made (since he'd rather do the new A_2 than the old A_1, and if he prefers doing one of the old alternatives (A_1) to doing the new A_2, he can still do it.) I shall claim later that this willingness or unwillingness to make the change marks an important difference between offers and threats.[15]

If a statement's being a threat or an offer depends upon how the carrying out of the statement affects the normal or expected course of events, one would expect that there will be situations where it is unclear whether a person is making a threat or an offer because it is unclear what the normal and expected course of events is. And one would expect that people will disagree about whether something is a threat or an offer because they disagree about what the normal and expected course of

---

[15] The notion discussed here should be distinguished from another in which both threatening Q with x if he does A and offering him y if he doesn't do A are said to predominantly involve an offer (threat) if for almost any action B, if Q is both threatened with x if he does B and offered y if he does B, Q will prefer to do B (not do B).

events is, which is to be used as a baseline in assessing whether something is a threat or an offer. This is indeed the case.

Consider the following example. Q is in the water far from shore, nearing the end of his energy, and P comes close by in his boat. Both know there is no other hope of Q's rescue around, and P knows that Q is the soul of honesty and that if Q makes a promise he will keep it. P says to Q 'I will take you in my boat and bring you to shore if and only if you first promise to pay me $10,000 within three days of reaching shore with my aid.' Is P offering to take Q to shore if he makes the promise, or is he threatening to let Q drown if Q doesn't make the promise? If one views the normal or expected course of events as one in which Q drowns without P's intervention, then in saying that he will save Q if and only if Q makes the promise, P is *offering* to save Q. If one views the normal or expected course of events as one in which a person in a boat who comes by a drowning person, in a situation such as this, saves him, then in saying that he will save Q if and only if Q makes the promise, P is *threatening* not to save Q. Whether P's saying that he will save Q if and only if Q makes the promise is an *offer* to save Q or a *threat* not to save Q depends upon what the normal or expected course of events is.

Since it is likely to be clear to the reader which course of events he wants to pick out as normal and expected as the background against which to assess whether P's statement is an offer or a threat (namely, the one that makes it a threat) we should sharpen the example. Suppose in addition to the foregoing that P knows that Q has greatly wronged P (or others), but that Q cannot be legally punished for this (no law covered the wrong, a legal technicality, the statute of limitations has run out, or some such thing). Or P knows that Q will go on to do monstrous deeds if rescued. In some such situations it will be unclear what P is morally expected to do, and hence unclear whether his statement is a threat or an offer. For other such situations it will be clear that P is morally expected to let Q drown, and hence his statement will be an offer.[16]

Thus far we have considered threats as introducing certain deviations from the normal and expected course of events. The question arises as to whether the normal or expected course of events itself can be coercive. Suppose that usually a slave owner beats his slave each morning, for no reason connected with the slave's behaviour. Today he says to his slave,

[16] I ignore problems arising from a divergence between what P believes to be the morally expected course of events and what is the morally expected course of events, e.g., where P believes he's morally required to let Q drown, although he's morally required to save Q.

'Tomorrow I will not beat you if and only if you now do A.' One is tempted to view this as a threat, and one is also tempted to view this as an offer. I attribute these conflicting temptations to the divergence between the normal course of events, in which the slave is beaten each morning, and the (morally) expected course of events, in which he is not. And I suggest that we have here a situation of a threat, and that here the morally expected course of events takes precedence over the normal course of events in assessing whether we have a threat or an offer.

One might think that in deciding whether something is a threat or an offer, the (morally) expected course of events always takes precedence over the normal or usual course of events, where these diverge. It is not obvious that this is so. I have in mind particularly the example mentioned earlier, where your normal supplier of dope says that he will continue to supply you if and only if you beat up a certain person. Here, let us suppose, the morally expected course of events is that he doesn't supply you with drugs, but the course of events which forms the background for deciding whether he has threatened you or made you an offer is the normal though not morally expected course of events (in which he supplies you with drugs for money); it is against this background that we can obtain the consequence that he's threatened you.

Thus, in both the slave and the addict examples the normal and morally expected courses of events diverge. Why do we pick one of these in one case, and the other in the other as the background against which to assess whether we have a threat or an offer? The relevant difference between these cases seems to be that the slave himself would prefer the morally expected to the normal course of events whereas the addict prefers the normal to the morally expected course of events. It may be that when the normal and morally expected courses of events diverge, the one of these which is to be used in deciding whether a conditional announcement of an action constitutes a threat or an offer is the course of events that the recipient of the action prefers.[17]

[17] Let me suggest as a fertile area for testing intuitions and theories, the following, where the normal and morally expected courses of events may diverge, and where it may not be clear what the morally expected course of events is. Suppose some nation N were to announce that it will in the future give economic aid to some other countries provided that these other countries satisfy certain conditions (e.g., do not vote contrary to N on important issues before the United Nations, do not trade with specific nations, do not have diplomatic relations with specific nations). Would this announcement constitute an offer to give these nations aid, or a threat not to do so? Relevant factors (to list just two of many) are whether or not

I have raised the question of whether the normal and expected course of events itself can be coercive, and was led to consider cases where the normal and (morally) expected courses of events diverged. I now would like to consider this question again, for cases where they do not diverge. Can P, by saying that he will bring about a consequence if Q does A (where this consequence is such that if Q does A, P would bring it about in the normal *and* (morally) expected course of events), coerce Q into not doing A? Suppose that in the normal *and* morally expected course of events, people get punished for theft. Aren't some people coerced into not stealing by the legal apparatus?

One might say that if a *type* of action or consequence is itself part of the normal and expected course of events if Q does A, one should use the normal and expected course of events minus this type of action or consequence as a background against which to assess whether a statement is a threat. If the consequences of an action would be worse, if the statement is carried out, than they would be in this *new* course of events (i.e. the normal and expected course of events without the type of action or consequence) then the statement is a threat. But who knows what the world would be like if there was no punishment for crimes? It might well be that things would be so bad that the institution of punishing crimes would improve the consequences of almost all actions, and hence count, according to this suggestion, as making offers to people.

An alternative procedure seems more reasonable; namely, to consider the normal and expected course of events, if Q does A, without P's particular act or without the particular consequence P will bring about, and against this background assess whether P's statement that if Q does A he will do a particular act or bring about a particular consequence constitutes a threat (i.e. whether P's statement, if carried out, makes Q's A worse than it would be in *this* new course of events).

There remain some problems about knowing what the course of events would be without this act, but these seem manageable. On this view, even though in the normal and expected course of events Q gets punished for theft, the statement that he will be punished for theft counts as a threat since the act of punishment, if Q steals, unfavourably affects the consequences of one act of Q's (stealing) against the background of

---

N has an obligation or is morally required to give these nations economic aid (independently of whether they satisfy the conditions), and whether or not N has previously given these nations economic aid independently of whether they satisfy the conditions

the normal and expected course of events minus *this* act of punishment.[18]

According to the account offered earlier of (the first sort of) coercion, threats are necessary for coercion. One might extend the account to include some offers, if there were clear situations in which Q is coerced into doing A even though Q does A because P offered to do B if Q did A. Despite my inclination to say that one is never coerced when one does something because of an offer, there is one sort of case, where the offer is closely tied to coercion or attempted coercion, which I find it difficult to decide about. Suppose that P knows that Q has committed a murder which the police are investigating, and knows of evidence sufficient to convict Q of this murder. P says to Q, 'If you give me $10,000 I will not turn over the information I have to the police.' Let us assume that were P unable to contact Q and present his proposal he would turn the information over to the police. Furthermore, in this situation P is (morally) expected to turn the information over to the police. So in the normal and expected course of events, P turns the information over to the police (whether or not Q gives him $10,000). It would seem, therefore, that P is *offering* not to turn the information over to the police, rather than *threatening* to turn it over. Yet one is strongly tempted to say, when Q pays P $10,000 because he accepts the offer, that Q was coerced by P into paying the $10,000.[19]

---

[18] Though this seems to me to be the correct thing to say, there is a problem, which I have not yet been able to solve, which I should briefly mention.

Letting P = you are punished
C = you commit a crime

the officials in the society might say

P if and only if C

or equivalently

not-P if and only if not-C.

Interpreted truth-functionally, each of these is equivalent to either (P and C) or (not-P and not-C). The two remaining possibilities are (P and not-C), and (C and not-P). The background we want to use in deciding whether a threat is involved is C and not-P. If we were to use the remaining possibility, P and not-C, as the background, then it would turn out that an offer is involved here. The problem is to formulate criteria, in cases where the biconditional is itself part of the normal and expected course of events, which pick out C and not-P rather than P and not-C in this and other threat cases, and which would pick out the appropriate background for offer cases as well.

[19] This is a case of blackmail which presumably should be legally forbidden because allowing it increases the probability that crimes will go undetected. Other reasons apply to other

If the following principle were correct, then this would be a case of coercion:

> If P offers to refrain from aiding the threatener of a coercive consequence for Q's A from bringing about this consequence, in exchange for Q's doing B, and if the credible threat of this consequence[20] if Q didn't perform B would coerce Q into doing B, then when Q does B because of the offer, Q was coerced into doing B.

A case similar to the previous one, is one in which the police arrest Q for a crime, believing that he has committed it and having sufficient evidence to convict him of it. In the course of questioning Q, they come to believe that Q knows who has committed some other crime, and they say that Q will not be prosecuted if and only if he tells them who has committed this other crime. Since if the police did not think Q knew who committed the other crime they would have prosecuted, and since they are morally expected to have him prosecuted, the police have *offered* not to have Q prosecuted rather than *threatened* to have him prosecuted. If Q names the person who committed the other crime, in order to escape being prosecuted, some are strongly tempted to say that he was coerced into giving the information. The above principle would yield this consequence. Though I do not deny that one may say, in some legitimate sense of these expressions, 'Q was forced to do what he did,' 'Q had no choice,' I am unable to decide whether, in the above cases, Q was coerced into doing so, and I leave this an open question.

The two previous cases are cases where P is morally expected or required to do the act, and would normally do so (turn the murderer over

---

cases, but note that it is not obvious that one wants to legally forbid all cases which fit the description: saying that one will make public some information about Q unless Q pays money. For example.
  (a) P's saying that he will make public the information that Q has not paid P the money Q owes him, unless Q pays the money.
  (b) P is writing a book, and in the course of his research comes across information about Q which will help sell many copies of the book. P tells Q he will refrain from including this information in the book if and only if Q pays him an amount of money equal to the expected difference in his royalties between the book containing this information and the book without the information.

[20] More precisely, the credible threat of raising the probability of this consequence from what it is without P's aiding in bringing it about, to what it would be with P's aid.

to the police, have Q prosecuted). It is worth mentioning cases where P has a legal and moral right to do the act, but would not decide to do so (even if Q didn't do A) were he not trying to get Q to do A. For example, P has a right to build on his land blocking Q's view, or foreclose Q's mortgage, or bring legal action against Q (on a valid and enforcible claim) but would not decide to do so (it's not worth the trouble, P has no pressing need for funds, etc.) were it not for his wanting Q to do A. P tells Q that unless he does A, he (P) will build on his land, foreclose Q's mortgage, bring legal action against Q, etc. Since P's action is not part of the morally expected course of events (not that P is morally expected *not* to do it) and since in the normal course of events P wouldn't do it, the account yields the result that one would wish: In these cases P is threatening to perform his actions rather than offering not to do so.

Threats and Warnings

In the section on Conditions for Coercion, because of the example of the SSRC people saying 'your money or your life,' we rejected the condition that P says or does what he does *in order* to get Q not to perform some particular action A. We substituted instead a condition requiring that (part of) P's reason for deciding to bring about the consequence if Q does A (or, if he hasn't decided, saying that he has) is that (P believes that) this worsens Q's alternative of doing A (or that Q would believe it does). And we mentioned the view that this is part of the notion of making a threat. This view illuminates the fact that some statements about one's future actions if Q does A, are not threats even though the acts you've stated you would do if Q does A worsen Q's alternative of doing A.

Such statements about one's future actions I shall call nonthreatening warnings (for short, just 'warnings'). The distinction between threats and nonthreatening warnings is crucial to some questions that arise in the law. For example, an election is about to be held in a factory to determine whether the employees will be represented by a labour union. The owner of the factory announces to his employees that if the union wins the election, he will close his factory and go out of business. Has he *threatened* the employees with loss of their jobs if the union wins, or merely *warned* them what will happen if the union wins? If a majority of the employees would have voted for the union if not for the announcement, and the union lost because of the announcement, were the employees *coerced* by their employer into rejecting the union?

We may view this situation as a game, represented by the following matrix:

	Employees	
	I. union wins	II. union loses
Employer A. Stays in business	(b)	(a)
Employer B. Goes out of business	(c)	(d)

The employees make the first move (pick a column) and the employer makes the second (picks a row) knowing what move the employees have first made. That is, first the employees choose to be represented by the union or not, and then the employer, knowing what choice his employees have made, decides to stay in business or go out of business. I shall assume that each of the members of some particular majority of the employees preferentially ranks the outcomes as follows:

(b)
(a)
(c)
(d)

and shall call this the preference ordering of the employees. There seem to me to be at least four cases worth considering[21], corresponding to four different preference rankings of these alternatives by the employer.

[21] I consider here cases where the employer *could* stay in business (without running at a loss) even if the union wins. In the case where, if the unions wins, the employer cannot both stay in business and out of the red, it is clear that his statement is a warning and not a threat. (In the normal course of events he does go out of business if the union wins, and chooses to do so earlier than he must, in order to cut his losses.) I assume, for the cases discussed in the text, that the employer making the statement intends to close if the union wins. If he intends not to close, or has no settled intention either way, then in stating that he will close if the union wins he is making a threat.

I should note that I am assuming for some of the cases in which the employer could profitably stay in business if the union wins, that he does not have an obligation to and is not morally required to remain in business if the union wins the election. It may be that some disagreements about whether the employer is threatening or warning stem from disagreements about whether he is morally required to remain in business if the union wins (morally required not to close because of dislike of running a unionized business, etc.).

These are:

(1) (a)	(2) (a)	(3) (a)	(4) (c)—(a)
(b)	(c)—(b)	(c)	(b)
(c)	(d)	(b)	
(d)			

I assume, for each case, that the employer knows the preference ranking of the employees.

Case (1): The employer, if he were sure that the union would win the election, would not make his announcement, since he prefers continuing in business though the factory is unionized, to going out of business. That is, he prefers (b) to (c). However he commits himself to going out of business if the factory is unionized, and announces this decision (that is, rules out (b)), in the hope that this will lead his employees to reject the union. By ruling out (b) beforehand he leaves his employees (a), (c), and (d) among which to choose, and since *of these* (a) is highest in the preference ranking of the employees, they will presumably then act so as to realize (a), and this is the alternative which the *employer* ranks most highly. The employer is committing himself beforehand, for strategic reasons, to do something (B) in a situation (I) such that had he not committed himself to this he would be better off doing something else (A) in that situation when and if it arose. It seems clear that in this case, when the employer announces that he will go out of business if the union wins the election he is *threatening* his employees.[22] For in the normal course of events, he does not go out of business, given his preferences, if the employees vote for the union. Hence he's announcing that he will depart from the normal course of events in a way to the detriment of his employees, if they elect the union.[23] And also (part of) his reason for deciding to go out of business if the union wins is that he believes that

---

[22] Cf. T. Schelling, *The Strategy of Conflict* (Harvard, 1960). Note that according to contemporary utility theory, it will be reasonable for the employer to rule out (b) for strategic reasons even if he doesn't know the preference ranking of the employees, so long as

$p\ u(a) + (1-p)\ u(c) > u(b)$,

where p is the probability that the union will lose the election after he's announced that if they win, he will go out of business, and u(x) is the utility of x to the employer.

[23] I should note that I have done nothing here to argue, as I would wish to, that acting on such strategic considerations is not part of the normal or expected course of events which forms the background to discussing questions of coercion. Not doing something unless you'd first announced it in this sort of strategic situation, for strategic reasons, should be distinguished from not doing something without prior announcement for other sorts of reasons; cf. discussions of ex post facto laws.

this worsens his employees alternative of electing the union (and he thereby hopes to influence them to reject the union). Hence his announcement is a threat, and he has threatened to go out of business if the union wins the election.

Case 2: The employer announces that he will go out of business if the union wins the election, thus ruling out (b), and leaving the employees a choice between (a) and (c). He makes this announcement hoping that because of it, his employees will reject the union. Note that in this case, unlike the first one, there is not something the employer would *rather* do than go out of business if the union wins the election. (For he is indifferent between (c) and (b), whereas in the first case, the employer preferred (b) to (c).) Though there aren't exactly the same strategic considerations as in the first case, still strategic considerations are involved. And this employer, too, has threatened his employees. For in the normal or expected course of events he wouldn't have made his announcement, and would, being indifferent between (c) and (b), decide whether or not to stay in business if and when the union won the election. We may suppose that before he decides there is some nonzero probability of his deciding to close the factory, and some nonzero probability of his staying in business. This being what one would expect in the normal course of events, his announcement and commitment to going out of business, for sure, if the union wins the election, changes the normal or expected course of events in the typical manner of a threat. For his being almost certain to go out of business is worse, from his employees' viewpoint, than there being some probability of his going out of business and some probability of his remaining in business. Since part of his reason for deciding to go out of business if the union wins is that (he believes) this worsens his employees' alternative of electing the union, this constitutes a threat.

But if in this case the employer does not announce that he will close if the union wins (which would be a threat), but instead announces truthfully that he is indifferent between closing and staying in business if the unions wins and will decide what to do afterwards (and if his employees voting for the union in the face of this announcement would not anger him and yield a larger probability of his closing than if the announcement hadn't been made), then the case may be significantly different. This issue is also raised by case 3, and is treated in the discussion of it.

Case 4: The employer tells his employees what his preferences are, and that he will go out of business if the union wins. We may suppose that he doesn't make his decision or tell them this in order to get them to reject the union, since he doesn't care whether they reject it or not. For even if they elect it, he can go out of business, and there is nothing he *prefers* to that. No strategic considerations are involved. He makes his announcement solely to inform his employees of what will be the consequences of their action. It was no part of his reason for deciding to go out of business if the union won, that this worsened his employees' alternative of electing the union, and no part of his reason for making the announcement was to get his employees to reject the union. It seems clear that this is not a case of coercion, and that the employer has not made a threat (even though his employees might sorrowfully tell the union representative that they had no choice) but has rather issued a nonthreatening warning.

Case 3: I have left case 3 for last because it is the most difficult. In this case, the employer announces what his preference ranking is, and says that he'll go out of business if the union wins the election. And indeed, unlike the employers in cases 1 and 2, but like the employer in case 4, he prefers going out of business if the union wins the election to staying in business with the union representing his employees. In the normal course of events, he would go out of business if the union wins, whether or not he has previously announced that he would do so. However, unlike the employer in case 4 but like the employers in cases 1 and 2, he prefers staying in business without the union to going out of business if the union wins the election, and makes his announcement in order to get his employees to reject the union. Has he threatened his employees, or just warned them? I am inclined to say that he has warned them rather than threatened them. (Note that a teacher can *warn* a student that he will fail unless his work improves, even if the teacher does so in order to get the student to work harder.) For he does not decide to close if the union wins in order to worsen the alternative of the union winning, and in making the announcement he does not worsen this alternative but rather makes known what its consequences will be. Furthermore, there seems to be no presumption against this employer's telling his employees that he will close if the union wins, whereas there is (normally) a presumption against making threats.[24]

These cases raise an interesting point relevant to the wider task of deciding what actions people should be free to do, and what actions they

[24] I wish here to exclude threats against certain acts which violate the rights of others. It is difficult to determine whether there is a presumption against threatening someone against (or coercing someone into not), e.g. murdering someone else, which is almost always easily overridden, or whether there is no such presumption in such cases. It is also difficult to determine exactly what the difference is between these two alternatives. For an attempt to describe the difference, see my 'Moral Complications and Moral Structures,' *Natural Law Forum*, Vol. 13, 1968, pp. 1–50, section 7.

should be unfree to do. It may be that, even if one picks out a particular pattern of freedom and unfreedom as optimal, there is no acceptable institutional arrangement available to one which realizes this pattern. One may lack the institutional means to realize exactly the optimal pattern of freedom and unfreedom, or certain ways of realizing this pattern, and publically distinguishing among persons, may be unacceptable to the society at large. So it may be that, given the available institutional means, the feasible patterns of freedom and unfreedom among which one must choose are suboptimal and nondominated patterns of the following forms:

> (a) Where some persons are unfree to do acts they should (according to the optimal pattern) be free to do.
> (b) Where some people are free to do acts they should be unfree to do.
> (c) Where some people are free to do acts they should be unfree to do, and some people are unfree to do acts they should be free to do.

A full theory of freedom would, as well as specifying the optimal pattern of freedom and unfreedom, concern itself with choices among such suboptimal patterns.

It may be that we have an example of such a choice here. For one may wish to make the case 1 and 2 employers unfree to make their announcements (threats) while leaving the case 3 and 4 employers free to make their announcements (warnings). However it may be difficult to devise an institutional arrangement which accomplishes this, for it may be difficult to distinguish case 1 and 2 employers from case 3 and 4 employers. (Note that if one attempts to distinguish them, there will be reason for case 1 and 2 employers to lie when asked about their preferences.) The actual institutional choice one faces may be to forbid all such announcements, to allow all such announcements, or to use some condition almost coextensive with the suitable preferences and forbid and allow announcements on the basis of whether this condition is satisfied, regretfully admitting that one cannot handle *all* the cases in the way one would wish.[25]

> [25] The Supreme Court held in Textile Workers Union v. Darlington Manufacturing Co. (380 U.S. 263 (1965)) that it is not an unfair labour practice for an employer to close his *entire* business, even if the closing is due to anti-union animus, but that closing *part* of a business is an unfair labour practice if *the purpose* is to discourage unionism in any of the employer's remaining plants, and if the employer may reasonably have foreseen such an effect. Given the difficulties in determining an employer's purpose, one suspects that the effect of this

Problems of choice among suboptimal patterns arise also and obviously for paternalistic legislation; legislation which, in order to prevent him from coming to harm, or to lessen the chance of this, or to enable him to realize some good, makes someone unfree to perform a particular act.[26] The feasible patterns will often require either making some persons, who do not need the paternalistic protection and might be better off without it, unfree to perform some acts, or leaving some people free to do acts it is thought they should be unfree to do (for their own protection). One will often have to choose among such patterns because there is no realizable and acceptable institutional arrangement which divides people up according to what is thought to be the optimal pattern with respect to particular acts. An important point emerges from this discussion; namely, that the statement that a particular piece of legislation makes some persons unfree to perform some acts they should not be unfree to perform (according to what is thought to be the optimal pattern of freedom and unfreedom), even if true, is not by itself a *conclusive* objection to the legislation. For it may be that no feasible and acceptable pattern of freedom and unfreedom is more optimal (or all other realizable patterns are less optimal) than the one yielded by this legislation.

I might mention the statement, which we might call a tip, which stands to an offer as a non-threatening warning stands to a threat; that is, P's statement which points out that P will bring about some consequence if Q does A which improves Q's alternative of doing A, though P's

---

decision will be to forbid all employers from closing part of their business because it has become unionized, if other parts of the business are not unionized.

[26] Note that some paternalistic acts can involve great self-sacrifice, as when drugs are legally forbidden in order to protect those who are not addicts who would be so under a system in which drugs were legal. The price *others* pay to protect them is increased risk of being robbed or assaulted by addicts trying to acquire money in order to pay the high prices on the illegal market, plus the diversion of resources into trying to enforce the law. Perhaps it is appropriate that others should all suffer for their original unjustified paternalistic intervention.

The reader might find it useful, in thinking about paternalism, to consider whether there are any limits to the severity of the penalty we would include in a paternalistic law, and how these limits are to be fixed. Could we, for example, have the death penalty for the offence of swimming at a beach when no lifeguard is present? Certain plausible-looking principles would allow this, because when the system including this penalty is instituted, it is the one of the alternatives which is expected to best operate for the person's own good. Surely something has gone haywire here.

believing that it improves or that Q would believe it improves Q's doing A is not part of P's reason for deciding to bring about the consequence if Q does A.

Building into the notion of P's making Q an offer to do A the requirement that (part of) P's reason for bringing about the consequence if Q does A is to improve Q's alternative of doing A, illuminates the following example: P comes up to Q and says, 'your money or your life.' Q resists and beats P up. Had P not said what he did and had he not confronted Q with a gun, and had Q just beaten P up, Q would have been a bully and people would have scorned him. But now the consequences of beating P up are made far more attractive to Q; Q becomes a hero if he does so. But P hasn't made Q an offer to beat him up, because though what P did improved the consequences of some action of Q's, bringing about this improvement was not part of P's reason for acting as he did. Has P tipped Q off to something? Highwaymen normally don't go on to say, 'And if you resist and beat me up you'll be a hero,' but if one did, he would have given his prospective victim a tip, however little appreciated. Note, incidentally, that one should not think for the case where Q beats P up after P makes his threat that Q was coerced into doing so, even though Q did so to avoid the threatened consequence. For not all of the other necessary conditions for coercion are satisfied.

Threats, Offers, and Choices

I have claimed that normally a person is not coerced into performing an action if he performs it because someone has offered him something to do it, though normally he is coerced into performing an action if he does so because of a threat that has been made against his not doing so. Writers who count offers as coercive do so, I suspect, because they accept something roughly like the following statement:

> If Q has available to him the actions in a set A, and as a result of what P has done or will do
> (a) act A_1 is significantly higher in utility to Q than the other actions in A
> (b) act A_2 is significantly lower in utility to Q than the other actions in A
> whereas it wasn't before, and Q
> (a) does A_1 because of this
> (b) refrains from A_2 because of this
> then Q was coerced into
> (a) doing A_1
> (b) not doing A_2

According to this view, any action of P's which results in A_1's being significantly greater or A_2's being significantly less in utility than the other actions in A may coerce Q. It makes no difference, according to this view, how the difference in utility is brought about; whether in (a) A_1 is absolutely raised in utility or all the other members of A are absolutely lowered in utility, or whether in (b) A_2 is absolutely lowered in utility, or all the other members of A are absolutely raised in utility. It is only the resulting *relative* positions, however arrived at, which count. This view is mistaken, and I shall assume that we can all think of examples that show to our satisfaction that this is so. I now want to consider whether anything illuminating can be said about *why* the notion of coercion isn't so wide as to encompass all bringing about of actions by the bringing about of difference in relative position. The question I'm asking may seem bogus. After all, there will be some terms which apply both to getting someone to do something via threats, and to getting someone to do something via offers, e.g., 'getting someone to do something.' And there will be some terms which apply to one and not the other. Am I just asking why the word 'coercion' is among those that apply to only one of these and not to both? And why expect the answer, presumably going back to the word's Latin roots, to be philosophically interesting? So let me state my task differently.

I would like to make sense of the following claims: when a person does something because of threats, the will of another is operating or predominant, whereas when he does something because of offers this is not so; a person who does something because of threats is subject to the will of another, whereas a person who acts because of an offer is not; a person who does something because of threats does not perform a fully voluntary action, whereas this is normally not the case with someone who does something because of offers; when someone does something because of offers it is his own choice, whereas when he does something because of threats it is not his own choice but someone else's, or not fully his own choice, or someone else has made his choice for him; when a person does something because of threats he does it unwillingly, whereas this is normally not the case when someone does something because of offers. (There are other ways to approach this area. One might ask why we say that we *accept* offers, but we go along with threats rather than accept them.)

I would like to make sense of these claims in the face of the following three roughly true statements, which seem to indicate that threat and offer situations are on a par so far as whose will operates, whether the act is fully voluntary, whose choice it is, and so forth.

(1) A person can be gotten to do something which someone else wants him to do, which he otherwise wouldn't do, by offers as well as by threats.

(2) A person can choose to do what there is a threat against his doing, just as a person can choose to do what there is an offer for him not to do. ('just as'?)

(3) Sometimes a threat is so great that a person cannot reasonably be expected not to go along with it, but also sometimes an offer is so great that a person cannot reasonably be expected not to go along with it (that is, not to accept it).

I shall consider only a partially described person, whom I shall call the Rational Man, and unfortunately shall not get to us. The Rational Man, being able to resist those temptations which he thinks he should resist, will normally welcome credible offers,[27] or at any rate not be unwilling to have them be made. For he can always decline to accept the offer, and in this case he is no worse off than he would have been had the offer not been made. (Here I ignore the 'costs' of making decisions, e.g. time spent in considering an offer.) Why *should* he be unwilling to be the recipient of an offer? On the other hand, the Rational Man will normally not welcome credible threats, will normally be unwilling to be threatened even if he is able to resist going along with them. It is worth mentioning some cases which are or seem to be exceptions to this. A person might not mind threats if he was going to do the act anyway. But, since in this case he (probably) wasn't coerced, he needn't concern us here. A person might welcome threats which restrict the acts he can reasonably be expected to perform, and therefore improve his bargaining

---

[27] I omit consideration of offers to do acts such that, if the offer is made, the act cannot be done without accepting the offer, e.g. one cannot work at certain government jobs without receiving a salary of at least one dollar per year. The Rational Man may sometimes prefer doing the act without the offer's having been made, so that it will be clear to others, and perhaps himself, *why* he does the act (e.g. not for the money). I also shall not consider the case of a person's not welcoming an offer for him to perform a malicious act because of what it shows about the person making the offer. Note the importance of our restricting our attention here to the Rational Man. Another person might not, for example, welcome an offer of $50,000 for him to kill Jones, because he's afraid he may be tempted to (and unable to resist the temptation to) accept the offer. In considering only the Rational Man, I am leaving part of my task undone. For I do not argue, as I would wish to, that even for someone who sometimes succumbs to temptations which he believes he ought to resist, there is a significant difference between offers and threats.

position with a third party, e.g. an employer negotiating with a labour union might welcome publicly known threats against raising wages by more than n per cent. But what he welcomes is not his being coerced into not raising wages by more than n per cent (he is not coerced), but its looking to others as though he is coerced. This needn't concern us here.

But there are other cases which are somewhat more difficult. For example, P tells Q that he'll give Q $10,000 if in the next week someone, without prompting, threatens Q. Someone does and Q welcomes the threat. Or, P is jealous of Q's receiving certain sorts of offers and tells Q that if he (Q) receives another offer before P does, then P will kill Q. Q cringes when the next offer comes. Or Q believes that having at least five threats (offers) made to one in one week brings good (bad) luck, and so is happy (unhappy) at the coming of the fifth threat (offer) in a week. Or for tax purposes Q welcomes a threat to illegally take some of his money. And so forth. I want to say that in such cases when threats are welcomed and offers shunned, they are done so for extraneous reasons, because of the special context. (One is tempted to say that in these contexts what would normally be a threat (offer) isn't really one.) I find it difficult to distinguish these special contexts from the others, but the claim that threats are normally unwelcome whereas offers are not, is not meant to apply to contexts where some special 'if-then' is believed to obtain, where it is believed to be the case that if a threat (offer) is made, resisted (accepted), or carried out then something good (bad) will happen to the recipient of the threat (offer) (where this good (bad) consequence is not 'internal' to the threat (offer)), and this belief on the part of the recipient of the threat (offer) overrides other considerations. It is along such lines that I suggest viewing the person who welcomes a threat because it affords him the opportunity to prove to others or test for himself his courage. Finally, let me mention the case where a person is in an n-person prisoners' dilemma situation. In this case, he may most prefer everyone *else's* being coerced into performing a dominated action while he is left free to perform the dominant action. He may also prefer everyone's being coerced into performing a specific dominated action (e.g. paying taxes) to no one's being so coerced. And since he realizes that the policy he most prefers, which treats him specially, isn't a feasible alternative, he may welcome the threat to everyone including himself.[28] But

---

[28] For a discussion of the prisoners dilemma, cf. R. D. Luce and Howard Raiffa, *Games and Decisions* (New York, 1957), pp. 94–102. On dominance principles, see my 'Newcomb's Problem and Two Principles of Choice' in N. Rescher *et. al.*, eds., *Essays in Honor of Carl G. Hempel* (Reidel, 1969). One often finds this argument applied to questions about the provision of a public good for a group. For example, each

though he welcomes the system which threatens everyone, he might still be coerced into performing his particular action (e.g. paying his taxes). This too seems to me not to be a counter-example to the claim that threat are unwelcome, but one of the special contexts, with special if-thens tagged onto the making of the threat, to which the claim is not meant to apply.

I have said that the Rational Man would normally be willing to have credible offers made to him, whereas he would not normally be willing to be the recipient of credible threats. Imagine that the Rational Man is given a choice about whether someone else makes him an offer (threatens him). For example, the Rational Man is asked, 'Shall I threaten you (make you an offer)?' If he answers 'yes', it is done. I am supposing that no offer is made the Rational Man to say 'yes' to this question, and no threat is made against his not saying 'yes'; i.e. that no threats of offers are involved in *this* choice about whether a threat (offer) is to be made. Let us call the situations before a threat or offer is made, the presituation. (I shall speak of the prethreat and preoffer situations, in anticipation of what is to come.) And let us call the situations after a threat or offer is made the threat and the offer situations respectively.

Looking first at offers:

> (a) The Rational Man is normally willing to go and would be willing to choose to go from the preoffer to the offer situation.
> (b) In the preoffer situation, the Rational Man is normally willing to do A if placed in the offer situation.

inhabitant of an island might prefer that others contribute to the construction of barriers against the sea while he does not, yet prefer everyone's being forced to contribute to contributions being left purely voluntary in which case, let us suppose, the barriers won't get constructed. (For a discussion of the conditions under which a public good will be provided, cf. Mancur Olson, *The Logic of Collective Action* (Harvard, 1965). James M. Buchanan and Gordon Tullock, in *The Calculus of Consent* (Michigan, 1962), argue that public goods for a group will be provided more often than one might think.)

One must be wary of concluding too quickly from this line of argument that there will be unanimous consent to the provision of the public good by forcing everyone to contribute. For there will generally be alternative ways in which the public good can be provided, and individuals even if they all agree that each of these ways is preferable to the purely voluntary situation, may differ about which of the ways should be used. Should the good be paid for from funds gathered via a system of proportional taxation, or one of progressive taxation? And so forth. It is not obvious how unanimous consent to one *particular* way of providing the good is supposed to arise.

(c) The Rational Man, in the preoffer situation, is unwilling to do A. (We're concerned with the case where he does A [partly] because of the offer.)
(d) The Rational Man, when placed in the offer situation, does not normally prefer being back in the preoffer situation.

Turning to threats:

(a) The Rational Man is normally unwilling to go and unwilling to choose to go from the prethreat situation to the threat situation.
(b) In the prethreat situation, the Rational Man is normally willing to do A if placed in the threat situation.
(c) The Rational Man, in the prethreat situation, is unwilling to do A, and would not choose to do it. (We're concerned with the case where he does the act [partly] because of the threat.)
(d) The Rational Man, when placed in the threat situation, would normally prefer being back in the prethreat situation, and would choose to move back.

The two significant differences between these two lists are:

(1) The Rational Man would be willing to move and to choose to move from the preoffer to the offer situation, whereas he would normally not be willing to move or to choose to move from the prethreat situation to the threat situation.
(2) The Rational Man, once in the offer situation, would not prefer being back in the preoffer situation, whereas the Rational Man in the threat situation would normally prefer being back in the prethreat situation.

If we concentrate solely on the choices made in the threat and offer situations, we shall be hard put to find a difference between these situations which seems to make a difference as to whose will is operating, whose choice it is, whether the act is fully voluntary, done willingly or unwillingly, and so forth. If, however, we widen our focus and look not only at the choices made in the postsituations, but look *also* at the choice that would be made about moving from the presituation to the postsituation, then things look more promising. For now we face not just two choices but two pairs of choices:

(1) To move from the preoffer to the offer situation, and to do A in the offer situation.
(2) To move from the prethreat to the threat situation, and to do A in the threat situation.

And the Rational Man would (be willing to) make both choices in (1), whereas he would not make both choices in (2). This difference in what choices are or would be made (when other factors are appropriately the same) seems to me to make the difference, when someone else intentionally moves you from the presituation to the postsituation, to whose choice it is, whose will operates, whether the act is willingly or unwillingly done, and to whether or not the act is fully voluntary.

One would like to formulate a principle that is built upon the preceding considerations, but I find it difficult to formulate one that I am confident is not open to very simple counter-examples. Very hesitantly and tentatively, I suggest the following plausible-looking principle:

> If the alternatives among which Q must choose are intentionally changed by P, and P made this change in order to get Q to do A, and before the change Q would not have chosen (and would have been unwilling to choose) to have the change made (and after it's made, Q would prefer that it hadn't been made), and before the change was made Q wouldn't have chosen to do A, and after the change is made Q does A, then Q's choice to do A is not fully his own.

Notice that I have *not* said that the feature I am emphasizing which is mentioned in the principle, namely, being willing to choose to move from one situation to another, is by itself sufficient for a choice in the latter situation to be not fully one's own, but instead I have said that this feature, *in conjunction* with the other features listed in the antecedent of the principle, is sufficient.

Since this principle presents a sufficient condition for Q's choice not being fully his own, it does not yield the consequence that in the offer situation, normally Q's choice is fully his own. A detailed discussion of when choices *are* fully one's own, or fully voluntary, yielding this consequence, would take us far afield. Here I just wish to suggest that the crucial difference between acting because of an offer and acting because of a threat *vis-à-vis* whose choice it is, etc., is that in one case (the offer case) the Rational Man is normally willing to move or be moved from the presituation to the situation itself, whereas in the other case (the threat case) he is not. Put baldly and too simply, the Rational Man would normally (be willing to) choose to make the choice among the alternatives facing him in the offer situation, whereas normally he would not (be willing to) choose to make the choice among the alternatives facing him in the threat situation.

The principle seems to me to be on the right track in concentrating not *just* on the choice of whether or not to do A, but also on the choice to move into the threat or offer situation. But it is difficult to state a principle, which gets all the details right, and which is not trivial and unilluminating (as one would be which said: if P moves Q from S_1 to S_2 via threats then . . .). It seems that rather than speaking (just) of act A being fully one's own choice, one should speak of its being fully one's own choice to do A rather than B. I have in mind the following sort of case. P intentionally breaks Q's leg (intentionally moving him from S_1 [no broken leg] to S_2 [broken leg]). Q would prefer not making this move, and afterwards would prefer not having made it. But once Q has a broken leg, he chooses to have a decorated cast put on it, rather than a plain white one. If we just look at the act of wearing a decorated cast, we will have difficulties, for surely it is not Q's own choice (he was forced into a position where he had to wear a cast, etc.), yet in some sense it is. It seems to me more illuminating to say that wearing a cast rather than none was not fully Q's own choice, wearing a decorated cast rather than a plain one *was* fully Q's own choice, and wearing a decorated cast rather than none was not fully Q's own choice. It is not clear how to state a principle which takes this and similar complications into account, and is not open to obvious difficulties. I do, however, want to suggest that we shall not be able to understand why acts done because of threats are not normally fully voluntary, fully one's own choice, etc. where as this is not normally the case with acts done in response to offers, if we attend only to the choice confronting the person in the threat and offer situations. We must look also at the (hypothetical) choice of getting (and willingness to get) into the threat and offer situations themselves.

We have said that if P coerces Q into not doing A then (part of) Q's reason for not doing A is to avoid or lessen the likelihood of P's threatened consequence. Assuming that all of the conditions in the first section of this paper are satisfied, then

> (a) In the case where Q's whole reason for not doing A is to avoid or lessen the likelihood of P's threatened consequence (ignoring his reasons for wanting to avoid this consequence), P coerces Q into not doing A.[29]
> (b) In the case where P's threatened consequence is not part of Q's reason for not doing A (even if it is a reason Q has for not doing A) then P does not coerce Q into not doing A.

But the case is more difficult when P's threatened consequence is part of Q's reason for not doing A, and other reasons which Q has for not doing A (which do not involve threats) are also part of his reason for not doing A. For in this case, Q contributes reasons of his own; it is not solely because of the threat that he refrains from doing A. If we had to say either that this situation was one of coercion, or was not one of coercion we would, I think, term it coercion.[30] But, I think, for such cases

[29] Even if Q has other reasons for not doing A. We distinguish between 'Q has a reason *r* for not doing A,' and '*r* is (part of) Q's reason for not doing A.'
[30] This indicates an asymmetry between doing something (partly) because of a threat, and doing something partly

one is inclined to want to switch from a classificatory notion of coercion to a quantitative one.

Let me indulge in a bit of science fiction. Suppose that one were able to assign weights to the parts of Q's reasons for not doing A, which indicated what fraction of Q's total reason for not doing A any given part was. One might then say, if P's threat was n/mth of Q's total reason for not doing A, that Q was n/m-coerced into not doing A. If P's threat is Q's whole reason for not doing A (no part of Q's reason for not doing A) then Q is 1-coerced (0-coerced) or, for short, coerced (not coerced). And, in the absence of precise weights, one might begin to speak of someone's being partially coerced, slightly coerced, almost fully coerced into doing something, and so forth. Furthermore, without claiming that a person is *never* to be held responsible for an act he was coerced into doing, we might, for some cases in which his reasons (other than the threat) for doing an act aren't sufficient to get him to decide to do the act, be led to speak of a person's being (held) partially responsible for his act; not completely responsible because he did it partly because of the threat, and not complete absence of responsibility because he didn't do it solely because of the threat, but contributed some reasons of his own. I would end by saying that the consideration of such a view of responsibility, and the tracing of the modifications in what has been said thus far introduced by a thorough-going use of the notion of n/m-coerced, would require another paper – were it not for the thought that some readers might take this as a threat.[31]

---

because of an offer. For suppose that the other reasons Q has for not doing A which are part of his reasons for not doing A, include an offer by R for Q not to do A. Using a classificatory notion of coercion, doing A partly because of a threat shows the person was coerced, whereas doing something partly because of an offer does not show that he was not coerced.

[31] *Note added in* 1972: Since 1966 when this essay was written, my views on coercion have undergone some changes, which I hope to state elsewhere. A portion of the intellectual descendant of the larger study of liberty contemplated in the opening sentence, is my forthcoming book, tentatively titled *Anarchy, The State, and Utopia: An Essay in Libertarian Political Philosophy.*

6 'Social Meaning' and the Explanation of Social Action[1]

Quentin Skinner

I

A social action may be said to have a meaning for the agent performing it. The acceptance of this rather vague claim represents the one major point of agreement in the continuing debate between those philosophers who wish to assert and those who wish to deny the naturalist thesis[2] to the effect that social actions can sufficiently be accounted for by the ordinary processes of causal explanation. The significance of the fact that social actions have a 'meaning' has of course been emphasized in each of the three main traditions of anti-naturalist opposition to the idea of a social science. Thus the followers of Dilthey, and of the whole tradition which has insisted on the importance of *verstehen*, stress that the special feature of 'the human studies' is their concern 'with a world which has meaning for the actors involved'.[3] Similarly, the phenomenologists stress that the aim of the social sciences must be to gain 'insight into the meaning which social acts have for those who act'.[4] And the followers of Wittgenstein stress that the 'forms of activity' studied in the social sciences will characteristically be those 'of which we can sensibly say that they have a *meaning*'.[5]

This emphasis on the meaning of social actions has been no less marked, however, in the various strands of thought which have converged in accepting the theoretical possibility of establishing a causal and predictive science of human action. Those who have wished to vindicate a generally 'scientific' approach to the study of social action

---

[1] I am particularly indebted to Dr John Burrow, Mr John Dunn, Mr Geoffrey Hawthorn and my co-editors for comments on earlier drafts of this paper.
[2] Here and throughout I adopt the terminology suggested by Sidney Morgenbesser, 'Is it a Science?', *Social Research* 33 (1966), p. 255.
[3] H. P. Rickman, *Understanding and the Human Studies* (London, 1967), p. 23.
[4] Alfred Schutz, 'The Social World and the Theory of Social Action', *Social Research* 27 (1960), p. 203.
[5] Peter Winch, *The Idea of a Social Science* (London, 1958), p. 45.

still concede the need to take account of 'the meaning of people's movements[6].' Similarly, those who have wished to claim that even an agent's reasons may be the causes of his actions still allow for the fact that such agents will characteristically see 'a point or meaning' in their actions.[7] And even those who have wished to maintain the strictest thesis of positivism, to the effect that an individual action must always be explained by deducing it from some known general law covering such movements, continue to concede that 'what distinguishes a mere bodily movement from an action' is 'the *meaning* of that movement'.[8]

It is in fact possible, as I shall next seek to show, to see the entire debate between the social science naturalists and their opponents in terms of the different conclusions which the two sides of the debate have drawn from their common stress on the fact that 'the acting individual' (as Weber put it) 'attaches a subjective meaning to his social behaviour'.

The anti-naturalists have traced a logical connection between the meaning of a social action and the agent's motives for performing it. And they have seen the recovery of the agent's motives for acting as a matter of placing the agent's action within a context of social rules. This view of social meaning has led them to the following two conclusions about the explanation of social actions. First, they have claimed that to decode the meaning of a social action is equivalent to giving a motive-explanation for the agent's performance of that action. (Thesis A). Secondly, they have claimed that since the recovery of an agent's motives for acting is a matter of placing the agent's action in a context of rules rather than causes, so to cited the social meaning and the motives of an action is to provide a form of explanation which stands in contrast with, and is in fact incompatible with, a causal explanation of the same action. (Thesis B.)

These anti-naturalist conclusions about the idea of a social science have in part derived, and have gained great strength, from the powerful impact of Wittgenstein's later philosophy upon recent philosophical psychology. This is most clearly evident in a work such as A. I. Melden's *Free Action* – with its stress on 'making sense' of the meaning of actions (p. 102), its insistence that this is essentially a matter of recovering the agent's motives (pp. 87–8), by way of grasping the 'background against

---

[6] Quentin Gibson, *The Logic of Social Enquiry* (London, 1960), p. 52.
[7] A. J. Ayer, 'Man as a Subject for Science' in P. Laslett and W. G. Runciman, eds., *Philosophy, Politics and Society* Series III (Oxford 1967), p. 23.
[8] May Brodbeck, 'Meaning and Action', *Philosophy of Science* 30 (1963), p. 309.

which both the man and his action can be understood' (p. 104), and its conclusion that this process makes causal explanation 'wholly irrelevant to the understanding' of social actions (p. 184).

There is also a much longer tradition of analysis, however, lying behind this type of anti-naturalist commitment. In the philosophy of history it is best represented by Collingwood's insistence, in *The Idea of History*, that to explain an action is always 'to discern the thoughts' of its agent, and that this study of individual motivation means that the historian who seeks to 'emulate the scientist in searching for the causes or laws of events' is simply 'ceasing to be an historian'. (pp. 214–15). This contrast, moreover, between understanding actions in terms of motives and explaining events in terms of causes looks back to Croce and Dilthey, and forward to the development of this argument by Dray, Donagan and others. And in the philosophy of social science a similar commitment has always informed the Weberian tradition of analysis. Weber himself never wished to suggest that the concepts of *verstehen* and causal explanation are incompatible. But he did begin the *Wirtschaft und Gesellschaft* by discussing motive-explanations, and he did at that point specifically equate the 'understanding of motivation' with the business of 'placing the act in an intelligible and more inclusive context of meaning'. (tr. Henderson and Parsons, p. 95.) Since then, moreover, a much more strongly anti-naturalist case has been developed by at least two schools of thought which have acknowledged Weber's influence. On the one hand the phenomenologists (such as Schutz, at least in certain moods) have gone on to insist both that an understanding of 'the meaning which social phenomena have for us' is a matter of recovering 'typical motives of typical actors', and that this is a form of understanding 'peculiar to social things'. (*loc. cit.*, pp. 206, 211, 214.) And on the other hand the Wittgensteinians (such as Winch) have insisted both that 'the notion of meaningful behaviour is closely connected with notions like *motive* and *reason*', and that the explanation of such behaviour, by way of relating the agent's motives to a context of social rules, requires 'a scheme of concepts which is logically incompatible with the kinds of explanation offered in the natural sciences'. (*op. cit.*, pp. 45, 72.)

The naturalists, by contrast, have given an account of social meaning from which they have drawn two conclusions opposed to those I have just set out. First, they have claimed that the decoding of the meaning of a social action merely provides a method of redescribing it. And they have insisted that since mere redescription cannot in itself be explanatory, so it must be a mistake to suppose that the placing of a social action in its context, or the decoding of its social meaning, can ever serve in itself as an explanation of the given action. (Thesis C.) Secondly, they have claimed that if the idea of decoding the meaning of an action is so much extended that it becomes equivalent to recovering the agent's motives for performing it, then there is no incompatibility between the ideas of social meaning and of causal explanation, since the provision of an explanation by way of citing an agent's motives, or even his intentions, is itself a form of causal explanation. They have thus concluded that there is nothing in the fact that a social action may have a meaning or consist of the following of a rule from which it follows that such episodes may not be entirely explicable simply by the ordinary processes of causal explanation. (Thesis D.)

These naturalist conclusions, like those of their opponents, have been in part derived from, and have been greatly influenced by, a recent movement in philosophical psychology. This is the current and increasing movement of reaction against the Wittgensteinian assumption that motives and intentions cannot function as causes of actions. This has already generated some powerful arguments (best stated by Davidson),[9] and has caused several philosophers (notably Hamlyn and MacIntyre) to recant their previously published anti-naturalist views about the explanation of action. The implications of the reaction can be seen at their clearest in an essay such as Ayer's on 'Man as a subject for science' – with its insistence both that to redescribe a phenomenon cannot be 'in any way to account for it', and that to cite either a motive or an intention to explain an action, as we do 'in the normal way', must always be ultimately to point to 'lawlike connections' which are causal in form. The conclusion is that even if we can 'estimate an action in terms of its conforming to a rule', and even if we need to understand such actions 'in terms of their social contexts', these factors affect the agent only as 'part of his motivation', and give us no grounds for doubting that the action can be sufficiently explained 'by means of a causal law'. There is thus said to be 'nothing about human conduct that would entitle us to conclude *a priori* that it was in any way less lawlike than any other sort of natural process'. (*op. cit.*, pp. 16, 17, 21, 22–3.)

As with the anti-naturalist commitment, there is a considerable tradition of analysis lying behind this type of claim. In the philosophy of history the idealist tradition represented by Dilthey and Collingwood has always been confronted by a positivist tradition stemming from the philosophy of science. This is perhaps best represented by Hempel's classic essay on 'The Function of General Laws in History', originally

---

[9] Donald Davidson, 'Actions, Reasons and Causes', *The Journal of Philosophy* 60 (1963), pp. 685–700.

published in the *Journal of Philosophy* for 1942. The attempt, it is there claimed, to explain the actions of historical individuals in an *ad hoc* manner, in terms of 'the circumstances under which they acted, and the motives which influence their actions' 'does not in itself constitute an explanation'. And the fact, it is claimed, that the historian may concern himself with 'the *"meanings"* of given historical events', as well as with motives and actions, does nothing to vitiate the claim that any genuine explanation of any historical phenomenon will have to consist of 'subsuming it under general empirical laws'. (pp. 44–5.) And similarly, in the philosophy of social science, the school of Weber has always been confronted by the school of Durkheim, with his dismissal of the need to study individual intentions and motives, and his insistence (in *The Rules of Sociological Method*) on the 'principle' that 'the determining cause of a social fact', in which he included social actions, 'should be sought among the social facts preceding it, and not among the states of individual consciousness'. (tr. Solovay and Mueller, p. 110.)

The two opposed theoretical traditions I have now sketched have both been represented in the two most recent volumes of *Philosophy, Politics and Society*. In Series II MacIntyre's essay made use of the antinaturalist approach, and he committed himself to theses A and B. (See especially pp. 56–7.) In Series III Ayer's essay put the case for the naturalist approach, and argued for theses C and D. (See especially pp. 21–3.) My aim in what follows will be to continue this feature of the series by attempting to do three things. I shall first try very briefly to make a new start (Section II) on the analysis of the required sense of 'meaning', and to give some examples of this analysis in action. I shall then try to show (Section III) that if this analysis is sound, then there seem to be some grounds for doubting each of the four theses I have now set out. (Here I shall in part attempt to adapt and apply an account of explaining social actions which I have already published.)[10] Finally, I shall try (Section IV) to suggest certain methodological implications of these conclusions for historians and social scientists, at least in so far as they are concerned with explaining the social actions of individual agents.

---

[10] See my article 'On Performing and Explaining Linguistic Actions', *The Philosophical Quarterly* 21 (1971), pp. 1–21. I make use of this material here by permission of the Editor.

II

There is a tendency, particularly amongst the anti-naturalists, to apply the concept of social meaning in a rather over-extended way. (This is perhaps evident from several of the quotations I have already given.) I shall begin therefore by restricting myself to considering the way in which the concept is used in the discussion of a single class of social actions. Later I shall try tentatively to extend the application of this analysis. But at first I shall concentrate on the class of social actions in which the concept of somebody meaning something (in or by saying or doing something) has its clearest and most obvious application, namely in the class of *linguistic* actions.

The classic analysis of the concept of a linguistic action has been provided by J. L. Austin in his William James Lectures, edited and published by J. O. Urmson as *How to Do Things with Words*. Austin's central contention is that any agent, in issuing any serious utterance, will be doing something as well as merely saying something, and will be doing something *in* saying what he says, and not merely as a consequence of what is said. Austin reached this conclusion by way of claiming that to issue any serious utterance is always to speak not only with a certain meaning but also with a certain intended force, corresponding to what Austin dubbed the 'illocutionary' act being performed by the agent in issuing his given utterance. Austin's claim is thus that to gain 'uptake', as he put it, of this element of illocutionary force co-ordinate with the ordinary meaning of the locution will be equivalent to understanding what the agent was *doing in* issuing that given utterance.

A single example will make clear the sense in which the issuing of any serious utterance constitutes, according to Austin, the performance of a type of social action. Consider the case of a policeman who sees a skater on a dangerous pond and issues to the skater the following serious utterance: 'The ice over there is very thin.'[11] Here the policeman is obviously issuing a meaningful utterance: he is saying something and

[11] Here I adopt an example from P. F. Strawson, 'Intention and Convention in Speech Acts', *The Philosophical Review* 73 (1964), pp. 439–60. I also follow the argument of this article (i) in extending (and in this sense rejecting) Austin's concept of a convention and (ii) in relating Grice's theory of meaning to Austin's theory of illocutionary force. I have tried to defend both these commitments in my article 'Conventions and the Understanding of Speech Acts', *The Philosophical Quarterly* 20 (1970) pp. 118–38.

the words mean something. But Austin's further point is that the utterance also has an illocutionary force, corresponding to the fact that the policeman will be doing something in issuing this meaningful utterance: he may for example be performing the illocutionary act of *warning the skater*.

I now wish to suggest that this account of linguistic action may be used to establish two crucial claims about the sense of 'meaning' with which I am concerned in discussing the meaning of social actions. The first is that the idea of decoding the meaning of an action seems, at least in the case of linguistic actions, to be equivalent to gaining uptake of the nature of the illocutionary act performed by the agent in issuing that particular utterance. To understand, that is, that the policeman, in issuing his utterance 'The ice over there is very thin' was performing the illocutionary act of warning seems equivalent to understanding the meaning of issuing the utterance itself. It is to understand what the policeman (non-naturally)[12] meant by performing his given (linguistic) action.

The second point is that to ask about this non-natural sense of meaning, at least in the case of linguistic actions, seems to be equivalent to asking about the agent's intention in performing his given social action. It is perhaps necessary to be more precise, and to stress that to ask this question is to ask about the agent's *primary* intention. It is arguable that Austin's way of stating his theory encourages the belief that there must be a correspondence between single intentions and single actions. But an agent may well have several different intentions in performing a single social action, some of which may be less important than others from the point of view of characterizing what the agent is doing, all of which may nevertheless form part of a complex set of intentions which are realized in the given action. It remains true, however, that to understand (in the example I am considering) that what the policeman meant to do in issuing his utterance 'The ice over there is very thin' was to warn the skater is equivalent to understanding what the policeman's primary intention was in performing that particular (linguistic) action.

It might be doubted, of course, whether this analysis of 'social meaning' in terms of understanding the intended illocutionary force of an agent's (linguistic) action can possibly be applied in the case of ordinary non-linguistic social actions. If we accept Austin's own claim, however, that certain illocutionary acts are invariably performed non-verbally (p. 118), there seems some reason to suppose that the analysis

---

[12] See H. P. Grice, 'Meaning', *The Philosophical Review* 66 (1957), pp. 377–88 and his revisions in 'Utterer's Meaning and Intentions', *The Philosophical Review* 78 (1969), pp. 147–77.

can be used at least to decode the meaning of the 'ritual and ceremonial' acts in which Austin was chiefly interested, even if many of these turn out to be non-linguistically performed. If we accept Strawson's argument, moreover, to the effect that the account which Austin gave of the conventions of illocutionary force may have been excessively narrow in scope, then there seems some reason to assume that the analysis can also be used to decode the meaning of a whole range of ordinary non-ritual as well as non-linguistic actions. Finally, it is relevant to recall that the main aim of Grice's original discussion of non-natural meaning was 'to show that the criteria for judging linguistic intentions are very like the criteria for judging non-linguistic intentions', and thus to show 'that linguistic intentions are very like non-linguistic intentions'. (*loc. cit.*, p. 388.)

These suggestions may be corroborated by considering some examples of such non-linguistic as well as linguistic actions. Consider first a case of a ritual but non-linguistic social action. (Hollis has popularized the following example.)[13] Certain Yoruba tribesmen 'carry about with them boxes covered with cowrie shells, which they treat with special regard'. Hollis's interest in this example (concerned with the need for the Yoruba to have rational thought-processes) is not relevant to my argument at this point. My interest is in the meaning of this social action and in the nature of the questions we need to ask and answer in order to decode it. In the first place, the crucial question to ask certainly seems to be about what the agent may be *doing in* performing just this action. The answer (Hollis tells us) is that the tribesmen believe 'that the boxes are their heads or souls' and that what they are doing in treating the boxes in a reverent way is protecting their souls against witchcraft. This in turn suggests that to ask and answer this question about the illocutionary force of the action is, as I have suggested, equivalent to asking about the intentions of the agent in acting in this way. Notice that we do not learn the nature of the motive which prompts (and perhaps causes) the Yoruba to treat his box with special regard – although we may now infer that the motive is likely to be respect or fear for the power of unknown forces. What we learn is the Yoruba's primary intention in acting in this way – that it is to protect his soul.

Consider next a case of a non-ritual, non-linguistic social action. (I derive the following example from one of the case-histories reported by R. D. Laing and A. Esterson in *Sanity, Madness and the Family* [2nd. edn. London, 1970].) An adolescent girl becomes an apparently compulsive reader, 'burying herself in her books' and refusing to stop

[13] Martin Hollis, 'Reason and Ritual', *Philosophy* 43 (1968), p. 231.

or allow herself to be interrupted (p. 46). Laing and Esterson's interest in the case lies primarily in their suggestion that the behaviour can be seen as a strategy, a deliberate social action, and not just as the symptom of an illness. My interest is again in the meaning of the behaviour, and in the appropriate questions to ask in order to determine whether it has any meaning, and if so how it should be decoded. Again it seems that the crucial question to ask is what the girl may be doing in performing just this action. The answer (Laing and Esterson suggest, p. 35) is that she is 'taking refuge' and preventing what she takes to be 'intrusions' by an overdemanding family. And again it seems that to ask and answer this question about the illocutionary force of the action is equivalent to asking about the girl's intentions in acting in this way. Notice again that this does not tell us the motives which prompted (and perhaps caused) the girl's behaviour. Laing and Esterson suggest (p. 34) that the motive may have been a desire for what they call 'autonomy', but one might infer other motives as well – such as a kind of pride, a degree of hatred, and so on. The point is that what we do learn is the girl's intentions in acting in this way – that they are to register a protest against, and to protect herself from, an excessively demanding social situation.

It may still seem, however, that to extend the discussion of non-natural meaning and illocutionary force to deal with such non-linguistic social actions is to give an illegitimate application to Austin's and Grice's theories. Consider finally, therefore, a further case of an ordinary (non-ritual) linguistic action – and not a dummy example this time, but a genuine (and historically important) utterance. Machiavelli, in Chapter 16 of *The Prince*, offers the following piece of advice: 'Princes must learn when not to be virtuous.' Several of his interpreters have asked what he may have meant by offering such advice. Here it cannot I think be doubted that the crucial question to ask, in order to answer this question, is what Machiavelli may have been doing in making this claim. One widely accepted answer (suggested by Felix Gilbert[14]) has been that Machiavelli was 'consciously refuting his predecessors' within the highly conventionalized genre of advice-books to princes (p. 477). Again it seems unquestionable that to ask and answer this question about the illocutionary force of Machiavelli's utterance is equivalent to asking about Machiavelli's intentions in writing this section of *The Prince*. Notice once more that this does not tell us the motives which prompted (and perhaps caused) Machiavelli to offer this advice. Gilbert suggests that the most likely motives might have been a mixture of frustration at

---

[14] Felix Gilbert, 'The Humanist Concept of the Prince and *The Prince* of Machiavelli', *The Journal of Modern History* 11 (1939), pp. 449–83.

the prevailing 'idealist interpretation of politics' combined with a simple desire to shock and a belief in the importance of giving genuinely practical political advice (p. 480). The point once more is that what we do learn is Machiavelli's intention in writing just what he did write. I do not wish to imply here, of course, that what we learn is the intention lying behind the writing of the particular sentence I have quoted, nor do I wish to imply that Machiavelli need have had any isolable intention in writing just that one sentence. But I do wish to claim that we learn the intention lying behind Machiavelli's argument at this point of his work – the primary intention (and the illocutionary force of his given utterance) being to challenge and repudiate an accepted moral commonplace.

III

I now turn to try to bring out the philosophical interest of these claims. This lies, as I have already indicated, in the suggestion that the argument I have now set out seems to give some grounds for saying that both the theses of the naturalists (C & D) as well as those of the anti-naturalists (A & B) may be mistaken. Consider first the two naturalist theses. Thesis C states that to redescribe an action is in no way to explain it. I have now sought to show, however, that for at least certain classes of social actions there can be a unique form of (illocutionary) redescription which, by way of recovering the agent's intended illocutionary act, may be capable of explaining at least certain features of the agent's behaviour. This conclusion can perhaps be most readily corroborated by reverting to the dummy example of the policeman issuing to the skater the utterance 'The ice over there is very thin.' This episode might be witnessed by a puzzled bystander who for some reason fails to grasp the policeman's primary intention in issuing this utterance. One request for an explanation might then take the form of asking 'Why did he say that?' (Or more exactly, 'Why did the policeman issue that given utterance?') And one reply, providing an explanation of the policeman's action, might be 'He said it to warn the skater.' (Or more exactly, 'The policeman's reason for issuing that given utterance was to give notice to the skater of the potential danger of skating where the ice is very thin.') The illocutionary redescription serves as an explanation of the (linguistic) action.

There seems no doubt, moreover, about the way in which such illocutionary redescriptions may serve as genuine explanations of at least some puzzles about a fairly wide range of social actions. For it is one thing if the bystander understands what the policeman's utterance to the skater means, so that he may be able to give an account of what the policeman said. But it is another and further thing if the bystander understands what the policeman's issuing of an utterance with that meaning was itself intended to mean on the given occasion, so that he may be able to give an account of why the policeman said what he said. Colloquially, we may say that what an illocutionary redescription will characteristically explain about a social action will be its *point*.

Consider next thesis D, that there is nothing in the fact that a social action may have a meaning from which it follows that the action may not be entirely explicable by means of the ordinary processes of causal explanation. I have now suggested, however, that while it may be essential in a wide range of cases to recover the meaning of a social action in order to be able to explain it, to supply this redescriptive form of explanation is certainly to supply something other than a causal explanation. Again this can most readily be corroborated by reverting to the dummy example of the policeman warning the skater. The explanation for the policeman's issuing of his given utterance is supplied by way of recovering what the policeman meant, in the non-natural sense of understanding not just what his utterance itself meant (for as Ziff has stressed it is not even necessary that the utterance should in that sense have a meaning at all) but of understanding what the act of issuing an utterance with that meaning might itself have meant in the given circumstances. This is supplied in turn by way of decoding the conventions governing the illocutionary force attaching to the policeman's utterance itself. But this can scarcely be to provide a causal form of explanation. For this is to focus on a *feature* of the policeman's action, and not on an independently specifiable condition of it, in the way that any causal form of explanation requires. Yet this is still to provide an explanation of the given action. For to know in the required sense what the agent meant is to know how he intended his utterance (or other action) to be taken. But this in turn is to know the agent's intention in performing that action. And this in turn is to know why he performed that particular action. We thus have a genuine form of explanation of the given action, even though it is clear that we cannot construe these sorts of intentions (intentions *in* acting) as causes of which the agent's corresponding actions can then be seen as effects.

Next consider the two anti-naturalist theses. Thesis A states that the reason the concept of social meaning can be explanatory is because it tells us the agent's motives for performing his given action. I have now sought to show, however, first that a sharp line needs to be drawn between an agent's motives and his intentions in acting, and secondly that it is these intentions, and not the agent's motives, which we need to recover in order to decode the meaning of a social action.

The possible need for this sharp division between motives and intentions does not seem to have been admitted by any of the anti-naturalist or the naturalist theorists I have cited. The anti-naturalists (such as Melden, Rickman and Winch)[15] as well as the naturalists (such as Ayer, Davidson and MacIntyre in his recent work)[16] write about motives and intentions in this connection – and often about reasons and purposes as well – as if they believe these concepts to be virtually interchangeable. This seems to be a mistake in itself, but it also seems to be a mistake of some consequence when we come to try to explain social actions, since it encourages the elision of what I take to be a necessary stage in the explanation of a certain range of actions. It is this extra stage, and the need to begin by considering it, which I have chiefly been concerned to emphasize – the stage, that is, at which it may be appropriate, before asking either about the agent's motives or about any deeper causes of his behaviour, to ask whether the performance of his given action itself bears any conventional element of (non-natural) meaning or (illocutionary) force.

The possible significance of isolating this extra stage can be conveniently illustrated by reconsidering the main example of a social action which Ayer chooses in his essay on Man as a subject for science. He takes the case (pp. 9–10) of a man drinking a glass of wine, and claims that this action might be explained, according to its context, either as '(1) an act of self-indulgence, (2) an expression of politeness, (3) a proof of alcoholism, (4) a manifestation of loyalty, (5) a gesture of despair, (6) an attempt at suicide, (7) the performance of a social rite, (8) a religious communication, (9) an attempt to summon up one's courage, (10) an attempt to seduce or corrupt another person, (11) the sealing of a bargain, (12) a display of professional expertise, (13) a piece of inadvertence, (14) an act of expiation, (15) the response to a challenge'.

It is true that my argument is not altogether easy to make good in terms of Ayer's particularly elaborate and eccentric list. In cases (3) and (13) it is not clear that the *explicans* yields the explanation of anything that could be called a voluntary action. In cases (6), (10) and (12) it is not clear how the *explicans* is to be understood. (It is hard to see, that is, how any of these answers could be offered as possible explana-

---

[15] Melden, *op. cit.*, pp. 83–9; Rickman, *op. cit.*, p. 69; Winch, *op. cit.*, pp. 45–51.
[16] Ayer, *op. cit.*, p. 9; Davidson, *loc. cit.*, p. 699; Alasdair MacIntyre, *Against the Self-Images of the Age* (London, 1971) p. 226.

tions for the action *simply* of drinking a glass of wine.) Furthermore, in cases (1), (7), (9), and (14) it does seem necessary to concede that the question of distinguishing the motives of the agent from his intentions in acting scarcely seems to arise. There scarcely seems, that is, to be any question to ask in these cases about the meaning of the given action, and it seems that, if we were to ask in these cases about the intentions of the agent in performing his given action, this would scarcely explain anything about the given behaviour. This still leaves us, however, with cases (2), (4), (5), (8), (11) and perhaps (15). The explanation in these cases, *pace* Ayer's assimilation of intentions to motives, seems to take the form of a redescription which directs us not primarily to the agent's motives, but rather to his intentions *in* performing the given action of drinking the glass of wine. Thus it does seem possible, at least in these cases, to insist on the need to begin by considering a stage of explanation which is prior to any attempt to elucidate the agent's motives, and which consists of an attempt to recover the unique illocutionary redescription of the action itself, in terms of which the agent's performance of it can be shown non-naturally to mean something. It seems therefore that the anti-naturalists must be mistaken when they equate the recovery of social meaning with the elucidation of the agent's motives for action.

Consider finally thesis B – that to explain an action by citing its meaning and the agent's motives is to provide a form of explanation incompatible with causality. This thesis is contradicted rather than sustained by the way in which I have sought to vindicate the possibility of giving non-causal explanations of social actions. I have sought only to argue that to explain a social action in terms of the agent's intentions in performing it constitutes one stage in the explanation of a certain range of social actions. I have at no point suggested that to provide such non-causal explanations is in any way incompatible with the subsequent provision of further and arguably causal explanations of the same action. One such further stage might be to provide an explanation in terms of the agent's motives. A yet further stage might be to provide an explanation in terms of the grounds for the agent's possession of just those motives. It will normally be indispensable to go on to both these further stages in order to be able to provide anything like a complete explanation of any social action. And I should wish to claim that it is strongly arguable in the case of the first of these further stages, and unquestionable in the case of the second, that to provide these further explanations will be to provide causal explanations for the performance of the given social action.

IV

I turn finally to consider the practical implications of the thesis I have argued.[17] There is a special interest in trying to make this point, first because of the tendency amongst some recent philosophers of social science to deny that their views about the logic of explanation entail any methodological recommendations,[18] and secondly because of the more obvious tendency amongst practising historians as well as social scientists to deny that the acceptance of any particular philosophical viewpoint could possibly have any practical bearing on the study of their subjects. I now wish to suggest that if the conceptual scheme I have set out is sound, it entails at least three methodological recommendations, all of which tend, moreover, to be ignored or even explicitly denied in a good deal of current writing in history and social science. I concede, of course, the difficulty of deriving anything except negative methodological injunctions from my *a priori* arguments. Perhaps any such injunctions, if they are to stand any chance of being sensible as well as sufficiently general to be of practical value, are bound in effect to consist of injunctions not to heed methodological injunctions based on mistaken *a priori* arguments. I hope nevertheless that it may be possible to see in this section the beginnings, if only the negative beginnings, of an answer to the critic of the last volume of *Philosophy, Politics and Society* who refused to see how the issues raised in Ayer's contribution to that volume could possibly have anything to do with the methodology of the social sciences.[19]

Consider first the classes (the non-linguistic as well as linguistic classes) of what Austin called 'ritual and ceremonial' actions. There are two methodological recommendations which seem, at least in these cases, to follow from the argument I have advanced. The first is the need to raise questions about the agent's ritual *beliefs* in order to be able to explain such actions. This claim appears to have been explicitly denied in some recent social anthropology,[20] and is certainly by-passed by

[17] For discussions about this section I am very greatly indebted to Dr John Burrow.
[18] See for example Peter Winch, 'Mr Louch's Idea of a Social Science', *Inquiry* 7 (1964), p. 203.
[19] D. D. Raphael in *The Philosophical Quarterly* 19 (1969), p. 185.
[20] For example, I. C. Jarvie and Joseph Agassi speak of 'a general criticism' in current social anthropology of 'the entire assumption that people's actions can be explained by their

those who have written as if they believe that ritual actions can sufficiently be explained in terms of their place in a given social structure and by reference to their social effects.[21] It is clear, however, that since there is obviously a crucial logical link between the nature and range of the intentions it makes sense to ascribe to an agent in acting, and the nature and range of that agent's beliefs, it must follow that in order to explain a ritual action by way of recovering the agent's intentions in performing it, we must necessarily be prepared to examine and allude to the ritual beliefs informing the intentions with which the agent performed his given ritual action.

The second recommendation is that as soon as we concede the need to enter the realm of the agent's beliefs in order to explain his social actions, it also becomes essential to raise questions about the *rationality* of these beliefs. This has of course been recently stressed, as I have mentioned, by Hollis and others. They have primarily been concerned, however, with the linguistic and logical elements in the concept of rationality. It seems clear, as they have argued, that we must be prepared to make some *a priori* assumptions about the universality of the laws of thought if we are going to be able correctly to identify (and so to translate) the nature of the speech-acts, as well as to explain the nature of the ritual actions, which may be performed in an alien culture. It also seems clear, however, that the analysis of the concept of rationality requires us to consider a further question, concerned with the nature of the procedures which will have to be followed, and the nature of the criteria met, before we can say of a given empirical belief that it is rationally held.

It might be doubted whether my basic theme – that of intentionality in relation to the explanation of action – necessarily requires an examination of this further point. To be concerned, however, with explaining actions, and thus with the examination of intentions as the means both of identifying those actions and of establishing whether they may be said to have a meaning, is to commit oneself not only (as I have just stressed) to examining the beliefs of which such intentional actions form the expression. It is also to commit oneself to asking about the rationality of the agent's beliefs, since the answer to this question must in turn affect our assessment of his intentions and actions.

It is true that the strong influence, until recently, of a positivist theory of knowledge upon the philosophy of social science has made it rather

---

beliefs' in Bryan R. Wilson, ed., *Rationality* (London, 1970), p. 179. (But this is denied by J. H. M. Beattie, *ibid.*, p. 246).
[21] Hollis, *loc. cit.*, pp. 235-6 criticizes this type of explanation.

easy to oversimplify, and perhaps to overstress, the significance of this point. It has been usual to define the concept of a rational belief in terms of the agent's capacity and willingness to recognize 'that there is sufficient evidence in its favour' (Gibson, *op. cit.*, p. 156), 'that it is based on good evidence' (Wilson, ed., *op. cit.*, p. 173) and so on. It is clear, however, that this fails to acknowledge something problematic in the very notion of holding a belief in the light of rather than in the face of 'the available evidence', since it fails to acknowledge that the question of what is to count as good or sufficient evidence in favour of holding a belief can never be free from cultural reference. This anti-positivist objection can be developed as follows. We can imagine an alien system of beliefs in which the paradigms used to connect the system together are such that none of the evidence which we should regard as evidence in favour of abandoning those beliefs is taken to count as decisive evidence either for or against them. We can then imagine an agent, operating within this belief-system, who accepts on trust these prevailing paradigms (and these prevailing canons of evidence), recognizing and following only the moves accepted as rational within the given system, but never challenging the rationality of any part of the system itself. It might now be argued, of the beliefs held by someone in this type of situation, that provided they are coherently connected together, and provided the agent recognizes their implications, they may be said to be held in an entirely rational way. There seems to be no space left for this possibility, however, if we insist on defining rational belief in terms of each individual believer's continual willingness to examine 'the available evidence' for and against each belief he holds.

A positivist might still wish to insist, however, that such an agent's beliefs cannot be rationally held, since it cannot be rational for anyone to accept on trust what are to count as the canons of evidence in favour of holding any given belief. Such an answer seems to be given, in effect, even by some of the most recent and avowedly anti-positivist writers on the topic of rationality. MacIntyre, for example, in his most recent essay on the topic, continues to rest his definition of rational belief on the (unanalysed) claim that to hold a belief rationally must be to hold the belief in the light of having engaged in a 'relevant process of appropriate deliberation', conducted according to 'the appropriate intellectual norms and procedures'.[22]

This type of reply, however, scarcely meets the original objection to the positivist way of connecting rational belief with evidence. It is clear that we all accept and act upon a large number of beliefs (particularly

[22] MacIntyre, *op. cit.*, p. 247.

of a technical or theoretical character) eithout ever trying – or even being in a position seriously to try – either to decide in an independent spirit on the 'appropriate procedures' for falsifying them, or to re-assess 'the available evidence' in favour of holding them. We accept such beliefs on trust, on the grounds that we know no better, that they look inherently plausible, and that most other people feel the same. There does not necessarily seem, however, to be anything irrational about accepting many of our empirical beliefs on trust in this way, both with respect to the alleged evidence in favour of holding them, and with respect to what should count as evidence. It would indeed be extremely irrational in many cases if we refused to accept a number of such conventional beliefs, and always insisted on the need to try to reconsider for ourselves the status of the alleged evidence for believing them, in order to arrive at our own far more untutored conclusions.

It is true that these sorts of objections to the analysis of rational belief simply in terms of evidence and refutability have gained considerable ground in recent discussions. They have perhaps drawn some of their strength from their apparent connection with Quine's attack on the alleged distinction between analytic and synthetic statements, a distinction which underlies the positivist way of connecting rational belief with the idea of examining the facts of the case. More recently, the attack has been popularized in such methodological studies as those of Kuhn and Winch, which have converged in rejecting the assumption that we ever construct or examine our theories in the light of anything like unvarnished evidence. As the idea that our theories really act as paradigms rather than as straightforward conjectures has gained ground, however, so a contrasting danger seems to have developed, which the positivists – with their simple application of a correspondence theory of truth to elucidate the concept of rational belief – at least managed to avoid.

This new danger arises with the tendency to suppose that in order to vindicate the rationality of an alien belief-system, *all* the investigator need do is to examine what counts as evidence within the given system, to assure himself that the alleged reasons which the agents may give for acting are genuinely reasons within the system, and in general to assure himself that each particular belief is connected with other beliefs in such a way as to make up a coherent and integrated cultural system. The danger with this type of emphasis lies in the tendency to assume that it must follow from this that there cannot be any trans-cultural or trans-historical criteria for applying the concept of rationality at all. Thus it has been explicitly insisted, for example by Winch, that the attempt to apply any such criteria must be altogether improper methodologically, and in any case 'not open to us', since the result will only be to contaminate our explanations with our own parochial standards of rationality.[23]

This argument between the positivists and these newly-fashionable relativists has left the topic of rationality in more or less complete disarray. Perhaps it is by now appropriate, however, to think in terms of trying to make at least a partial defence of a more positivist point of view. It may be proper, that is, first to try to stress the value of attaching *some* weight to the idea of examining and rejecting empirical beliefs in the light of the available evidence, and secondly to try to show the way in which this approach (however question-begging it may seem) may still yield a methodological injunction to the historian or the social scientist concerned with the explanation of individual social actions.

Suppose it were possible to combine the elements of a correspondence with a coherence theory of truth in the way that such an approach would seem to require. Why would this be worthwhile, from the point of view of trying to explain individual social actions? Because a belief which an agent holds rationally in this sense – in the sense of holding it in the light of considering the evidence available to him for refuting it – will generate a quite different range of social actions from the range generated out of a belief which he holds irrationally, in the sense of holding it in the face of rather than in the light of the available evidence. The reason is that the agent will have a quite different perception in each case of the appropriate action to perform. In the first type of situation, the investigator will need to find the means to assure himself that the agent's beliefs are in fact rationally held. This may require an extremely sensitive analysis of 'the available evidence', since the state of the evidence may be such that the agent's beliefs can be seen by the investigator to be false, and may nevertheless have been rationally held. (Some recent discussions have arguably failed to keep the ideas of rational and of true belief sufficiently separate.)[24] In the second type of situation, a further and different type of investigation becomes necessary if the agent's social action is to be explained. The investigator needs to be able to discover why the agent continues irrationally to hold a given belief if the evidence to refute it is in some clear sense available to him. It follows in each case that if the investigator fails to raise the question of the rationality of an agent's beliefs, in relation to the facts, he will not have

---

[23] This is the position taken up in Peter Winch, 'Understanding a Primitive Society', *The American Philosophical Quarterly* 1 (1964), p. 316.
[24] They seem, for example, to be conflated in Steven Lukes, 'Some Problems about Rationality', *The European Journal of Sociology* 8 (1967), p. 262.

established exactly what there is to be explained about the given action. He will thus be unable to avoid the danger of giving a wholly inappropriate type of explanation.

I turn finally to consider the wider class of social actions which I have suggested can in part be explained by decoding the agent's intentions in performing them. I wish to suggest that a further methodological injunction follows in these cases from my general argument. This would be to begin by focusing not on the individual action to be explained, but rather on the *conventions* surrounding the performance of the given type of social action in the given social situation. The sense of grasping what is conventional which is relevant here is not limited to the strict sense in which we speak of understanding that a given action is being performed according to a convention of which the agent is aware, and which he deliberately follows. The relevant sense includes the wider idea of understanding what the established, conventional standards are which we may expect to see followed in the case of various types of social action within a given culture. The methodological injunction then becomes: begin not by trying to recover the agent's motives by studying the context of social rules, but rather by trying to decode the agent's intentions by aligning his given social action with a more general awareness of the conventional standards which are generally found to apply to such types of social action within a given social situation.

This injunction appears to hold good even in the case of the type of abnormal social behaviour I have mentioned – such as the example out of Laing and Esterson's work on schizophrenia. It seems, that is, that the appropriate injunction to follow, in the attempt to discover whether the apparent autism of an allegedly schizophrenic adolescent may not be a case of deliberate and meaningful behaviour, must be to begin not by making an intensive study of the particular case and its possible aetiology. It must be to begin instead by trying to relate the particular case to other instances of adolescent withdrawal, in order to try to assess the extent to which the given degree of autism may not after all represent a fairly conventional form and degree of adolescent protest, rather than a straightforward set of pathological symptoms awaiting a straightforward causal explanation.

The same injunction applies even more clearly in the case of the types of linguistic action I have mentioned – such as the example out of Machiavelli's *Prince*, where there is not only a highly conventionalized genre of writing against which to measure Machiavelli's contribution to it, but also the clear presumption that Machiavelli was aware both of the genre and of the conventions usually applying in it. Here it seems unquestionable that the appropriate injunction to follow, in the attempt to disclose the meaning of such a work, must be to begin not by making an intensive study of the text in itself, but rather by trying to see what relations it bears to these existing conventions.

It is true that this injunction has been explicitly attacked by a prevailing school of historians of social and political thought, who have wished to insist that it must be possible, simply by reading such works 'over and over', to arrive at a sufficient understanding of them.[25] It will be clear by now, however, that to adopt such an approach must usually be to follow an inadequate methodology. It is surely clear (to keep to the Machiavelli example) that the fact that *The Prince* was in part intended as a deliberate attack on the moral conventions of advice-books to princes cannot be discovered simply by attending to the text, since this is not a fact contained in the text. It is also clear, however, that no one can be said fully to understand Machiavelli's text who does not understand this fact about it. To fail to grasp this fact is to fail to grasp the *point* of Machiavelli's argument in the latter Chapters of his book. It seems then, that some other form of study besides that of reading the text itself 'over and over' must be indispensable to an understanding of it. And it seems that this will at least need to take the form of adding a study of the general conventions and assumptions of the genre, from which the intentions of any particular contributor to it may then – by a combination of inference and scholarship – be decoded.

V

It will be clear by now that my thesis occupies a middle ground which has I believe been somewhat overlooked in the course of the current philosophical debate about the explanation of action in history and in social science. I have not been particularly concerned with exegesis, but I believe my position to be similar, at least in certain important respects, to that taken up – though by a very different route – in Weber's *Wirtschaft und Gesellschaft*. Those who have emphasized (correctly, I believe) the importance of intentions and conventions in the explanation of social action have usually written as though it follows that the attempt to explain such actions causally must represent a confusion, even a 'pernicious confusion'; that it must in any case be 'wholly irrele-

---

[25] This is the commitment of the methodological introduction to J. P. Plamenatz, *Man and Society* 2 vols. (London, 1964), 1, p.x.

vant'; and that the whole vocabulary of causality ought accordingly to be 'expunged' from discussions about the explanation of social action.[26] Conversely, those philosophers who have insisted (again correctly, I believe) on the absurdity of this commitment have usually written (as I have shown in the case of all the naturalists I have examined) as though it follows that intentions and conventions must themselves be treated simply as causal conditions of social actions. What I have essentially sought to argue is that neither of these alleged implications follows, and that both these claims seem to be mistaken.

It might finally be asked what relation these conclusions may bear to the issue of determinism with respect to voluntary human actions. This would be a vertiginous question even to broach, were it not that several proponents of the two naturalist theses I have examined seem to suggest that they lend an immediate strength to the thesis of determinism. This belief emerges, for example, at the end of Ayer's essay on Man as a subject for science. It is first pointed out there that we ordinarily explain human actions by citing the agent's motives and intentions and the social context of his behaviour. It is then argued that all these conditions must be construed as causes of which the agent's actions are effects. It is then said to follow that there is 'no reason why the reign of law should break down' when we come to explain such actions. This is 'the strength of the determinists'. (*op. cit.*, p. 24.)

I have sought to argue, however, that while there can undoubtedly be successful causal explanations of voluntary human actions, there can also be successful explanations of voluntary human actions which operate simply by recovering the illocutionary redescription of the given action, which are neither causal nor reducible to a causal form. If this argument is sound, then it seems possible to suggest two conclusions about the relations between the naturalist theses I have examined and the idea of the social determinism of actions, without having to commit oneself on the vexed question of the meaning of the thesis of determinism itself. The first, which must obviously be put very tentatively, is that if it is in fact essential for the defence of the thesis of the social determinism of actions that it should be possible to construe all the mental states of agents as causes of their actions, then there may be something inherently doubtful about the thesis. But the main conclusion, which can I think be expressed more confidently, is that in so far as the current arguments in favour of the thesis of social determinism have to depend

---

[26] For these claims see respectively A. R. Louch, *Explanation and Human Action* (Oxford, 1966), p. 238; Melden, *op. cit.*, p. 184; Raziel Abelson, 'Because I Want To', *Mind* 74 (1965), p. 541.

upon the truth of theses C and D – including the assumption contained in thesis D that an agent's intentions must always be construed as causes of which his actions are effects – the thesis of social determinism has not yet been strengthened at all.

7 The Identity of the History of Ideas[1]

John Dunn

Two types of criticism are frequently levelled at the history of ideas in general and the history of political theory in particular. The first is very much that of historians practising in other fields; that it is written as a saga in which all the great deeds are done by entities which could not, in principle, *do* anything. In it, Science is always wrestling with Theology, Empiricism with Rationalism, Monism with Dualism, Evolution with the Great Chain of Being, Artifice with Nature, *Politik* with Political Moralism. Its protagonists are never humans, but only reified abstractions – or, if humans by inadvertence, humans only as the loci of these abstractions. The other charge, one more frequently levelled by philosophers, is that it is insensitive to the distinctive features of ideas, unconcerned with, or more often ineffectual in its concern with, truth and falsehood, its products more like intellectual seed-catalogues than adequate studies of thought. In short it is characterized by a persistent tension between the threats of falsity in its history and incompetence in its philosophy.

At first sight both these charges seem plausible. One might well suppose that the status of propositions about the history of thought would be at issue both in the accuracy of their location of a particular event in the past and in the adequacy of their understanding of the nature of the event so located. Statements about a type of event in the past, statements that event X took place at time P, may be mistaken in their claims that (the event that took place at time P) was an event of X-type or that (an event of X-type) *did* take place at time P. Concentration on the identification of some types of event (e.g. in the history of ideas, the subtler sorts of analysis of classics of philosophy) may well lead to greater concern for analytical complexity and force than for mere historicity,[2] and concentration on mere historicity may well lead to an inferior understanding of what it was that did exist in the past. In this way the two types of criticism can readily be seen as the advocacy of different forms

---

[1] A slightly longer version of this essay first appeared in *Philosophy*, XLIII, April 1968, 85–116.

[2] It seems to be the case that the interpretation of the famous passage in Hume's *Treatise of Human Nature* on deducing 'ought' from 'is' has been distorted in just this way. Cf. W. D. Hudson, ed., *The Is/Ought Question* (London, 1969) Part One.

of enquiry within the common subject-matter. This would make the issue between them not one of truth or falsity but merely of the tactical choice between competing simplifications. And if such a choice between competing evils is necessary, it must be equally legitimate to represent it as a choice between competing goods. This painless resolution is in fact that which most practitioners adopt, in so far, that is, as they see any need for resolution. For them, this is at worst a matter of discounting risks (not, of course, a matter of making statements which are deliberately false, whether historically or philosophically). After one has chosen the aspect of a subject-matter which most concerns one, the criticisms of those whose interest in it is very different are discounted. If choice is necessary and some sort of failure certain, then one *should* plainly choose to discount the costs of the type of failure one has chosen. Such axioms about the necessary limitations of human skills are nothing but the most ordinary common sense.

What I wish principally to argue in this paper is that the costs of such self-abnegation are much higher than is normally recognized; that the connection between an adequate philosophical account of the notions held by an individual in the past and an accurate historical account of these notions is an intimate one, that both historical specificity and philosophical delicacy are more likely to be attained if they are pursued together than if one is deserted for the other at an early stage of the investigation. In other words, I wish to claim that the disagreements over the appropriate subject-matter and form of explanation for the history of ideas, though they are indeed persuasions to choose to examine one form of description of intellectual acts in the past rather than another, are also something more. What is in question is not merely a choice between true (or false) stories but a problem intrinsic to the attempt to tell stories about this type of data. More precisely, I wish to claim (1) that the completion of both types of investigation is a necessary preliminary to the construction of an indefeasible explanation of either type, and (2) that a sensitive exercise of both types of explanation and a realization of the sort of problems which an audience would have in following the story will tend to produce a convergence of tactic in this pursuit – that is, that a rational explanation of a past philosophical dilemma, a causal explanation of a past philosopher's enterprise and an account of either of these rendered intelligible to an ignorant layman will display a considerable symmetry of form and that most of the unsatisfactory features of the history of ideas as written comes from its notable lack of resemblance to any such form.

There is nothing very obscure about the notion that much of the history of ideas as written displays a certain philosophical crassness. But what exactly are we to make of the complaint about the 'bloodlessness' of the history of ideas? I shall attempt to dramatize this charge in what follows, in order to make its appeal more obvious. The point, in essence, is simple enough. Apart from odd examples in the history of religious development or scientific discovery, few branches of the history of ideas have been written as the history of an *activity*. Complicated structures of ideas, arranged in a manner approximating as closely as may be (frequently closer than the evidence permits) to deductive systems have been examined at different points in time or their morphology traced over the centuries. Reified reconstructions of a great man's more accessible notions have been compared with those of other great men; hence the weird tendency of much writing, in the history of political thought more especially, to be made up of what propositions in what great books remind the author of what propositions in what other great books. Key principles of the explanatory thought-systems of social groups, of communities, and of whole countries have been pursued through the centuries. As a make-weight to this type of analysis, we have biographies of great thinkers which identify the central arguments of their more important works, sketch in their social background in some detail and expatiate upon their merits or moral relevance to the present day. Finally we have formal philosophical analyses of the works of great philosophers or scientists which tell us what Hobbes's theory of obligation or Plato's theory of justice or Galileo's theory of motion is and how far we should accept it.[3] All of these enterprises are recognized, and properly recognized, as forming part of a pursuit which can be labelled as the 'history of ideas'. Yet none of them is necessarily bound to (and few ever in fact do) provide any sort of historical account of an activity which we would recognize, in common sense terms, as 'thinking'. The history of thought as it is characteristically written is not a history of men battling to achieve a coherent ordering of their experience. It is, rather, a history of fictions – of rationalist constructs out of the thought processes of individuals, not of plausible abridgments of these thought processes. It consists not of representations, but, in the most literal sense, of reconstructions, not of plausible accounts of how men thought, but of more or less painful attempts to elaborate their ideas to a degree of formal intellectual articulation which there is no evidence that they ever attained.

Because of these features, it is often extremely unclear whether the history of ideas is the history of anything which ever did actually exist

[3] It is important to emphasize, in order to avoid misunderstanding, the very remarkable quality of much of the work which has been done in these subjects by Cassirer, Koyré, Kemp Smith, Lovejoy and many others.

in the past, whether it is not habitually conducted in a manner in which the relationship of evidence to conclusion is so tenuous that it provides no grounds at all for assent. For there are certain banal truths which the customary approaches appear to neglect: that thinking is an effortful activity on the part of human beings, not simply a unitary performance; that incompleteness, incoherence, instability and the effort to overcome these are its persistent characteristics; that it is not an activity which takes its meaning from a set of finished performances which have been set up in type and preserved in libraries, but an activity which is conducted more or less incompetently for most of their waking life by a substantial proportion of the human race, which generates conflicts and which is used to resolve these, which is directed towards problem-solving and not towards the construction of closed formal games; that the works in which at a single point in time a set of problems issue in an attempt at a coherent rational ordering of the relevant experience are in some sense unintelligible except in terms of this context; that language is not a repository of formal truths donated by God to Adam but simply the tool which human beings use in their struggle to make sense of their experiences. Once talking and thinking are considered seriously as social activities, it will be apparent that intellectual discussions will only be fully understood if they are seen as complicated instances of these social activities.

All of this is, of course, to beg the question at issue; but it has its plausibility. Whether it has anything else is what I shall try to show. May the charge perhaps amount to nothing more interesting than a pun on the word 'understanding'? The notions of understanding and explaining historical events have recently received a considerable amount of philosophical attention. Complicated issues of epistemology and of the logical forms of explanations have been extensively explored and the practice of historians somewhat clarified. But the extent of the disagreement which remains is still considerable and its precise character frequently elusive.

Consider the following plausible historians' assignments: (1) Explain why Plato wrote the *Republic*; (2) Explain why Plato's ideal state has an authoritarian political structure; (3) Explain why Plato criticizes Thrasymachus's account of justice in the *Republic*; (4) Explain why the Roman empire in the west collapsed; (5) Explain why there was a French Revolution between 1750 and 1820; (6) Explain why there was a French Revolution in 1789; (7) Explain why there was not an English Revolution in 1831.

Some of these seem to be problems about the states of consciousness of agents; others do not. Some seem to demand an account of the set of premises which make a given argument or set of arguments seem cogent. Some seem to be answerable by a detailed narrative of a period of time in the past. Others do not seem to be susceptible of narrative treatment at all. That is to say, a story of the periods in point seems to leave the question raised quite unanswered. What story could possibly explain why there was a French Revolution between 1750 and 1820? It would need a most remarkable story of 1789 to seem an appropriate answer to that question. Why should one wish to assimilate one set of these questions to another, still less reduce them all to one sort? Or, to put the issue differently, why should one suppose that the venerable dispute between idealist and positivist philosophers of history, or its more recent avatar, that between the exponents of causal and those of 'rational' or narrative explanations, between the notions of history as applied general sociology or as stories which happen to be true, is a real dispute at all? Is it not rather an attempt to legislate for the type of historical explanations which should ideally be given, a lengthy exercise in the persuasive definition of the adjective 'historical'? Beneath what conceivable set of causal laws could (3) be subsumed? Or what narrative or set of reasons could constitute an answer to (4) or (5)? Giving reasons for why an argument seemed cogent or an act appropriate to an individual in the past is not an instance of subsuming anything under a causal law, though there are certainly causes for the appearance of cogency in the argument or appropriateness in the act. No explanation of the persistence and change of a complex social system over time can be adequately provided by a story. But both of these last two enterprises, whether or not they have ever been carried out in a definitively satisfactory manner represent intelligible and characteristic *explanatory*[4] enterprises of historians and the attempt to reduce them to the same type of enterprise is absurd. But to insist that there is a correct model for historical explanation implies that one or other of these, causal or rational, must be merely provisional, preliminaries to the construction of an explanation of the approved form. In any case, does either of them provide an appropriate form of explanation for the history of ideas (surely an ideal example for those with a strong distaste for the more scientistic aspirations of historians)?

What *is* the subject-matter of the history of ideas: past thinking,

[4] Most historical writing, for better or worse, does not in the main consist of explanation. This lends an adventitious force to the arguments of critics of the 'deductive-nomological' paradigm. But if the narratives of historians are claimed to be true, some sort of concern for causality seems to be inexpugnable. The most elegant literary constructs in history do come to grief on aesthetically trivial facts.

philosophy, ideas, ideologies? And what indeed is its form: a set of narratives, a set of subsumptions of individual instances under covering laws, a set of reconstructed rationalia for specific philosophical performances? Most urgently, how far does causality intrude into this sensitive intellectualist enquiry and how far are its permitted intrusions a matter of intellectual taste on the part of the historian and how far a matter of professional obligation; how far, in short, is the meaning of any set of ideas irreducibly infected by the conditions of its birth?

One might want to say that any statement made by any individual at any time could only be said to be *fully* understood if one knew the conditioning-history and the set of present stimulus conditions which elicited it. And yet human beings do to some extent understand each other, and by the time they reach the age of speech the very notion of such a history of their conditioning seems to elude our pictures of them. It is not just that no one has ever been able to provide such a specification; but who would seriously claim to be able to imagine what it would be like to know such a story and then confront the individual whose story it was? What would the logical relations between such a story and our own descriptions of actions be like? Clearly, if this were a necessary condition for understanding a statement we could not have acquired the very notion of understanding statements. Indeed, one might say that to suppose anything so implausible is simply to make the familiar mistake of confusing psychology with epistemology, to mistake the genetics of a statement for its logical status. But the initial proposition was not that one could not understand statements *at all* but that one could not *fully* understand them; that any understanding was in principle liable to be exposed as including a specific misunderstanding of some feature of what it is claimed to understand. But what sort of feature? For, any explanation of a given linguistic act in terms of its history can only give at best the necessary and sufficient conditions of its occurrence. It cannot account for its truth-value. This does not mean that such an explanation cannot include an account of why X thought it to be true (in so far as he did do so) – plainly this must be included – nor even an account of why X thought it was true though many with the same values as X and greater specific skills would have been able to show conclusively why it was false. What the explanation cannot give in purely historical terms is an account of why it is true or false. To put the point most simply, in the history of science, the full set of statements about the sufficient conditions of Aristarchus of Samos's heliocentrism does not serve to tell us the senses in which his theory was true or false.

If this assertion is correct, important conclusions follow. In the history of philosophy, for example, the only account of a past philosophical performance which could be said to be complete at any one time must comprise the complete story of its behavioural genesis[5] and the best available assessment of its truth-value. Furthermore it implies that every complete account in the history of philosophy is implicitly dated. (Not, of course, every *statement* in the history of philosophy, as, for example, 'Plato wrote the *Republic*' or even, 'Locke's *Essay* contains criticisms of a doctrine that there are innately known truths'). For its truth is contingent on the adequacy of this philosophical assessment; and the criteria for the adequacy of the assessment change over time. Perhaps, though, the point is trivial. So, after all, do the criteria for truth claims in psychology; say, from Aquinas to Descartes to Bain to Skinner. In the nineteenth century the idea of a complete physics did not seem fatuous and hence a complete psychology at least in principle conceivable. Today, where the idea of indefeasible physical truth is so puzzling, the idea of an indefeasible psychology seems grotesque. Perhaps it is grotesque. In which case the claim collapses into the banality that all explanations are implicitly dated. One could also perhaps argue for a necessary time-specificity in the philosophical account on lines parallel to those which Danto uses[6] to distinguish between contemporary- and future-specific descriptions of events. But it seems equally plausible today to argue for a time-specificity in the causal story. It's not simply what true statements there are to make about the past (the contemporary- or future-specific descriptions of the past) which alters, but what one knows the past to have been like. In the same way, changes in physical or chemical knowledge may have effects in geology which alter the geological story, while the history of the human race as such at most alters the labels attached to different areas of the geological subject-matter.

Even at this level of abstraction the argument clearly implies that there are two necessary components to the *identification* of every past performance of philosophical importance, two descriptions of the act which require very different verificatory procedures. A major argument of this paper is that much of the incoherence and implausibility in the history of ideas stems from the failure to separate these adequately and that most abstract methodological arguments in the subject depend upon an effort

---

[5] I have no wish to foreclose on any form of attained causal explanation of behaviour. But I do not wish, particularly in the face of Charles Taylor, *The Explanation of Behaviour* (London, 1964), to assert that the explanations must be ultimately reducible to statements in a 'physical-object data language'.

[6] Arthur C. Danto, *Analytical Philosophy of History* (Cambridge, 1965).

to make one of the two descriptions of the act all-important and the other trivial. They err in proffering one description as the overriding, the *correct*, description of the performance in place of the other. It seems clear that both descriptions are in principle correct, that they constitute answers to different questions about the nature of the act. What is much less clear (perhaps, even, not always true in practice) is the claim that they cannot be brought off perfectly well separately. The causal story is clearly a very intricate piece of historical explanation whereas the philosophical analysis may well seem simpler. May we not follow a suggestion of Alan Ryan's[7] in leaving to the historian the question of 'what Locke intended' and confining our attention to 'what Locke said'? The question then is simply how we may know 'what Locke said'. Perhaps, if we examine the history of political theory we shall contrive to discover such a temporally inviolate entity.

What is it that the history of political thought is the history of? Two things, at least: the set of argued propositions in the past which discuss how the political world is and ought to be and what should constitute the criteria for proper action within it, and the set of activities in which men were engaged when they enunciated these propositions. The precise degree of abstraction which places a given proposition inside or outside the category is obviously pretty arbitrary. But the identification of the continuum on which this break occurs is simple enough – roughly from the *Republic* or *Social Choice and Individual Values* to the single expletive 'Fascist'. To the two types of history there correspond two sorts of integral explanation, 'rational' and causal. Between the two, and punningly encompassing both, there lies a third, narrative, which is 'rational' without the humility and causal without the criteria of achievement. The first looks like a history of political arguments; the second a history of political arguing. One develops the coherence which a set of political propositions seems to have held for its proponents and comments on the status of this coherence (places it within criteria of rationality and irrationality to which we accede today); it maps the logic of arguments and sets these out against its own prescriptive logic, so that their structure can be grasped clearly. All the statements contained in it are statements about the relationships of propositions to propositions. But history, surely, is about the world and not about propositions. Where, in the world, do these propositions have their place? In what does their historicity consist? The answer plainly is that they are not merely propositions, logical structures; they are also statements. Men have said (or at least written) them. So the men appear again in the story,

[7] Alan Ryan, 'Locke and the Dictatorship of the Bourgeoisie', *Political Studies* VIII (1965), p. 219.

appear as speakers. It is in the role of the speaker that this disembodiment of the proposition begins to be threatened.

For there are three ways in commonsense terms that one may misunderstand what it is that a man has said. The meaning one attributes to his words may not be a meaning that can properly be attributed to them in his public language (in which case the only way the interpretation could be correct would be if he characteristically misused his language in this particular way). The meaning which one attributes to them may not have been that which he intended them to bear; and this in more than the peripheral sense that he committed a malapropism or a Freudian slip. Or the meaning which one attributes to his act in saying them may be mistaken. One's identification of the speech act may fail in its grasp of the lexical possibilities, of the historical actuality of the proposition which he intended to enunciate (usually one of the lexical possibilities), or of what he was doing in saying it. The failure to grasp a set of propositions correctly may be due to what is necessarily a mistranslation (an error about language), in fact a misinterpretation of what someone has said (an error about a propositional enterprise of a human being) or a misinterpretation of his behaviour in saying it (an error about the nature of a complex action).

If the historicity of the history of philosophy or political theory consists in the fact that the statements *were* made at a particular date by a particular person, then it seems that the enterprise of identification can be confined to the avoidance of the first two types of misunderstanding. Surely, one might say, it matters what Socrates said, not just what words he used but what he was saying in using them – what he meant. But it does not matter, as far as the history of philosophy is concerned, what he was *doing* in saying them. No description of the psychological state of the philosopher can infect the truth or falsity of what he maintains. Philosophy is about truth not about action. It may be a profound sociological truth (well, it *might*, anyway) that socialism is a cry of pain.[8] But this tells us nothing of the truth-value of such propositions and arguments as constitute Socialism.

The problem, however, is more pressing than this. There are occasions on which one cannot know what a man means unless one knows what he is doing. Suppose a person were to give a parody of the sort of argument normally produced in favour of a position which he particularly detests – say, in an argument about the justification for punishing homosexual acts as such, to describe an alleged causal relationship between changes in the sexual mores of the Roman aristocracy and the

[8] Emile Durkheim, *Socialism and Saint-Simon* (New York, 1958), p. 41.

military collapse of the Roman empire in the West. If, at the end of the recital, a listener were to be asked what the speaker in question had said, it might be possible for him to provide a full record of the words used and in the correct order and with perfect understanding of the rules for the use for each particular word and yet still not have *understood* what was said. Of course, such a misapprehension could readily be described as a failure to grasp what the speaker was doing in saying those words; and this is clearly an apt description. But it does seem at least equally natural to describe it as not understanding 'what he was saying'. 'Doing things with words' is saying things, just as saying things is doing things with words.[9] Parody or even irony are not just acts which hold the world at a respectful distance. They are ways of saying things about the world. It would surely be impossible to write a coherent account of Plato's ideas in the *Gorgias* or Hume's in the *Dialogues concerning Natural Religion* without taking note of the fact that some of the propositions which they contain are highly ironical in character. On the other hand, clearly a coherent account of the arguments in these works does not necessarily itself contain lots of ironical propositions. The point that needs emphasis is only that the identification of what Plato's or Hume's arguments are is contingent on understanding what they were doing in enunciating certain propositions at particular points in their works. But the sort of specific and primitive failure of identification here in question is hardly the most frequent danger. Must it not in any case be possible to elicit the correct identification of the meaning from the text itself? For, it would be most embarrassing if it *is* the case that we need some accurate emotional and cognitive chart of Plato's experiences while writing the work, or some sort of abridged story of his intellectual career beforehand, in order to grasp it fully, since we manifestly know almost nothing about these except from the pages of the dialogues. But, to take a vulgar example from the causal story as we have had it told, just what sort of light does it shed on the arguments of the *Republic*, supposing that it were in some sense true, to say that it is an instance of the ideology of the declining Athenian political élite?

Clearly it does not tell us whether any particular argument in the work is true or false. But if the claim about the causal story can be sustained, it must to some degree improve our identification of the arguments as arguments. At first sight this seems implausible. For, what sort of acts can we adequately identify in terms of their social causation? Crudely, one can provide an account of the social causation of acts which can be specified as the performance of socially defined roles (this is circular).

[9] See J. L. Austin, *How to Do Things with Words* (Oxford, 1962), *passim*.

These can be widely differentiated and may not look as though they have any social component at all: attacking the government, defending (or affirming the rationality of) the social structure, loving one's wife, praising God, philosophizing. The sole necessary condition is that the act must appear only as an instance of the role (contrast 'loving one's wife' with 'how one loves one's wife'), and the role must be specified in the description of the general social order. The only particulars which appear in the account must appear as instances of universals. No description of a social structure, taken by itself and without the addition of a huge number of dated statements about the individual, could enable one to deduce the complete life story of the individual. This is quite irrelevant to the issue of whether one can in principle predict all human behaviour; it is merely a logical feature of any explanation of individual acts in terms of a social structure. This manifestly does not mean that one cannot improve one's understanding of an individual act by improving the social description of it (cf. Why is he kneeling in discomfort in the gloom consuming that tasteless food and ill-flavoured wine? Answer, he is partaking of the Body and the Blood of Christ. But compare the complexity today of the demand: 'Describe just what he is doing in "worshipping God" in that way'). But what would it mean if it were true, ignoring the vulgarity of the chosen phrasing, that the *Republic* was ideology for the declining Athenian political élite, as it were, an acceptable substitute for being Critias? It clearly would not mean that any description of the social role of the declining Athenian political élite would have written the Republic for you. It is a very abstract description of the book and what we are interested in, if we are interested in the history of philosophy or political theory, is a very concrete description. What could be said to be socially caused about the *Republic* is at most certain features of it. The authoritarian political structure of Plato's Utopia is not the *Republic*, is not why it appears in the history of political thought, let alone philosophy.

But here again, we have clearly rejected too much. For, those features of the *Republic* for which we might attempt to sketch causal explanations in terms of the social history of Athens can certainly tell us something about the arguments of the book as such. It is when we come to look for the unstated premises of Plato's arguments or attempt to understand why the stated premises seemed to him to need no further extrinsic justification, that we see their relevance. All arguments have to start somewhere. Different sorts of explanations of the plausibility of a premise to an individual provide different sorts of blocking-off points to the account which can be given of his argument. The constant threat of anachronism, the wholly spurious transparency which sometimes characterizes what men have said in the past, makes the correct identification of the premises of arguments and the explanation of these the basic precondition for an adequate account, whether historical or philosophical. If we are to understand the criteria of truth or falsehood implicit in a complex intellectual architectonic, we have to understand the structures of biographical or social experience which made these criteria seem self-evident. To abstract an argument from the context of truth-criteria which it was devised to meet is to convert it into a different argument. If, in our insistent urge to learn from the arguments of the past, we assume that its consequently enhanced intelligibility will teach us more, we merely guarantee that what it teaches us must be something different from what it says and furthermore that what it teaches us must be much closer to what we already know. If the effort to learn from philosophers of the past is a plausible philosophical heuristic, it would be most odd if it can be best carried out *in general* by failing to grasp their actual arguments.

If we wish to exploit the causal story, the history of philosophizing, for such a purpose, and if we are never granted access to the very special causal stories previously suggested as paradigms for explanation, from what sort of stories can we benefit? Motive-explanations and ideological explanations can both be made causal in form (the former with some difficulty) and both could under some circumstances lend greater intelligibility to a complex structure of ideas; but they certainly raise problems. Even a sociological theory like functionalism is wildly evasive when given consistent causal interpretation, and there have been psychological experiments about emotions designed to establish empirically what are necessary logical truths. Even if they are to function as blocks to further rational explanation, they must be rationally-connected motives or ideologies or no explanation can be provided of the specific intellectual explicandum, just a description of it which suppresses its intellectual specificity. Clearly the sort of jejune retrospective sociology of knowledge or random biographical information which we have at our disposal before, say, the nineteenth century are not going to help very much. But even if this is a counsel of perfection, or despair, it is not one which we can honourably avoid. There must be a point in any argument at which a man stops being able to give reasons – and at that point the organism has to give them for the man. Some, very general, seem almost biological data; like the demand to give general reasons for the practice of self-preservation. Such a request, while it is intelligible enough to some (and could even be said to have a whole modern philosophy devised as an attempted answer), must simply seem a category mistake to most people. A few such teleological laws are widely credited as axioms. In describing a philosophical project coherently some of the premises must be authenticated in this way, extra-intellectually. Any deductive system must have some axioms and there are some claims for anyone which are simply axioms, where a request for a reason for the statement will only be met by a causal explanation of its axiomatic status, that it is one of the stipulations of this man's history. '*I* just do think eating people is wrong'. Such causal explanations may be hard indeed to find in the past. Even if our explanatory accounts come to include explicit fictions as explanatory terms (and after all most historical accounts contain more or less discreet fictions), at least this will enable others to attempt to test their truth or falsity. Only if we learn to make our fictions explicit are we ever likely to escape from our present conceptual morass, from the persisting problem of never knowing just what we are talking about.

Having in this disheartened way evaded the question of what sort of stories to look for in the history of philosophizing, there remains the question of what to look for the stories of. The history of philosophy must necessarily be written in terms of current philosophical interests. This does not mean that it has to be falsified in terms of our current philosophical tastes, because the causal story, in so far as we can still discover it, has always to be elaborated first. Its historicity is its sufficient and its sole legitimate immunity from our philosophical prejudices. To call these arbitrary is vacuous. A man for whom the philosophical articulations of a society, thinned out in the tortuous distillations of rationality from 'the fury and the mire of human veins', appear arbitrary is a man whose inadvertence takes in both the philosophical and the causal stories, a man for whom everything must be arbitrary. And in the insight that every human interest is arbitrary (as with the story that all human experience is a dream) we do not gain a truth, we merely lose a word. If we did not write it in terms of these current philosophical interests there would be no interests in terms of which to define it. A philosophical analysis of the *Republic* seems apt, where one of the *Iliad* or the *Gortyn Code* does not, and this scarcely raises a problem. Epics and law codes in primitive societies simply are not philosophical – even though one might be a little embarrassed by being pressed on the status of – say – Blake, or Milton, or Dante; and even though Peter Winch[10] writes as though any sociological analysis of the *Gortyn Code* was necessarily 'philosophical'.

No doubt there are true claims to be made in these areas by somewhat stretching the meaning of the word 'philosophical'. But the central point

---

[10] Peter Winch, *The Idea of a Social Science* (London, 1958).

remains that epics and law codes are conceptually set in well-defined areas of activity, whatever one can learn *from* them about the history of philosophy, and appeal explicitly or implicitly for their standing to many criteria altogether discrete from the nature of truth.[11] The history of philosophy, like the history of science, must needs be Whig as to subject-matter, just as, like all history, it must be Tory as to truth. This does not mean that one should *necessarily* study Kant rather than Christian Wolff; only that one should select philosophically interesting philosophy, after one has identified what philosophy there is to study. The criteria for selecting this, as indeed in a broader sense the criteria of what in the identified past is philosophy at all, are provided by philosophy today. But the criteria provided by philosophy today need never be merely those of philosophy yesterday. The criterion of future philosophical interest is the achievement of the investigator, not the tradition of the Schools. What we can learn from the past is always what we can succeed in learning; and the educative past can change – as if some disused Mendip lead-working were one day to disclose a new and precious sort of uranium.

But this hardly provides any very helpful direction. To bring together the threads of Utopian persuasion, we must return to the contexts of the utterances which men produce. If a statement is considered in a fully open context, its meaning may be any lexically possible set of colligations of the uttered propositions. A man might mean by it anything that a man might mean by it. The problem of interpretation is always the problem of closing the context. What closes the context in actuality is the intention (and, much more broadly, the experiences) of the speaker. Locke, in talking, talks about what he talks about. The problem of the historian is always that *his* experience also drastically closes the context of utterance; indeed all too readily turns a fact about the past into a fact about the intellectual biography of the historian. If in the seventeenth century Locke and Hobbes are the two English political theorists whom we all read and if, had we been writing Locke's major work, we should surely have wished to address ourselves mainly to the works of Hobbes, it is a very simple ellipse to suppose that Locke must surely have been addressing himself to Hobbes. Indeed it is so simple that men will go to the most extraordinarily intricate theoretical lengths to rescue this

---

[11] Not that one would not employ philosophical notions at any point in the attempt to explain and assess them; only, that most of the operation of understanding them, even after the story of how they come to be there is told completely, has nothing to do with philosophy.

somewhat subjective 'appearance'.[12] The solution to the historian's problem is formally simple, to substitute the closure of context provided by the biography of the speaker for that provided by the biography of the historian. But such a project is not merely, in a trivial sense and *pace* Collingwood, logically impossible. It is also in a more pragmatic sense overwhelmingly difficult. But the difficulty is not one which we can consciously agree to evade. Communicating what Locke said and understanding what Locke said both involve making comprehensible the utterance of *Locke*. It is here that the symmetry between understanding, explaining and giving an account of a philosophical claim becomes strongest. For any of these activities must necessarily include what are in effect abridgments of the other two activities and any of them which fails to do so may be in principle corrigible by either of the other two. The problem of communicating, for instance, the meaning of Plato's *Republic* to an audience, the sort of problem which the dim privacy of our writing in the history of ideas so notably fails to solve, is the prototypical problem for the historian of ideas. For it demands not the sort of flashing of professional credit cards, the Great Chain of Being, associationism, Vico, which serve well enough inside the profession when we all feel tired, that rigid and dead reaction to recognized points which, as Professor Wisdom complained of aesthetics, is 'sometimes found in dog fanciers and characteristic of the pharisees',[13] but grasping the point of the original intellectual enterprise. In the reconstitution of this enterprise, the identification of the problem, the identification, again *pace* Collingwood, of why it was a problem for its proponent (and why many things which would be for us were not for him – firmly a part of the causal story), and in the critical judgment of the solution, we turn a theorem about an intellectual enterprise in the past into an intellectual enterprise in the present. All the premises in our own understanding and representation are inserted firmly into the past as hypotheses for historical adjudication. When the audience can think of no more questions to ask and when we can think of no new questions to ask and can get no more answers to our old questions from the evidence, such an investigation is completed; until the next investigation follows in due course. What I wish to emphasize is that such an investigation, if

---

[12] See Peter Laslett, ed., John Locke, *Two Treatises of Government* (Cambridge, 1960) pp. 67–76, and John Dunn, *The Political Thought of John Locke* (Cambridge, 1969).
[13] John Wisdom, 'Things and Persons', Arist. Soc. Suppl. Vol. XXII, quoted by John Passmore, 'The Dreariness of Aesthetics', in William Elton, ed., *Aesthetics and Language* (Oxford, 1959), p. 40.

at any time it were carried to a conclusion, would be the only sort of explanation which would necessarily meet both those types of criticism of the history of ideas in general or the history of philosophy or political theory in particular which I began by noting. All this indeed is whistling to keep our courage up and in no immediate danger of instantiation. But unless we have a picture of the possible shape of success, it will be hard to see why we do it all so badly.

8 Negative and Positive Freedom[1]
Gerald C. MacCallum Jr.

This paper challenges the view that we may usefully distinguish between two kinds or concepts of political and social freedom – negative and positive. The argument is not that one of these is the only, the 'truest', or the 'most worthwhile' freedom, but rather that the distinction between them has never been made sufficiently clear, is based in part upon a serious confusion, and has drawn attention away from precisely what needs examining if the differences separating philosophers, ideologies, and social movements concerned with freedom are to be understood. The corrective advised is to regard freedom as always one and the same triadic relation, but recognize that various contending parties disagree with each other in what they understand to be the ranges of the term variables. To view the matter in this way is to release oneself from a prevalent but unrewarding concentration on 'kinds' of freedom, and to turn attention toward the truly important issues in this area of social and political philosophy.

I

Controversies generated by appeals to the presence or absence of freedom in societies have been roughly of four closely related kinds – namely (1) about the nature of freedom itself, (2) about the relationships holding between the attainment of freedom and the attainment of other possible social benefits, (3) about the ranking of freedom among such benefits, and (4) about the consequences of this or that policy with respect to realizing or attaining freedom. Disputes of one kind have turned readily into disputes of the other kinds.

Of those who agree that freedom is a benefit, most would also agree that it is not the *only* benefit a society may secure its members. Other benefits might include, for example, economic and military security, technological efficiency, and exemplifications of various aesthetic and spiritual values. Once this is admitted, however, disputes of types (2) and (3) are possible. Questions can be raised as to the logical and causal relationships holding between the attainment of freedom and the attain-

[1] Reprinted with permission from: *The Philosophical Review*, 76 (1967), pp. 312–34.

ment of these other benefits, and as to whether one could on some occasions reasonably prefer to cultivate or emphasize certain of the latter at the expense of the former. Thus, one may be led to ask: *can* anyone cultivate and emphasize freedom at the cost of realizing these other goals and values (or vice versa) and, secondly, *should* anyone ever do this? In practice, these issues are often masked by or confused with disputes about the consequences of this or that action with respect to realizing the various goals or values.

Further, any of the above disputes may stem from or turn into a dispute about what freedom *is*. The borderlines have never been easy to keep clear. But a reason for this especially worth noting at the start is that disputes about the nature of freedom are certainly historically best understood as a series of attempts by parties opposing each other on very many issues to capture for their own side the favourable attitudes attaching to the notion of freedom. It has commonly been advantageous for partisans to link the presence or absence of freedom as closely as possible to the presence or absence of those other social benefits believed to be secured or denied by the forms of social organization advocated or condemned. Each social benefit is, accordingly, treated as either a result of or a contribution to freedom, and each liability is connected somehow to the absence of freedom. This history of the matter goes far to explain how freedom came to be identified with so many different kinds of social and individual benefits, and why the status of freedom as simply one among a number of social benefits has remained unclear. The resulting flexibility of the notion of freedom, and the resulting enhancement of the value of freedom, have suited the purposes of the polemicist.

It is against this background that one should first see the issues surrounding the distinction between positive and negative freedom as two fundamentally different kinds of freedom. Nevertheless, the difficulties surrounding the distinction should not be attributed solely to the interplay of Machiavellian motives. The disputes, and indeed the distinction itself, have also been influenced by a genuine confusion concerning the concept of freedom. The confusion results from failure to understand fully the conditions under which use of the concept of freedom is intelligible.

II

Whenever the freedom of some agent or agents is in question, it is always freedom from some constraint or restriction on, interference with, or barrier to doing, not doing, becoming, or not becoming something.[2] Such freedom is thus always *of* something (an agent or agents), *from* something, *to* do, not do, become, or not become something; it is a triadic relation. Taking the format 'x is (is not) free from y to do (not do, become, not become) z,' x ranges over agents, y ranges over such 'preventing conditions' as constraints, restrictions, interferences, and barriers, and z ranges over actions or conditions of character or circumstance. When reference to one of these three terms is missing in such a discussion of freedom, it should be only because the reference is thought to be understood from the context of the discussion.[3]

Admittedly, the idioms of freedom are such that this is sometimes not obvious. The claim, however, is not about what we say, but rather about the conditions under which what we say is intelligible. And, of course, it is important to notice that the claim is only about what makes talk concerning the freedom of agents intelligible. This restriction excludes from consideration, for example, some uses of 'free of' and 'free from' – namely, those not concerned with the freedom of agents, and where, consequently, what is meant may be only 'rid of' or 'without'. Thus, consideration of 'The sky is now free of clouds' is excluded because this expression does not deal with agents at all; but consideration of 'His record is free of blemish' and 'She is free from any vice' is most probably also excluded. Doubt about these latter two hinges on whether these expressions might be thought claims about the freedom of agents; if so, then they are not excluded, but neither are they intelligible *as* claims about the freedom of agents until one is in a position to fill in the elements of the format offered above; if not, then although probably

---

[2] The need to elaborate in this unwieldy way arises from the absence in this paper of any discussion of the verification conditions for claims about freedom. The elaboration is designed to leave open the issues one would want to raise in such a discussion.

[3] Of writers on political and social freedom who have approached this view, the clearest case is Felix Oppenheim in *Dimensions of Freedom* (New York, 1961); but, while viewing social freedom as a triadic relation, he limits the ranges of the term variables so sharply as to cut one off from many issues I wish to reach. Cf. also T. D. Weldon, *The Vocabulary of*

parasitic upon talk about the freedom of agents and thus perhaps viewable as figurative anyway, they fall outside the scope of this investigation.

The claim that freedom, subject to the restriction noted above, is a triadic relation can hardly be substantiated here by exhaustive examination of the idioms of freedom. But the most obviously troublesome cases – namely, those in which one's understanding of the context must in a relevant way carry past the limits of what is explicit in the idiom – may be classified roughly and illustrated as follows:

(a) *Cases where agents are not mentioned*: for example, consider any of the wide range of expressions having the form 'free *x*' in which (*i*) the place of *x* is taken by an expression not clearly referring to an agent – as in 'free society' or 'free will' – or (*ii*) the place of *x* is taken by an expression clearly not referring to an agent – as in 'free beer'. All such cases can be understood to be concerned with the freedom of agents and, indeed, their intelligibility rests upon their being so understood; they are thus subject to the claims made above. This is fairly obvious in the cases of 'free will' and 'free society'. The intelligibility of the free-will problem is generally and correctly thought to rest at least upon the problem's being concerned with the freedom of persons, even though the criteria for identification of the persons or 'selves' whose freedom is in question have not often been made sufficiently clear.[4] And it is beyond question that the expression 'free society', although of course subject to various conflicting analyses with respect to the identity of the agent(s) whose freedom is involved, is thought intelligible only because it is thought to concern the freedom of agents of some sort or other. The expression 'free beer', on the other hand (to take only one of a rich class of cases some of which would have to be managed differently), is ordinarily thought intelligible because thought to refer to beer that *people* are free *from* the ordinary restrictions of the market place *to* drink without paying for it.

For an expression of another grammatical form, consider 'The property is free of (or from) encumbrance'. Although this involves a loose use of 'property', suppose that the term refers to something like a piece of land; the claim then clearly means that *owners* of that land are free *from* certain well-known restrictions (for example, certain types of

---

Politics (Harmondsworth, 1953), esp. pp. 157ff.; but see also pp. 70–2.

[4] Indeed, lack of clarity on just this point is probably one of the major sources of confusion in discussions of free will.

charges or liabilities consequent upon their ownership of the land) *to* use, enjoy, dispose of the land as they wish.

(*b*) *Cases where it is not clear what corresponds to the second term*: for example, 'freedom of choice,' 'freedom to choose as I please'. Here, the range of constraints, restrictions, and so forth, is generally clear from the context of the discussion. In political matters, legal constraints or restrictions are most often thought of; but one also sometimes finds, as in Mill's *On Liberty*, concern for constraints and interferences constituted by social pressures. It is sometimes difficult for persons to see social pressures as constraints or interferences; this will be discussed below. It is also notoriously difficult to see casual nexuses as implying constraints or restrictions on the 'will' (the person?) in connection with the free-will problem. But the very fact that such difficulties are the focus of so much attention is witness to the importance of getting clear about this term of the relation before such discussions of freedom can be said to be intelligible.

One might think that references to a second term of this sort could always be eliminated by a device such as the following. Instead of saying, for example, (*i*) 'Smith is free *from* legal restrictions on travel *to* leave the country', one could say (*ii*) 'Smith is free *to* leave the country *because* there are no legal restrictions on his leaving'. The latter would make freedom appear to be a dyadic, rather than a triadic, relation. But we would be best advised to regard the appearance illusory, and this may be seen if one thinks a bit about the suggestion or implication of the sentence that nothing hinders or prevents Smith from leaving the country. Difficulties about this might be settled by attaching a qualifier to 'free' – namely, '*legally* free'. Alternatively, one could consider which, of all the things that might still hinder or prevent Smith from leaving the country (for example, has he promised someone to remain? will the responsibilities of his job keep him here? has he enough money to buy passage and, if not, why not?), could count as limitations on his freedom to leave the country; one would then be in a position to determine whether the claim had been misleading or false. In either case, however, the devices adopted would reveal that our understanding of what has been said hinged upon our understanding of the range of obstacles or constraints from which Smith had been claimed to be free.

(*c*) *Cases where it is not clear what corresponds to the third term*: for example, 'freedom from hunger' ('want', 'fear', 'disease', and so forth). One quick but not very satisfactory way of dealing with such expressions is to regard them as figurative, or at least not really concerned with anybody's freedom; thus, being free from hunger would be simply being rid of, or without, hunger – as a sky may be free of clouds (compare the discussion of this above). Alternatively, one might incline toward regarding hunger as a barrier of some sort, and claim that a person free *from* hunger is free *to* be well fed or to do or do well the various things he could not do or do well if hungry. Yet again, and more satisfactorily, one could turn to the context of the initial bit of Rooseveltian rhetoric and there find reason to treat the expression as follows. Suppose that hunger is a feeling and that someone *seeks* hunger; he is on a diet and the hunger feeling reassures him that he is losing weight.[5] Alternatively, suppose that hunger is a bodily condition and that someone seeks it; he is on a Gandhi-style hunger strike. In either case, Roosevelt or his fellow orators might have wanted a world in which these people were free from hunger; but this surely does not mean that they wanted a world in which people were not hungry despite a wish to be so. They wanted, rather, a world in which people were not victims of hunger they did not seek; that is, they wanted a world without barriers keeping people hungry despite efforts to avoid hunger – a world in which people would be free *from* barriers constituted by various specifiable agricultural, economic, and political conditions *to* get enough food to prevent hunger. This view of 'freedom from hunger' not only makes a perfectly good and historically accurate sense out of the expression, but also conforms to the view that freedom is a triadic relation.

In other politically important idioms the *range* of the third term is not always utterly clear. For example, does freedom of religion include freedom *not* to worship? Does freedom of speech include *all* speech no matter what its content, manner of delivery, or the circumstances of its delivery? Such matters, however, raise largely historical questions or questions to be settled by political decision; they do not throw doubt on the need for a third term.

That the intelligibility of talk concerned with the freedom of agents rests in the end upon an understanding of freedom as a triadic relation is what many persons distinguishing between positive and negative freedom apparently fail to see or see clearly enough. Evidence of such failure or, alternatively, invitation to it is found in the simple but conventional characterization of the difference between the two kinds of freedom as the difference between 'freedom from' and 'freedom to' – a characterization suggesting that freedom could be either of two dyadic relations. This characterization, however, cannot distinguish two genuinely different kinds of freedom; it can serve only to emphasize one or the other of two features of *every* case of the freedom of agents. Consequently, anyone who argues that freedom *from* is the 'only' freedom, or that freedom *to* is the 'truest' freedom, or that one is 'more important than'

---

[5] I owe this example to Professor James Pratt.

the other, cannot be taken as having said anything both straightforward and sensible about two distinct kinds of freedom. He can, at most, be said to be attending to, or emphasizing the importance of only one part of what is always present in any case of freedom.

Unfortunately, even if this basis of distinction between positive and negative freedom as two distinct kinds or concepts of freedom is shown to collapse, one has not gone very far in understanding the issues separating those philosophers or ideologies commonly said to utilize one or the other of them. One has, however, dissipated one of the main confusions blocking understanding of these issues. In recognizing that freedom is always *both* freedom from something and freedom to do or become something, one is provided with a means of making sense out of interminable and poorly defined controversies concerning, for example, when a person really is free, why freedom is important, and on what its importance depends. As these, in turn, are matters on which the distinction between positive and negative freedom has turned, one is given also a means of managing sensibly the writings appearing to accept or to be based upon that distinction.

III

The key to understanding lies in recognition of precisely how differing styles of answer to the question 'When are persons free?' could survive agreement that freedom is a triadic relation. The differences would be rooted in differing views on the ranges of the term variables – that is, on the ('true') identities of the agents whose freedom is in question, on what counts as an obstacle to or interference with the freedom of such agents, or on the range of what such agents might or might not be free to do or become.[6] Although perhaps not always obvious or dramatic, such differences could lead to vastly different accounts of when persons are free. Furthermore, differences on one of these matters might or might not be accompanied by differences on either of the others. There is thus a rich stock of ways in which such accounts might diverge, and a rich stock of possible foci of argument.

[6] They might also be rooted in differing views on the verification conditions for claims about freedom. This issue would be important to discuss in a full-scale treatment of freedom but, as already mentioned, it is not discussed in this paper. It plays, at most, an easily eliminable role in the distinction between positive and negative freedom.

It is therefore crucial, when dealing with accounts of when persons are free, to insist on getting *quite* clear on what each writer considers to be the ranges of these term variables. Such insistence will reveal where the differences between writers are, and will provide a starting point for rewarding consideration of what might justify these differences.

The distinction between positive and negative freedom has, however, stood in the way of this approach. It has encouraged us to see differences in accounts of freedom as resulting from differences in concepts of freedom. This in turn has encouraged the wrong sorts of questions. We have been tempted to ask such questions as 'Well, who *is* right? Whose concept of freedom *is* the correct one?' or 'Which *kind* of freedom do we really want after all?' Such questions will not help reveal the fundamental issues separating major writers on freedom from each other, no matter *how* the writers are arranged into 'camps'. It would be far better to insist that the same concept of freedom is operating throughout, and that the differences, rather than being about what *freedom* is, are for example about what persons are, and about what can count as an obstacle to or interference with the freedom of persons so conceived.

The appropriateness of this insistence is easily seen when one examines prevailing characterizations of the differences between 'positive' and 'negative' freedom. Once the alleged difference between 'freedom from' and 'freedom to' has been disallowed (as it must be; see above), the most persuasive of the remaining characterizations appear to be as follows:[7]

1. Writers adhering to the concept of 'negative' freedom hold that only the *presence* of something can render a person unfree; writers adhering to the concept of 'positive' freedom hold that the *absence* of something may also render a person unfree.

2. The former hold that a person is free to do *x* just in case *nothing due to arrangements made by other persons* stops him from doing *x*; the latter adopt no such restriction.

3. The former hold that the agents whose freedom is in question (for example, 'persons', 'men') are, in effect, identifiable as Anglo-American law would identify 'natural' (as opposed to 'artificial') persons; the latter sometimes hold quite different views as to how these agents are to be identified (see below).

The most obvious thing to be said about these characterizations, of course, is that appeal to them provides at best an excessively crude

[7] Yet other attempts at characterization have been offered – most recently and notably by Sir Isaiah Berlin in *Two Concepts of Liberty* (Oxford, 1958). Berlin also offers the second and (more or less) the third of the characterizations cited here.

justification of the conventional classification of writers into opposing camps.[8] When one presses on the alleged points of difference, they have a tendency to break down, or at least to become less dramatic than they at first seemed.[9] As should not be surprising, the patterns of agreement

[8] A fair picture of that classification is provided by Berlin (*op. cit.*) who cites and quotes from various writers in such a way as to suggest that they are in one camp or the other. Identified in this manner as adherents of 'negative' freedom, one finds Occam, Erasmus, Hobbes, Locke, Bentham, Constant, J. S. Mill, Tocqueville, Jefferson, Burke, Paine. Among adherents of 'positive' freedom one finds Plato, Epictetus, St Ambrose, Montesquieu, Spinoza, Kant, Herder, Rousseau, Hegel, Fichte, Marx, Bukharin, Comte, Carlyle, T. H. Green, Bradley, Bosanquet.

[9] For example, consider No. 1. Perhaps there is something to it, but the following cautionary remarks should be made. (*a*) The so-called adherents of 'negative' freedom might very well accept the *absence* of something as an obstacle to freedom. Consider a man who is not free because, although unguarded, he has been locked in chains. Is he unfree because of the *presence* of the locked chains, or is he unfree because he *lacks* a key? Are adherents of 'negative' freedom prohibited from giving the latter answer? (*b*) Even purported adherents of 'positive' freedom are not always straightforward in their acceptance of the lack of something as an obstacle to freedom. They sometimes swing toward attributing the absence of freedom to the presence of certain conditions causally connected with the lack, absence, or deprivation mentioned initially. For example, it may be said that a person who was unable to qualify for a position owing to lack of training (and thus not free to accept or 'have' it) was prevented from accepting the position by a social, political, economic, or educational 'system' the workings of which resulted in his being bereft of training.

Also, in so far as this swing is made, our view of the difference mentioned in No. 2 may become fuzzy; for adherents of 'positive' freedom might be thought at bottom to regard those 'preventing conditions' counting as infringements of freedom as most often if not always circumstances due to human arrangements. This might be true even when, as we shall see is sometimes the case, the focus is on the role of 'irrational passions and appetites'. The presence or undisciplined character of these may be treated as resulting from the operation of certain specifiable social, educational, or moral institutions or arrangements. (Berlin, e.g., seems to acknowledge this with respect to the Marxists. See Berlin, *op. cit.*, p. 8, n.1, and the text at this point.) Thus one might in the end be able to say no more than this: that the adherents of 'negative' freedom are on the whole more inclined to require that the *intention* of the

and disagreement on these several points are in fact either too diverse or too indistinct to support any clearly justifiable arrangement of major writers into two camps. The trouble is not merely that some writers do not fit too well where they have been placed; it is rather that writers who are purportedly the very models of membership in one camp or the other (for example, Locke, the Marxists) do not fit very well where they have been placed[10] – thus suggesting that the whole system of dichotomous classification is futile and, even worse, conducive to distortion of important views on freedom.

But, even supposing that there were something to the classification and to the justification for it in terms of the above three points of difference, what then? The differences are of two kinds. They concern (*a*) the ('true') identities of the agents whose freedom is in question, and (*b*) what is to count as an 'obstacle' or 'barrier' to, 'restriction' on, or 'interference' with the freedom of such agents. They are thus clearly about the ranges of two of the three term variables mentioned earlier. It would be a mistake to see them in any other way. We are likely to make this mistake, however, and obscure the path of rewarding argument, if we present them as differences concerning what 'freedom' means.

Consider the following. Suppose that we have been raised in the so-called 'libertarian' tradition (roughly characterized as that of 'negative' freedom). There would be nothing unusual to us, and perhaps even nothing troubling, in conventional accounts of what the adherent of negative freedom treats as the ranges of these variables.

1. He is purported to count persons just as we do – to point to living human bodies and say of each (and only of each), 'There's a person.' Precisely what we ordinarily call persons. (And if he is troubled by non-viable fetuses, and so forth, so are we.)

---

arrangements in question have been to coerce, compel, or deprive persons of this or that. The difference here, however, is not very striking.

[10] Locke said: 'liberty . . . is the power a man has to do or forbear doing any particular action according . . . as he himself wills it' (*Essay Concerning Human Understanding*, Bk. 11, ch. xxi, sec. 15). He also said, of law, 'that ill deserves the name of confinement which hedges us in only from bogs and precipices', and 'the end of law is, not to abolish or restrain, but to preserve and enlarge freedom' (Second *Treatise of Government*, sec. 57). He also sometimes spoke of a man's consent as though it were the same as the consent of the majority.

Why doesn't all this put him in the camp of 'positive' freedom vis-à-vis at least points (2) and (3) above? Concerning the Marxists, see n.8, *supra*.

2. He is purported to mean much what we mean by 'obstacle'. and so forth, though this changes with changes in our views of what can be attributed to arrangements made by human beings, and also with variations in the importance we attach to consenting to rules, practices, and so forth.[11]

3. He is purported to have quite 'ordinary' views on what a person may or may not be free to do or become. The actions are sometimes suggested in fairly specific terms – for example, free to have a home, raise a family, 'rise to the top'. But, on the whole, he is purported to talk of persons being free or not free 'to do what they want' or (perhaps) 'to express themselves'.[12] Furthermore, the criteria for determining what a person wants to do are those we customarily use, or perhaps even the most naive and unsophisticated of them – for example, what a person wants to do is determined by what he *says* he wants to do, or by what he manifestly *tries* to do, or even *does* do.[13]

In contrast, much might trouble us in the accounts of the so-called adherents of 'positive' freedom.

1. They sometimes do not count, as the agent whose freedom is being considered, what inheritors of our tradition would unhesitatingly consider to be a 'person'. Instead, they occasionally engage in what has been revealingly but pejoratively called 'the retreat to the inner citadel';[14] the agent in whose freedom they are interested is identified as the 'real' or the 'rational' or the 'moral' person who is somehow sometimes hidden within, or has his seed contained within, the living human body. Sometimes, however, rather than a retreat to such an 'inner citadel', or sometimes in addition to such a retreat, there is an expansion of the limits of 'person' such that the institutions and members, the histories and futures

---

[11] The point of 'consent theories' of political obligation sometimes seems to be to hide from ourselves the fact that a rule of unanimity is an unworkable basis for a system of government and that government does involve coercion. We seem, however, not really to have made up our minds about this.

[12] These last ways of putting it are appreciably different. When a person who would otherwise count as a libertarian speaks of persons as free or not free to express themselves, his position as a libertarian may muddy a bit. One may feel invited to wonder which of the multitudinous wants of a given individual *are* expressive of his nature – that is, which are such that their fulfilment is conducive to the expression of his 'self'.

[13] The possibility of conflicts among these criteria has not been much considered by so-called libertarians.

[14] See Berlin, *op. cit.*, pp. 17ff. (though Berlin significantly admits also that this move can be made by adherents of negative freedom; see p. 19).

of the communities in which the living human body is found are considered to be inextricable parts of the 'person'.

These expansions or contractions of the criteria for identification of persons may seem unwarranted to us. Whether they are so, however, depends upon the strength of the arguments offered in support of the helpfulness of regarding persons in these ways while discussing freedom. For example, the retreat to the 'inner citadel' may be initiated simply by worries about which, of all the things we want, will give us lasting satisfaction – a view of our interests making it possible to see the surge of impulse or passion as an obstacle to the attainment of what we 'really want'. And the expansion of the limits of the 'self' to include our families, cultures, nations, or races may be launched by awareness that our 'self' is to some extent the product of these associations; by awareness that our identification of our interests may be influenced by our beliefs concerning ways in which our destinies are tied to the destinies of our families, nations, and so forth; by the way we see tugs and stresses upon those associations as tugs and stresses upon us; and by the ways we see ourselves and *identify* ourselves as officeholders in such associations with the rights and obligations of such offices. This expansion, in turn, makes it possible for us to see the infringement of the autonomy of our associations as infringement on our freedom.

Assessing the strengths of the various positions taken on these matters requires a painstaking investigation and evaluation of the arguments offered – something that can hardly be launched within the confines of this paper. But what should be observed is that this set of seemingly radical departures by adherents of positive freedom from the ways 'we' ordinarily identify persons does not provide us with any reason whatever to claim that a different concept of *freedom* is involved (one might as well say that the shift from 'The apple is to the left of the orange' to 'The seeds of the apple are to the left of the seeds of the orange' changes what 'to the left of' means). Furthermore, that claim would draw attention away from precisely what we should focus on; it would lead us to focus on the wrong concept – namely, 'freedom' instead of 'person'. Only by insisting at least provisionally that all the writers have the same concept of freedom can one see clearly and keep sharply focused the obvious and extremely important differences among them concerning the concept of 'person'.

2. Similarly, adherents of so-called 'positive' freedom purportedly differ from 'us' on what counts as an obstacle. Will *this* difference be revealed adequately if we focus on supposed differences in the concept of 'freedom'? Not likely. Given differences on what a person is, differences in what counts as an obstacle or interference are not surprising,

of course, since what could count as an obstacle to the activity of a person identified in one way might not possibly count as an obstacle to persons identified in other ways. But the differences concerning 'obstacle' and so forth are probably not due solely to differences concerning 'person'. If, for example, we so-called adherents of negative freedom, in order to count something as a preventing condition, ordinarily require that it can be shown a result of arrangements made by human beings, and our 'opponents' do not require this, why not? On the whole, perhaps, the latter are saying this: if one is concerned with social, political, and economic policies, and with how these policies can remove or increase human misery, it is quite irrelevant whether difficulties in the way of the policies are or are not *due to* arrangements made by human beings. The only question is whether the difficulties can be removed by human arrangements, and at what cost. This view, seen as an attack upon the 'artificiality' of a borderline for distinguishing human freedom from other human values, does not seem inherently unreasonable; a close look at the positions and arguments seems called for.[15]

[15] The libertarian position concerning the borderline is well expressed by Berlin in the following passage on the struggle of colonial peoples: 'Is the struggle for higher status, the wish to escape from an inferior position, to be called a struggle for liberty? Is it mere pedantry to confine this word to the main ("negative") senses discussed above, or are we, as I suspect, in danger of calling any adjustment of his social situation favoured by a human being an increase of his liberty, and will this not render this term so vague and distended as to make it virtually useless' (*op. cit.*, p. 44)? One may surely agree with Berlin that there may be something of a threat here; but one may also agree with him when, in the passage immediately following, he inclines to give back what he has just taken away: 'And yet we cannot simply dismiss this case as a mere confusion of the notion of freedom with those of status, or solidarity, or fraternity, or equality, or some combination of these. For the craving for status is, in certain respects very close to the desire to be an independent agent.' What first needs explaining, of course, is why colonial peoples might believe themselves freer under the rule of local tyrants than under the rule of (possibly) benevolent colonial administrations. Berlin tends to dismiss this as a simple confusion of a desire for freedom with a hankering after status and recognition. What need more careful evaluation than he gives them are (*a*) the strength of reasons for regarding rule by one's racial and religious peers as self-rule and (*b*) the strength of claims about freedom based on the consequences of consent or authorization for one's capacity to speak of 'self-rule' (cf. Hobbes's famous ch. xvi in *Leviathan*, 'Of Persons and Things Personated'). Cf. n.10, *supra*.

But again, the issues and arguments will be misfocused if we fail to see them as about the range of a term variable of a single triadic relation (freedom). Admittedly, we *could* see some aspects of the matter (those where the differences do not follow merely from differences in what is thought to be the agent whose freedom is in question) as amounting to disagreements about what is meant by 'freedom'. But there is no decisive reason for doing so, and this move surely threatens to obscure the socially and politically significant issues raised by the argument suggested above.

3. Concerning treatment of the third term by purported adherents of positive freedom, perhaps enough has already been said to suggest that they tend to emphasize conditions of character rather than actions, and to suggest that, as with 'us' too, the range of character conditions and actions focused on may influence or be influenced by what is thought to count as agent and by what is thought to count as preventing condition. Thus, though something more definite would have to be said about the matter eventually, at least some contact with the issues previously raised might be expected in arguments about the range of this variable.

It is important to observe here and throughout, however, that close agreement between two writers in their understanding of the range of one of the variables does not make *inevitable* like agreement on the ranges of the others. Indeed, we have gone far enough to see that the kinds of issues arising in determination of the ranges are sufficiently diverse to make such simple correlations unlikely. Precisely this renders attempts to arrange writers on freedom into two opposing camps so distorted and ultimately futile. There is too rich a stock of ways in which accounts of freedom diverge.

If we are to manage these divergences sensibly, we must focus our attention on each of these variables and on differences in views as to their ranges. Until we do this, we will not see clearly the issues which have in fact been raised, and thus will not see clearly what needs arguing. In view of this need, it is both clumsy and misleading to try to sort out writers as adherents of this or that 'kind' or 'concept' of freedom. We would be far better off to insist that they all have the same concept of freedom (as a triadic relation) – thus putting ourselves in a position to notice how, and inquire fruitfully into why, they identify differently what can serve as agent, preventing condition, and action or state of character vis-à-vis issues of freedom.

IV

If the importance of this approach to discussion of freedom has been generally overlooked, it is because social and political philosophers have, with dreary regularity, made the mistake of trying to answer the unadorned question, 'When are men free?' or, alternatively, 'When are men *really* free?' These questions *invite* confusion and misunderstanding, largely because of their tacit presumption that persons can be free or not free *simpliciter*.

One might suppose that, strictly speaking, a person could be free *simpliciter* only if there were no interference from which he was not free, and nothing that he was not free to do or become. On this view, however, and on acceptance of common views as to what counts as a person, what counts as interference, and what actions or conditions of character may meaningfully be said to be free or not free, all disputes concerning whether or not men in societies are ever free would be inane. Concerning such settings, where the use and threat of coercion are distinctively present, there would *always* be an air of fraud or hocus-pocus about claims that men are free – just like that.

Yet one might hold that men can be free (*simpliciter*) even in society because certain things which ordinarily are counted as interferences or barriers are not actually so, or because certain kinds of behaviour ordinarily thought to be either free or unfree do not, for some reason, 'count'. Thus one might argue that at least in certain (conceivable) societies there is no activity in which men in that society are not free to engage, and no possible restriction or barrier from which they are not free.

The burden of such an argument should now be clear. Everything *from* which a person in that society might ordinarily be considered unfree must be shown not actually an interference or barrier (or not a relevant one), and everything which a person in that society might ordinarily be considered not free to *do* or *become* must be shown irrelevant to the issue of freedom. (Part of the argument in either or both cases might be that the 'true' identity of the person in question is not what it has been thought to be.)

Pitfalls may remain for attempts to evaluate such arguments. For example, one may uncover tendencies to telescope questions concerning the *legitimacy* of interference into questions concerning genuineness *as* interference.[16] One may also find telescoping of questions concerning the *desirability* of certain modes of behaviour or character states into

---

[16] Cf. nn.10 and 14, *supra*.

questions concerning the *possibility* of being either free or not free to engage in those modes of behaviour or become that kind of person.[17] Nevertheless, a demand for specification of the term variables helps pinpoint such problems, as well as forestalling the confusions obviously encouraged by failure to make the specifications.

Perhaps, however, the claim that certain men are free *simpliciter* is merely elliptical for the claim that they are free in every important respect, or in most important respects, or 'on the whole'. Nevertheless, the point still remains that when this ellipsis is filled in, the reasonableness of asking both 'What are they free from?' and 'What are they free to do or become?' becomes apparent. Only when one gets straightforward answers to these questions is he in any position to judge whether the men *are* free as claimed. Likewise, only then will he be in a position to judge the *value* or *importance* of the freedom(s) in question. It is important to know, for example, whether a man is free from legal restrictions to raise a family. But of course social or economic 'arrangements' may be such that he still could not raise a family if he wanted to. Thus, merely to say that he is free to raise a family, when what is meant is only that he is free from legal restrictions to raise a family, is to invite misunderstanding. Further, the *range* of activities he may or may not be free from this or that to engage in, or the range of character states he may or may not be free to develop, should make a difference in our evaluations of his situation and of his society; but this too is not called for strongly enough when one asks simply, 'Is the man free?' Only when we determine what the men in question are free from, and what they are free to do or become, will we be in a position to estimate the value for human happiness and fulfilment of being free from *that* (whatever *it* is), to do *the other thing* (whatever *it* is). Only then will we be in a position to make rational evaluations of the relative merits of societies with regard to freedom.

V

The above remarks can be tied again to the controversy concerning negative and positive freedom by considering the following argument by friends of 'negative' freedom. Freedom is always and necessarily *from* restraint; thus, in so far as the adherents of positive freedom speak of persons being made free *by means* of restraint, they cannot be talking about freedom.

[17] E.g., is it logically possible for a person to be free to do something immoral? Cf. Berlin, *op. cit.*, p. 10, n.

The issues raised by this argument (which is seldom stated more fully than here) can be revealed by investigating what might be done to make good sense out of the claim that, for example, Smith is (or can be) made free by restraining (constraining, coercing) him.[18] Use of the format of specifications recommended above reveals two major possibilities:

1. Restraining Smith by means *a* from doing *b* produces a situation in which he is now able to do *c* becaues restraint *d* is lifted. He is thereby, by means of restraint *a*, made free from *d* to do *c*, although he can no longer do *b*. For example, suppose that Smith, who always walks to where he needs to go, lives in a tiny town where there have been no pedestrian crosswalks and where automobiles have had right of way over pedestrians. Suppose further that a series of pedestrian crosswalks is instituted along with the regulation that pedestrians must use only these walks when crossing, but that while in these walks pedestrians have right of way over automobiles. The regulation restrains Smith (he can no longer legally cross streets where he pleases) but it also frees him (while in crosswalks he no longer has a duty to defer to automobile traffic). Using the schema above, the regulation (*a*) restrains Smith from crossing streets wherever he likes (*b*), but at the same time is such as to (make it practicable to) give him restricted right of way (*c*) over automobile traffic. The regulation (*a*) thus gives him restricted right of way (*c*) because it lifts the rule (*d*) giving automobiles general right of way over pedestrians.

This interpretation of the assertion that Smith can be made free by restraining him is straightforward enough. It raises problems only if one supposes that persons must be either free or not free *simpliciter*, and that the claim in question is that Smith is made free *simpliciter*. But there is no obvious justification for either of these suppositions.

If these suppositions *are* made, however, then the following interpretation may be appropriate:

2. Smith is being 'restrained' only in the ordinary acceptance of that term; actually, he is not being restrained at all. He is being helped to do what he really wants to do, or what he *would* want to do if he were reasonable (moral, prudent, or such like); compare Locke's words: 'that ill deserves the name of confinement which hedges us in only from bogs and precipices'.[19] Because of the 'constraint' put upon him, a *genuine* constraint that *was* upon him (for example, ignorance, passion, the

---

[18] This presumes that the prospect of freeing Smith by restraining *someone else* would be unproblematic even for the friends of negative freedom.

[19] *The Second Treatise of Government*, sec. 57. As is remarked below, however, the proper interpretation of this passage is not at all clear.

intrusions of others) is lifted, and he is free from the latter to do what he really wishes (or would wish if . . .).

This interpretation is hardly straightforward, but the claim that it embodies is nevertheless arguable; Plato argues it in the *Republic* and implies such a claim in the *Gorgias*. Furthermore, insistence upon the format of specifications recommended above can lead one to see clearly the kind of arguments needed to support the claim. For example, if a person is to be made free, whether by means of restraint or otherwise, there must be something *from* which he is made free. This must be singled out. Its character may not always be clear; for example, in Locke's discussion the confinement from which one is liberated by law is perhaps the constraint produced by the arbitrary uncontrolled actions of one's neighbours, or perhaps it is the 'constraint' arising from one's own ignorance or passion, or perhaps it is both of these. If only the former, then the specification is unexceptionable enough; that kind of constraint is well within the range of what is ordinarily thought to be constraint. If the latter, however, then some further argument is needed; one's own ignorance and passion are at least not unquestionably within the range of what can restrain him and limit his freedom. The required argument may attempt to show that ignorance and passion prevent persons from doing what they want to do, or what they 'really' want to do, or what they *would* want to do if. . . . The idea would be to promote seeing the removal of ignorance and passion, or at least the control of their effects, as the removal or control of something preventing a person from doing as he wishes, really wishes, or would wish, and so forth, and thus, plausibly, an increase of that person's freedom.

Arguments concerning the 'true' identity of the person in question and what *can* restrict such a person's freedom are of course important here and should be pushed further than the above discussion suggests. For the present, however, one need observe only that they are met again when one presses for specification of the full range of what, on interpretation (2), Smith is made free to *do*. Apparently, he is made free to do as he wishes, really wishes, or *would* wish if. . . . But, quite obviously, there is also something that he is *prima facie not* free to do; otherwise, there would be no point in declaring that he was being made free *by means of* restraint. One may discover how this difficulty is met by looking again to the arguments by which the claimer seeks to establish that something which at first appears to be a restraint is not actually a restraint at all. Two main lines may be found here: (*a*) that the activities being 'restrained' are so unimportant or minor (relative, perhaps to what is gained) that they are not worth counting, or (*b*) that the activities are such that no one could ever want (or really want, and so forth) to engage in them. If the activities in question are so unimportant as to be negligible, the restraints that prevent one from engaging in them may be also 'not worthy of consideration'; if, on the other hand, the activities are ones that no one would conceivably freely choose to engage in, then it might indeed be thought 'idle' to consider our inability to do them as a restriction upon our freedom.

Admittedly, the persons actually making the principal claim under consideration may have been confused, may not have seen all these alternatives of interpretation, and so forth. The intention here is not to say what such persons did mean when uttering the claims, but only more or less plausibly what they might have meant. The interpretations provide the main lines for the latter. They also provide a clear picture of what needs to be done in order to assess the worth of the claims in each case; for, of course, no pretence is being made here that such arguments are always or even very often ultimately convincing.

Interpretation (2) clearly provides the most difficult and interesting problems. One may analyse and discuss these problems by considering them to be raised by attempts to answer the following four questions:

(*a*) What is to count as an interference with the freedom of persons?

(*b*) What is to count as an action that persons might reasonably be said to be either free or not free to perform?

(*c*) What is to count as a legitimate interference with the freedom of persons?

(*d*) What actions are persons best left free to do?

As was mentioned above, there is a tendency to telescope (*c*) into (*a*), and to telescope (*d*) into (*b*). It was also noted that (*c*) and (*d*) are not distinct questions: they are logically related in so far as criteria of legitimacy are connected to beliefs about what is best or most desirable. (*a*) and (*b*) are also closely related in that an answer to one will affect what can reasonably be considered an answer to the other. The use of these questions as guides in the analysis and understanding of discussions of freedom should not, therefore, be expected to produce always a neat ordering of the discussions. But it *will* help further to delimit the alternatives of reasonable interpretation.

VI

In the end, then, discussions of the freedom of agents can be fully intelligible and rationally assessed only after the specification of each term of this triadic relation has been made or at least understood. The principal claim made here has been that insistence upon this single 'concept' of freedom puts us in a position to see the interesting and important ranges of issues separating the philosophers who write about freedom in such different ways, and the ideologies that treat freedom so differently. These issues are obscured, if not hidden, when we suppose that the important thing is that the fascists, communists, and socialists on the one side, for example, have a different concept of freedom from that of the 'libertarians' on the other. These issues are also hidden, of course, by the facile assumption that the adherents on one side or the other are never sincere.

9 Why is Authority such a Problem?[1]

Richard Tuck

Many philosophers have felt that in the claim to possess political authority, or to act by virtue of it, there is a highly problematical element. It is a claim that very much needs explaining, in a way in which a claim to possess political power does not – the latter can after all be substantiated in the last resort by a pitched battle. By some analysts of the concrete social phenomenon of authority this problematical, mysterious element has been seen as an essential feature of the institution: authority involves 'the *legitimation* of power, an ideological elaboration and specification of the representation or halo; the "miranda" is elaborated into "doctrine", to the simple piety for emblems is added theology'.[2] But problems call for solutions; and philosopher after philosopher has tried to interpret claims to authority by reducing them to more straightforward claims, or assimilating political to non-political authority (for instance that of an academic in his chosen field). Even Hobbes was inclined to argue that governmental authority is the same as the authority an agent has from the man who authorized him to act, though if this were the case, the necessary reply to a claim by a ruler to have authority over his people would be 'authority from whom?' – which is not in fact an answer that generally occurs to anyone.

What is clear is that claims to authority occur in a wide variety of situations, and that there is no *prima facie* reason to suppose that the nature of the claim is in each case the same (though there will presumably be at least a tenuous connection between them). It is equally clear that the basic claim by an individual to possess authority is (partly for this reason) not the most helpful linguistic unit with which to work. I propose in this paper to talk instead about 'authority citations', by which I mean a claim that a particular action is to be permitted by someone who might want to oppose it, because either the speaker or someone on whom he is relying is in a position of authority. This covers claims like 'I have authority from A for action in this matter', since this is not entirely equivalent to 'A says I can act as his agent' – there is the implication (as

---

[1] I would like to thank Quentin Skinner for reading and commenting on an earlier draft of this paper; any mistakes which remain are of course entirely my responsibility.
[2] H. H. Gerth and C. Wright Mills: *Character and Social Structure* (London, 1954), p. 413. The Weberian roots of this view need no stressing.

Hobbes realized) that A has the right to act himself and so his agent is not only assuming A's role but exercising his right.

The difficulties involved in trying to reduce authority citations to claims about something else are well brought out by Peter Winch in one of the more extensive modern discussions of the concept. His position is the highly Wittgensteinian one that 'the acceptance of authority is not just something which, as a matter of fact, you cannot get along without if you want to participate in rule-governed activities; rather, to participate in rule-governed activities *is*, in a certain way, to accept authority. For to participate in such an activity is to accept that there is *a right and a wrong way of doing things*, and the decision as to what is right and wrong in a given case can never depend *completely* on one's own caprice'. We might reply that this could well be true of the authority of the known and agreed-on rules of a game, but what about politics, where such rules do not seem to operate? Winch admits that here 'general agreement on the right course of action is lacking' and that 'where we have no agreement about *what* is to be done, we must, unless we are to lapse into chaos, have some agreement about *who is to decide* what is to be done. But I still wish to maintain . . . that we have to deal with genuine authority, as opposed to bare power or ability to influence, only where he who decides does so under the idea of what he conceives to be the *right* decision . . . '[3]

Winch's argument, then, is that (a) in any rule-governed situation where the rules are generally knowable and promulgated, the novitiate will accept someone as an authority because he is known to know the rules; (b) in a situation presumed to be rule-governed where the rules are *not* generally known, a man can be an authority only if he conceives them to be knowable, and known to him personally, and if people have decided that his pronouncements are to be authoritative. There is an obvious dissymetry between these two positions: in (a) we (as novitiates) perform our actions because we believe them to be right on the basis of our authority's knowledge, but in (b) we (as citizens) perform them because we have agreed that there is to be only one person or institution deciding what should be done, and because we accept that he or they will decide it on the basis of what they think to be right. Suppose that in this case we also think we know what is right, and the authority has made a mistake: 'An authority can be allowed to make mistakes (up to a certain point) about what is the right course to follow, and still retain its authoritative character; but for it to be thought that it no longer cares about what

---

[3] P. Winch: 'Authority', *Proceedings of the Aristotelian Society* Supp. Vol. 32, 1958, pp. 228 and 235.

is right and what is wrong ... *is* for it to degenerate from authority into force.'[4] Thus a necessary condition for the authority-relationship in (a) is that we believe the authority to be right; for it in (b) that the authority believes itself to be right.

The discrepancy between (a) and (b) could be likened to that between a judge at the moment when he is expounding the details of the law and a judge at the moment when he is delivering sentence: in the first case he is an authority on the law, and in the second he is an authority in Winch's second sense. The individual in an authority-relationship of the first kind can argue: 'I do X because A says I should; A is my authority for the doing of X-like things. But A is my authority because what he says is right; hence I do X because it is right, and what A says is my evidence for its being right.' With such an argument, the concept of authority itself slips out of prominence, figuring as only one way of describing one reason why we should believe a particular action to be right. But it is because it cannot be slipped out of prominence in this way in (b) (as Winch found) that it is such a problem for the philosopher. Winch in fact sought to remove the thorniness of the concept by resting it solely on the two conditions above, of which the more important is that there must be some agreement that an authority shall be authoritative. This raises the important issue of agreement, a topic which has constantly recurred in discussions abut authority, but it does not really illuminate what the agreement is about.

Daniel Bell has recently argued that the concept *can* be slipped out of prominence in political discourse, by claiming (in effect) that people have political authority because they are generally right about political actions.[5] This position was (as it happens) precisely anticipated by Thomas White in his *The grounds of obedience and government* (1655); but neither White's nor Bell's interpretation fully takes into account the fact (to be discussed later) that a government may be meaningfully said to have authority to perform mistaken actions. Winch himself (on whom Bell explicitly relies), in a postscript to his paper when it was reprinted in 1967,[6] accepted that his attempt to combine the two senses of authority was mistaken. However, by trying to combine them he did bring out the critical difference between the two types, and he would presumably still be satisfied with the broad account of them presented above. His inclination in the postscript to look for a version of authority specifically located in the state seems, on the other hand, an awkward

---

[4] ibid p. 236.
[5] D. Bell: 'Authority', *Royal Institute of Philosophy Lectures* 1969–1970 (London, 1971), pp. 190–204.
[6] A. Quinton, ed.: *Political Philosophy* (Oxford, 1967), pp. 109, 110.

foundation for a new analysis: many structures which allow rights only to a particular person or persons, such as a family, generate this 'political' authority.

Although Richard Peters, in a companion piece to Winch's in the P.A.S. symposium, did not raise the issue of *agreement* so explicitly, he did so implicitly by arguing that authority has to do with 'the giving of commands, the making of decisions and pronouncements, as distinct from the use of force, incentives and propaganda': for what distinguishes the two categories except that in the former our active agreement can be observed? However, by pointing out in addition that the root of the concept is 'in the Latin word "auctoritas" which implies an originator in the sphere of opinion, counsel and command,'[7] he made life easier for himself than Winch did: for agreement on what is to be *originative* is easier to understand than agreement on what is to be authoritative. (Of course he did not thereby provide a satisfactory answer, for as Winch remarked in his paper, somehow or other 'rightness' must be involved in our concept of authority, and Peters did not fully take account of that.)

What this analysis does is to direct attention to the need that authority citations meet; the idea of agreement as a necessary condition of their meaningful employment is an attempt to explain how they both resemble and differ from other ways in which actions may be originated. 'Originate', however, implies a more direct connection with the action than is in fact the case (e.g. desires may be said to originate actions, and this is clearly not the sense that Peters intends). 'Justify' seems considerably nearer the mark Peters was aiming at: on the face of it, authority citations *are* justifications of claims or actions, and the implication of the Winch-Peters argument will then be that political authority citations are that class of justifications which work by alluding to an anterior agreement over someone's role. To appreciate why this should be an attractive way out of the problem, we must first consider the general nature of justifications, and the other ideas, including vindications, defences and exculpations, which move within its orbit. They are all in fact descriptions of the way in which language is used in a particular context, where doubt is thrown on a claim; as a consequence, they all involve an anterior statement which cannot by itself command assent: no justification can be a simple repetition of the original claim. It is true that it can take the form of redescribing an action, but the redescription will have to add *something* – for instance that in performing a certain action the agent is in fact switching on a light. It has also been argued (plausibly) by various

---

[7] P.A.S. vol. cit. pp. 223, 224.

people,[8] that strictly speaking there is no such thing as a *bad* justification: that to be a justification at all a statement must actually work so as to command assent to the anterior claim, and that a 'bad justification' is something which in fact fails to function as a justification at all.

There is obviously a problem in refining the notion of commanding assent: for instance, the statement 'I will give you £5,000 if you agree with me' may actually work so as to command assent to an anterior claim, but we would hesitate to say that it was a justification. That objection can be met most readily by talking about common belief in the claim's rightness, rather than simply assent to it; but what then is the status of sleight-of-hand arguments, which do convince but should not? It is clearly the case that we may say 'I thought yesterday your position was justified, but on thinking it over I concluded that it wasn't' – not that it was justified yesterday and is not today, which would have to be the case if the mere achievement of common conviction were the function of justifications. Instead, it must be that a statement functions as a justification if and only if it is such that it can secure a common belief, *based on adequate grounds*, in the rightness of a claim. Our view of what an adequate ground is, however, can of course alter, and when it does our view of what is or was a justification must alter too.

It is clear that authority citations in Winch's first sense function as justifications, though not by virtue of any previous agreement, and it is because they do so that the concept can be so evanescent. In the case where A is an authority for X in the sense that what A says on such matters is generally right, citing A to someone else who knows about his tendency that way is likely to secure a common belief that X is right. If it later appears on other, more adequate grounds that X is not right, those grounds by themselves are likely to secure a new common belief in its incorrectness, and A can be forgotten about. But if second sense citations are also justifications, they must work by securing common belief on the basis of anterior agreement about the role either of an agent, i.e. that his pronouncements shall originate action, or of a set of principles, for instance the authority of tradition. Tradition is however an awkward example, since it can act as an authority in both senses; but if it is the case that people simply accept that it should be originative in political matters, then its status does not seem to be any different (in terms of agreement over its role) from the agreed first principles of logical deduction. But, and this is the important part, the latter are not seen as *authorities* for a conclusion reached on their basis.

[8] E.g. A. O. Rorty: 'Wants and Justifications', *Journal of Philosophy*, 63 (1966), and J. Rachels: 'Wants, Reasons, and Justifications', *Philosophical Quarterly*, 18 (1968).

This objection can in principle be met by limiting the type of agreement: thus Day, approaching the problem of authority from the different angle of the traditional dichotomy between *auctoritas* and *potestas*, concluded that for someone or some institution to be meaningfully described as 'in authority' there should be previous agreement by the parties that his or its decisions should be grounds for action, and (the limiting condition) that this agreement should be *voluntary*. 'Whenever the word "authority" is used sociologically,[9] reference is made to the voluntary acceptance by one man or group of men of some decisions of another.'[10] To deal with the comparison between tradition and the first principles of deductive reasoning, such an argument would presumably include something about the difficulty of regarding our acceptance of such principles as *voluntary* – are there in fact any other options open to us?

But the problems involved in seeing even voluntary agreement as a necessary condition of the meaningful use of an authority citation emerge strongly if we consider the different ways in which a man can be enslaved. He can either voluntarily put himself under the command of an owner, or be taken by force, for instance as a prisoner of war. Day concedes that having chosen an authority one is not at liberty to regard it as such only when it suits oneself, so that on his argument a voluntary slave is presumably in an authority-relationship with his owner, and the compulsory slave is not. The snag about this is of course that they are both in fact treated in the same way; what are we to say happens when the owner forgets how he acquired each slave?

If it is thus not the case that political authority citations are justifications which function by virtue of an anterior agreement, the possibilities are that they are not justifications at all, or that they are, and function in some other (and probably rather peculiar) way. It seems difficult to argue that they are *not* justifications, as their paradigm use is to defend actions or assertions against real or potential criticism; yet it seems equally difficult to argue that they do so by securing common belief in the original claim's rightness. A man may have authority to do something which is widely – even universally – regarded as wrong, as for instance when a government is obliged by the pressure of a foreign power

[9] By 'sociological' authority, Day means authority *actually recognised as such*, rather than the authority to which someone may be legally entitled. In practice, this sort of distinction is one between a claim to authority being rightly accepted and a claim being wrongly rejected – i.e. it does not distinguish between two sorts of claim. Day is still talking about the conditions for the correct application of the term 'authority'.

[10] J. Day: 'Authority', *Political Studies*, 11 (1963), p. 258.

to tell its policeman to arrest innocent men. The government itself does not think such action is *right*, and while the foreign power does, it would not be true to say that it authorizes the policemen. In this instance it might be argued that the domestic government had made a decision that on balance, in view of all the consequences of defying the foreign power, the action was right; but my general line of argument is rebutted only if it were the case that every intentional action could be said to be right for us, because otherwise we would not have performed it. As long as there is the possibility that an individual, or a government, can deliberately perform actions which it does not think should be performed, then there is an equal possibility that it may *authorize* actions which it does not think should be performed. Winch would counter this by saying that if it went on long enough, the government would cease to be in authority; this may be a sociological truth, but it does not seem to be a logical one.

The difference between political authority citations and normal justifications may be brought out as follows: if I challenge a policeman in the act of arresting an innocent person, he can defend his action in terms of the general justification for the police having discretion in such matters, but he can also say 'I have authority to do so'. This is not a shorthand version of the general justification, for if it were, it would be impossible to say in return, 'OK, but you shouldn't have authority to do so', just as it sounds odd to say 'OK, but you shouldn't be justified in doing so'. A great deal of confusion has been caused precisely because it has been thought that an authority citation must be collapsible into some form of general justification; if it is the case that it cannot be, we must ask again what role they play, and why it seems not unlike that of the straightforward justification. Authority citations of the political kind were presumably called into being because of the deficiencies of the normal techniques of justification, and to understand what those deficiencies are it is most helpful to consider the case of a society where (at first) political authority citations are never used, and the consequent limitations on political action which are lifted after the evolution of the citation.

Such a society in fact existed among the North American Algonkian Indians of the seventeenth and eighteenth centuries. Nicholas Perrot, a fur-trader, wrote of them 1680 'subordination is not a maxim among these savages; the savage does not know what it is to obey... The father does not venture to exercise authority over his son, nor does the chief dare give commands to his soldier.' These early reports have been confirmed by the work of a modern anthropologist, W. B. Miller, who has remarked 'it would be difficult to point to a single role-relationship in

Algonkian society that was essentially analogous to the European type of authority relationship',[11] though he then misleadingly tried to put in its place a relationship based on a so-called Algonkian concept of authority – if it was not the European concept, it was presumably not a concept of authority.

As described by the anthropologists, the society appears to have taken communal decisions, and there appear to have been opinion leaders like chiefs; but each suggestion had to be justified to each tribesman, and if the justification did not work properly, the tribesman felt free to disregard the suggestion. Political argument at this stage is essentially the swapping of authentic justifications, including no doubt first-sense authority citations (e.g. the medicine man may be seen as an authority in the sense that what he says about rainfall is generally true). For the justifications to work, the society must have a concept of 'right action', and we may presume that as a consequence it has a primitive concept of 'rights'. H. L. A. Hart has argued in his paper on Natural Rights that societies able to evaluate actions as right or wrong do not necessarily know what having a right might be;[12] but if it is the case that it is right for A to perform X, it seems rather odd to say that he has not got a right to do it.

An examination of the relationships between the noun 'right' and the adjectives 'right' and 'all right' suggests the following: that 'It is right for A to do X' implies 'A has a right to do X', but that this is not an equivalence. 'A has a right to do X' implies instead 'It is *all right* for A to do X' (the essential difference between 'right' and 'all right' being that while describing an action as 'right' seems to involve an obligation on the agent to perform it if possible, describing it as 'all right' involves no such obligation). If this is correct, then talk of rights need not be the product of a sophisticated legal system, and can be seen as more deeply embedded in normal language than is often thought. A capacity to talk about right action would develop quickly into a capacity to talk about action as all right, though the idea of a formal system of *jus*, with rights as *property*, obviously depends on a whole host of ancillary concepts which are not necessarily present among a primitive people.[13]

---

[11] W. B. Miller: 'Two Concepts of Authority', *American Anthropologist*, 51 (1955), pp. 271 and 275.
[12] H. L. A. Hart: 'Are there any Natural Rights?' *Philosophical Review*, 64 (1955), p. 177.
[13] The term 'all right' is in fact found in English from almost as early a date as the term 'right', and a full analysis of its use might well serve as a new lead into the still vexed problem of rights.

Assuming that the Algonkians have this sort of ability to talk about rights, a right which is universal in the community will present no difficulties to them: at the very least, everyone has a right to perform actions which are intrinsically right. But what happens when someone claims that an action must be performed which not everyone *can* have the right to do – for instance who has the right to propose action which must be justified to the community? If there is a universal right to propose policy, which everyone exercises, and which it is known to everyone that everyone else wishes to exercise, it will be impossible actually to decide on any action until all the proposals have been heard, since to do otherwise would curtail the right. As a result, proposals that by their very nature involve speedy action will not be possible in a tribe with such a universal right; so we can assume that the Algonkians first generate a principle that only a limited or specified number of people may propose action to the tribe. The generation of such a principle is still within the framework of political argument conducted solely in terms of authentic justifications: it can easily be defended, on the grounds that there are kinds of action (particularly those to do – say – with war) which cannot be performed if everyone can propose them, and that there is no point in proposing an action which is inherently impossible, and known to be so to the rational proposer. Hence for these actions to be performed at all, they must be proposed by a limited number of people.

The next question to arise will be, what criteria do the Algonkians have to determine who that limited number of people should be? This is clearly going to be a critical problem, as at the moment A has as much right as B or C to be the one to propose action, and hence the right is in effect still universalized. There are two main ways in which they can argue about it: one is to point to features of the proposition, and argue from them to which members of the community should put it forward; the other is to point to features of the community, and argue from them that only by certain people proposing action will (for example) civil disturbance be avoided. In the first category belong particularly arguments like 'A is best at doing this sort of thing, and so he should do it,' and in the second belong arguments like 'Whoever the tribe decides should do it, for whatever reasons they have decided, should *ipso facto* do it'.

The first category of arguments runs into several difficulties: the major ones are that if it is necessary to consider what the proposition is before considering who should make it, the proposer's work has been pre-empted (in that what he has to say has already been a matter for discussion); and that if the proposer is specified in a general way, such as 'the best man at putting proposals before the assembly', then as the whole point is that we are dealing with a right in principle limited to certain people, the idea of 'best at doing' something cannot fit into our scheme. We cannot mean 'best of the whole tribe' – since to know he *is* best presupposes a universalized right, and a continuing one if he is to remain the best; nor can we mean 'best of a limited group of potential proposers' – since we still have to justify the limitation of the role to that group.

The other group of arguments are more important. They too, from the point of view of the excessively purist Algonkian, have the flaw that to say 'this is the only possible course to avert disaster' cannot carry complete conviction unless the other courses have been tried, but this is obviously something of a sledgehammer argument. We are clearly prepared to act on the basis of probability in affairs of this kind, and such an argument can function as a perfectly good justification for political action. But we can see the difficulties of this line of argument if we consider the possible natures of our postulated society: if it is postulated as a society of completely rational beings, then this way of specifying to whom the right should be limited cannot work. For the argument must boil down to saying something like 'Only by choosing our proposers in this way will disagreement in the tribe over how it should be done be prevented, and so the interests of the tribe advanced'. 'This way', on this line of argument, will be arbitrary, but must as a matter of fact be something the tribe agrees on. Agreement implies that the tribesmen must anteriorly have opinions on the matter, but if they are completely rational they will have perceived that there are no grounds on which to hold an opinion, other than that the tribe as a matter of fact hold the common opinion that a particular way is the right way to select proposers. We are faced with an infinite regress, and despite Strawson's words of caution against using such a regress too readily to demolish an argument,[14] it does seem to form an insurmountable barrier against this solution to the problem.

If we assume, on the other hand, that the tribesmen can have opinions on the matter which are not based on rational considerations, then it is simply unclear why they should be satisfied with an argument that says whoever in holding the proposer's post minimizes civil disturbance, *ipso facto* has a right to it. If they happen to think (on whatever grounds they use) that A has a right to it by virtue of those grounds, it is merely a subsidiary argument that his holding it will be the easiest way out of confusion for the community as a whole. If on the other hand they are of the minority who think B has a right to it, B does not in their eyes lose

---

[14] P. F. Strawson: 'Intention and Convention in Speech Acts', *Philosophical Review*, 74 (1964), p. 454.

this right if they are forced by the considerations of civil peace to accept A – such an acceptance they would doubtless categorize as 'unfortunately necessary'. The one person who might think considerations of civil peace gave A a *right* to the post is the rational tribesman who cannot conceive of any other grounds, but who observes that all his fellows can. But he must think the problem of who has a right to the post either as in principle soluble, in which case he must presumably think his solution correct, and his fellows' wrong – and hence be committed to at least trying to convert them to his way of thinking rather than in practice accepting the validity of their arguments; or as in principle insoluble, in which case he cannot think *he* has reached a solution. The position he might adopt is that of the man who realizes that everyone in a society has got the wrong ideas, and that he cannot convert them. He might then treat this state of affairs as given, and arrange the best outcome for the society as a whole by arguing that A should have the job. But such a man would still be committed to holding that the tribe *should* decide to give A the job on the grounds he thinks are correct: his position does not in fact seem at all different from that of the tribesmen who wanted B but put up with A, since they too will have held that the tribe *should* have decided on the grounds they thought were correct – the difference of course being that such a decision would have specified B and not A.

It would seem that it is extremely difficult, if not impossible, to find a way of determining who actually is justified in exercising a right which is in principle limited to specific people. Other solutions could be proffered, for instance that the tribesmen should have the right in rotation, but the justification for that must again be in terms of community interest and so come under the criticisms levelled above at this type of argument. If we accept that we do in fact have a paradox here, then we are faced with a new situation in Algonkian society: suddenly a political action has developed which is justifiable in principle, but the actual operation of which does not seem capable of a genuine justification, even though it is necessary in certain circumstances to the continued existence of the Algonkian community. What sort of claim is the operator of this right, the proposer of motions to the assembly, going to make to be the operator? He cannot use the justification which has hitherto been standard practice with the tribe, that is (typically) the justification of a particular agent's particular action, but instead will have to say that while the action is right if one person performs it, it is neither right nor wrong that he should be that one person: argument about it in the traditional manner of the tribe is impossible. He has no right to do what he is doing, but that is because the whole notion of *right* is inapplicable at this stage of his claim to continue in the role of proposer.

Is this sort of utterance what we have been looking for: can it be seen as essentially an authority citation? Certainly it meets our original criterion: it is a statement designed to kill criticism of a political action, which is nevertheless not an authentic justification. Moreover it also illuminates the tendency of writers on the concept of authority to talk about 'rights': for it is a necessary condition of this sort of claim (which we can call the Algonkian claim) being made meaningfully, that there is a limited right to the action in question, but the claim is not itself equivalent to an assertion by the agent that he personally has a right to the action.

However, I specified as a possible context for a political authority citation one in which a man could meaningfully use it to defend an action universally thought to be wrong, and this might seem to threaten the equation between an authority citation and an Algonkian claim. But for a government (for example) to say 'we have authority to do this wrong action' is in fact for it to say 'we are the only men who can take action in this sort of area; you have no right to stop us, even if you think it is wrong'. And this latter assertion is easily interpretable in terms of an Algonkian claim, with its talk of limited rights. A comparable example would be that of the husband who feels that he has no right to stop his wife from committing adultery with intent solely to cause him pain, but who feels also that he *has* a right to stop her from committing murder. The wife is the only person who has a right to stop herself from committing or permit herself to commit adultery, but everyone has a right to stop anyone from committing murder. One can have a limited right to decide whether the right course of action should be followed or not, and that right is not dependent on a decision that the right course should be followed. (This should of course be distinguished from Winch's view that the right to decide depends on the fact that the decision will (generally) be the right one.)

Furthermore, the comparison between an Algonkian claim and a political authority citation goes some way towards clearing up the complications involved in argument about the legitimacy of governments founded on *coups*. The problem has always been that if a given government has authority because of what it is or does, then that authority either continues or disappears accordingly as the government's actions continue or cease. If they are the sort of actions (e.g. protecting citizens) which only organizations with definite power in the community can perform, then that sort of power is a necessary condition of their authority, while if they are not, then governments in exile still have their original authority. Unfortunately, people seem to feel both that a new government has authority, and that in some sense the old has too (holding either that the return of the original government will not be another *coup* or, less usually, the idea represented by the Royalist judge David Jenkins's remarks on Parliament, that the King might be 'at *Holmby*, with guards upon him, and yet they governe by the virtuall Power of their Prisoner').[15]

Now, for an Algonkian claim to be made there have to be three separate assertions: (1) There is a limited right to do X; (2) There is no way of specifying to whom that right is limited; (3) I am doing X. (1) is the assertion correctly repeated by the old government – it was never the case that there could be two people with the right to do X, and never the case that anyone had the right to compel another to stop doing it so that they could start. (This is obviously not a logical impossibility, but it is rather difficult to see what kind of right to X a man might have, if someone else has an equal right to stop him doing X whenever they choose.) (3) is the assertion correctly made by the new government, and (2) is tacitly accepted by both sides, in so far as they cannot use the nature of X as an argument to specify conclusively who should perform it. The new government, in taking over, in effect (or in so many words) denied the limited nature of the right; but at the point at which it can start to assert (1) (which is generally the point at which its original denial has been forgotten) it can start making correct Algonkian claims, and if their identity with authority citations is true, it will correctly be in authority. The time lag observable before a new government is thought to have complete authority, and an old one none at all, is thus a practical condition to allow part of the necessary claim to be made without undue embarrassment.

My elucidation of an Algonkian claim also goes some way towards explaining why the *word* 'authority' should be used in the two senses which we originally examined; for a fundamental element in an Algonkian claim is the existence of a right limited to one (or a few) agents, and this is precisely what is involved in a first-sense (i.e. non-political) authority relationship. The man who is (say) an academic authority has a right, limited no doubt largely to himself, that his views should legitimate other people's utterances. But in his case, his possession of this right is not problematical: it is the case that he is more often correct about what he is concerned with than other people, and hence the authority citation does not lead to the sort of argument that political authority citations lead to.

While the explanatory advantages of assimilating the Algonkian claim to an authority citation are considerable, it could be argued that with

[15] D. Jenkins: *The vindication of Judge Jenkins* (London, 1647), p. 8.

the method I have adopted it cannot be said finally that an Algonkian claim *is* an authority citation, but merely that their functions closely resemble each other. But the point is that while an authority citation is used (for instance) to kill criticism of an action, this is not the crucial area in which it resembles an Algonkian claim. What is important is that it kills criticism *in the same way*, by pointing to the same features of the agent's situation, and that it generates the same kinds of problems and arguments as a result. It is true that to show two illocutionary acts have the same object is not to say very much about the different concepts in-involved,[16] but I have tried to show that in this case not only do they have the same object, but they hit it in the same way: and that tells us a great deal about the concepts. Moreover it enables us to understand rather better the kind of arguments which have gone on over authority, to see why people should have said the kind of things they did; and such an insight into the history of argument over a concept is in many ways as important as an insight into the nature of the concept itself.

---

[16] Cf. e.g. J. R. Searle: *Speech Acts* (Cambridge 1969), pp. 152, 153.

10 Collective Decisions and Collective Action

James Coleman

Several years ago, I was sitting on the edge of a cliff, and in front of me was a swarm of insects. The swarm hovered in front of me, darted to the left and to the right, expanded and contracted, hovered again, and then finally darted away. The sight fascinated me then, and the thought has continued to fascinate me. I was willing to take as given that an insect could direct his motion, could act in one or another direction. I was not willing to take as given that a set of insects could act as a body: could dart this way and that, could hover motionless in a body (though each insect was in rapid motion), could carry out actions as if it were a single entity. I might add parenthetically that if I were English, I might not see it that way. For one of the interesting differences between the English and American languages is that the English language treats a collectivity as third person plural, while the American language uses third person singular. Thus if I were English, I would have said that the swarm carried out actions as as if *they* were a single entity.

This problem of collective action is the fundamental question of organization that occurs in any scientific field. The biologist would be willing to take as given the behaviour of the insects' cells – or at least, some biologists would – but would not take as given the organization of cells into a functioning body. And so on down to the lowest level of organization of matter. The special concern of sociologists is with this question of organization or collective action among men: how is it that men act as a body? How is it that collectivities act? A sociologist is willing to take as given that a man can direct his action; but he is not willing to take as given that a collectivity of men can act. Yet just as the swarm of insects darts this way and that, collectivities do act – and social scientists treat them as actors. The acting units in much sociological investigation are groups and organizations; in political science, the acting units are often governments, sometimes political parties, sometimes nations; in economics, households or families are ordinarily treated as the consuming unit, and firms as the producing unit.

At the very outset, we could solve the problem by fiat, as some sociologists do, and merely accept that men sometimes do act collectively, and begin with the units of our investigation as collectivities themselves. Sociologists take this approach when they take as a starting point in their analysis the 'norms of a group', the 'goals of an organization', the actions of an association. Political scientists do so as well when they examine only the actions of governments or nations. Even economists, whose classical theory is based on the idea of a rational individual actor, leave unexamined the question when they take families as consuming units and firms as producing units, assuming that a family – as a unit – has utilities for certain goods and a firm – again as a unit – has the goal of maximizing profit.

Yet if we fail to take at some point the actions of these units as problematic, then we fail to examine the most important questions of social organization: how governments come to take an action, when parties split, the conditions under which community conflict occurs, the conditions of revolution or civil war, the way leaders are selected in groups, the emergence of norms in a group, the processes of collective decisions.

One way of posing the intellectual problem is to start with a framework that forms the basis of economic theory. That is, one may begin with rational individual actors, acting as free agents. Then, how does this lead to collective actors, in which two or more men carry out an action as a single actor? Much of economic theory is based on a satisfactory answer to that question in a very restricted case of two actors. When each has a good, and each values his good less than he values the other's good, then both can benefit from an exchange. There exists the possibility of a collective action, exchange of goods, in which both will be better off than they were before. Yet even in this restricted situation, problems arise. There are other conditions under which no action will occur. If both value the good they hold more highly than that of the other, by mutual consent, no exchange would occur. Or if only one values the other's good more highly than his own, one will want to make the exchange, but the other will not. Obviously, with two free agents, the exchange would not occur in this case either, since only one sees a benefit. But now the failure to exchange is not by mutual consent: one desires the exchange, and the other does not. It is this last situation that finds its analogue in larger collectivities. In a collectivity larger than two actors, the condition in which all will benefit can become very unlikely indeed. For if there are n actors, all free agents, and a decision of whether to carry out a given collective action or not, there are 2^n possible patterns of preference. For only two of these, all preferring not to act, or all preferring to act, do all agree. Thus if both preferences are equally likely for the n actors, the probability that all will agree is $2/2^n$. For a collectivity of ten actors, the probability is $2/1024$ that all will agree. For the other 1022 patterns of preference, we have no basis for saying which decision the collectivity will make. For example, there are ten patterns out of these 1022 in which 9 of the 10 favour the action. Can we say that the action will occur? Hardly, for we know that one actor prefers not to act. But can we say that the action will not occur? Again hardly, for the failure to act goes against the preference of 9 of the 10, and the ten may very well have bound themselves in by a majority rule.

The first point to recognize, then, is that the simple principle of rational man can serve to account for collective action only in the most restricted cases: when the free preferences of all lead to the same choice. In economics, these collective actions are given special recognition as 'Pareto-optimal' actions, since they constitute the one kind of collective action that economic theory is equipped to handle. For in economic theory, every actor (whether an individual, a household, or a firm) is a wholly free agent, and all collective action must derive from the voluntary choice of these free agents. A Pareto-optimal action is one which will make at least one person better off without making anyone worse off. But if anyone prefers the present state to the proposed action, the action is not Pareto-optimal.

The second point to recognize stems directly from this: that only in so far as men bind themselves so that on any action they are not wholly free agents, but are bound either by a constitution, by long-range calculations of self-interest, or by another means, will they take action when there is less than unanimity. This is a rather simple and self-evident proposition, but one which has implications for the kinds of decision rules members of a collectivity establish – decision rules ranging from action at the command of a single leader to action dependent on unanimity. The degree to which members of a collectivity retain their autonomy as free agents is measured by the inclusiveness of the decision rule in the collectivity. For example, collectivities have less inclusive decision rules for certain actions, such as temporal legislation, which usually require only a majority vote of the legislature, than for others, such as changes in the constitution, which often require a greater-than-majority agreement in the legislature, and sometimes ratification by a referendum. Furthermore, this question is closely related to a perennial question in the relation between the individual and society: the power of the individual relative to that of the society. Obviously, if all actions require unanimity, the individual has all the power, and the collectivity none; if all actions require only the decision of a single leader, the collectivity has all the power and the individual none.

I should note, to prevent confusion, that there is an extreme case that appears to be the precise antithesis to this. There are collectivities, ordinarily the most communal and solidary, for example some communities established by religious groups, in which all collective actions require unanimity. These communities appear to present a paradox, because of all collectivities, they most fully submerge individuality. But the paradox is only apparent: in such communities, there is seen to be no distinction between the individual and the collectivity. This is explicit in the dogma of many such communities, which have such phrases as 'the absorption of the self into the community', or 'the total abdication of self'. The unanimity rule here is not a means for insuring that all retain their autonomy, but quite the opposite: an insurance to the collectivity that all individuals have fully submerged themselves in the collective will, and are fully bound by it. In such communities, a variety of social psychological processes occur to insure that the individual does in fact give up his full autonomy to the collectivity. This is a fundamentally different and more primitive form of social organization than the one I shall discuss here. In the form of organization I discuss here, the individuals maintain distinct selves with distinct self-interests, outside the collectivity. The communal form of collective action, though important, is best reserved for a separate discussion.

Examples of the relation between a decision rule and the power of the collectivity relative to the individual may be easily found in current affairs. An interesting case has occurred recently in the U.S. that illustrates especially well this uneasy balance between the power of the individual and the power of the collectivity. The decision is the decision to fluoridate the water system. In many communities, this decision was taken by the city council, a small body of elected representatives. But in many communities, the decision by the council was then upset by petition followed by referendum. This gave rise to pressure in state legislatures which in some states has resulted in legislation forbidding a city council to take action fluoridating the water without a referendum. Thus the members of these communities, acting through their state legislatures, withdrew power from the city government on this action, by making a change in the decision rule to require consent of the individuals themselves through a referendum.

The general question of how decision rules and the procedural rules that govern collectivities arise is a complex one, as the above comments indicate. It is a problem that I will merely note here, however, and will turn instead to the processes through which rational individuals can carry out collective action, even given a set of rules. The first point noted above is that the idea of the rational man, acting voluntarily as a free agent, can account only for unanimous action. But given that this is so, one may ask whether an extension of this principle of rational individuals can lead to a more powerful theoretical approach to collective actions. As a start to answering this question, I will give two illustrations, one to show what I believe is not a fruitful approach to extending the idea of rational man, and the other to show what I believe is the correct approach. Both examples are from economics, and both are designed to develop the theoretical basis of collective action, beginning with the idea of a rational man. The first approach, which I believe is the wrong way to proceed, is that by Kenneth Arrow in a famous monograph published in 1950, *Social Choice and Individual Values*. Arrow shows, in a contribution to welfare economics, that no decision rule can be established that, beginning with the preferences of rational men, would necessarily give a 'rational' social choice. That is, even though the preferences of individuals obeyed the requirements of rationality, the choices of the collectivity could not be guaranteed to do so. In particular, the principle of transitivity would not be maintained: in a three-alternative choice, a situation could arise in which alternative A would win over B, and B over C; but then C would win over A. Arrow's theorem is correct, and indeed, it has stimulated an enormous body of work; rather, it is his goal that I believe to be wrong: to attempt to establish a parallel between the rational individual and the rational collectivity, in which the collectivity is merely an analogue or parallel, governed by the same principle of rationality as the individual. Indeed, as some further work has shown, and as I will discuss shortly, rational behaviour on the part of individuals may lead to systematic deviations from 'rationality' by the collectivity, quite apart from the Arrow paradox.

The second illustration is in the work of Knut Wicksell, in a contribution to the theory of public finance in 1898. Wicksell's effort was the opposite of Arrow's: it was unsuccessful, but the goal was correct. He was concerned with the question of a just tax: how could one be sure that the benefits of the tax outweighed its costs? Wicksell began with the premise that the only sure criterion was that for each individual the benefits outweighed the tax. Thus the decision rule should be unanimity. But this alone would lead to a rejection of nearly all tax proposals. Wicksell proposed a sequence of adjustments in the tax bill, so that those whose costs outweighed their benefits, and thus oppose the tax, would have their tax costs reduced, by the increase of others to whom the benefit was worth more than their proposed tax. Wicksell's proposal was similar in some respects to the compensation principle introduced later by Nicholas Kaldor in an attempt to solve the problem of interpersonal comparison of utility in welfare economics. In Wicksell's scheme, after appropriate adjustments, either the benefits to all would outweigh the costs, and the tax-and-benefit could be passed unanimously, or the costs would outweigh the benefits for some, in which case the tax would, appropriately, be defeated. The flaw in this procedure is that individuals will understate or underestimate their benefits, attempting to escape the costs and still enjoy the benefits. The consequence is that the tax would not be passed, even if benefits did outweigh costs for each individual. The correctness of Wicksell's goal, despite the faults of the technique, lay in his attempt to use the principle of rational action at the individual level in order to give a result for the collectivity derivative from this – not to establish a parallel 'principle of rationality' at the collectivity level.

This, I suggest, should be the goal of this direction of theory: to begin with the principle of rationality at the individual level, and derive from this the consequences for action at the level of the collectivity. This entails recognition of a number of points that have implications for the collective decision.

First, the fact that a collective action is a single action, derivative from the actions of the several members (say in voting), means that each individual cannot act merely according to the principle of rationality under certainty; the collective action is related only probabilistically to his own action. He must act according to expected utility, using the calculus of rationality under risk. Thus a rational individual will not blindly vote his preference, as rationality under certainty would predict, but will consider also the probability of each outcome under various possible actions he can take. The full implications of this difference become evident in conjunction with subsequent points.

The second element in a theory of collective decisions is the fact that no collective action stands alone, and none can be considered alone. A collectivity by its very definition consists of a set of interdependencies continuing over a period of time. For each type of collective action engaged in by this collectivity, each individual has a resource, his degree of control over the action, as specified by the formal constitution or the unwritten norms and customs of the collectivity. The rational individual thus considers his total resources in the collectivity, in conjunction with the interest he has in each collective action.

The implications of this point are extremely important for political processes. One implication is that an individual can, and a rational individual will, concentrate his resources so as to gain control of those actions most important to him. In particular, rational individuals will engage in barter, giving up their control – for example, their votes – over actions less important to them in return for control over actions of more importance. More precisely, they will make an exchange whenever they stand to gain in expected utility by doing so. It can be shown in addition that such exchange behaviour tends to lead – though not under all conditions – to an increase in the social welfare.[1]

[1] The fact that a vote – considered as a good being exchanged between two parties – has external benefits and costs for those

The process of political exchange or barter can be seen as a process by which potential conflict is reduced in a collectivity. For if some members feel intensely about an action, but do not have the votes or formal power to pass it, they can gain such power by giving up power over things that matter less. For example, in the passage of the Civil Rights Act of 1964 in the United States, agreement not to filibuster by Southern Senators was needed, to pass the legislation. The administration used a variety of inducements and pressures to gain this agreement. One was the design and passage of a Cotton Act in the same year, which gave benefits to cotton-growing states. The end result was that both the Civil Rights Act and the Cotton Act were passed, with both sides getting their way on issues of great interest to them. Note that this is more than a simple exchange of votes: it involves first the design of a second action, the Cotton Act in this case, that allows such exchange to take place.

Another major way in which the continuity of the collectivity affects the collectivity's action is by the creation of *compound actions* that can gain enough power to pass under the given decision rule, while the single action alone could not. In Congress, for example, at one stage in recent medicare legislation, a bill was introduced containing legislation favourable to tobacco interests, and *also* an 'amendment' introducing a physicians' supported medicare bill. This tactic was designed by the supporters of the latter to gain the votes of legislators from the tobacco states. More often, the bill will contain a multitude of related points designed to make it beneficial for a majority of the relevant interests. Again, in the medicare legislation: the final bill contained provisions that made it beneficial to the Blue Cross – Blue Shield Insurance Societies, giving them, rather than a government agency, power to establish rates. Thus by incorporating such a point in the bill itself, the conflict was reduced; and enough power was gained to pass the legislation.

One of the important conditions allowing such a transformation process that changes potential conflict into consensus is what may be termed a resource-expansion in the system at hand. Heuristically, the matter can be seen quite simply: if the resources of a given system are static or contracting, then any collective action that concerns these resources must make some members worse off, for any action producing a shift of resources, however slight, will cause some to lose. However, if there is an expansion of resources, then there are many actions that would make

---

other than the two parties to the transaction makes this exchange different from exchange of pure private goods, not necessarily increasing social welfare.

most members better off, and perhaps even some that would make everyone better off. In economists' terms, one could say that there are many possible actions toward Pareto-optimality in an expanding system. Such resources are not wholly economic, though the expanding portion may be principally economic. The example of the Civil Rights Act involved a redistribution of political resources, giving more political resources to blacks and certain other minorities than they had previously enjoyed. But the expanding economic resources made possible the Cotton Act, thus making a combined action that was more nearly Pareto-optimal.

More generally, in a period of economic expansion, an astute policymaker can greatly reduce conflict on a whole set of public-expenditure issues by a process of successive linking, or political credit-creation. One measure that gives benefits to one group gains consensus because support is 'borrowed' from other groups, in return for promises to pay in future legislation. The second legislation, in turn, gains votes from the first group because of the credit the administration has gained through passage of the first. And so on – with subsequent legislation. The crucial question from the policy-initiator's viewpoint is, as in financial transactions, whether in a given legislation, a profit is turned: is more credit gained from the benefited party than debt is incurred to the legislators whose support was borrowed? This corresponds roughly to the crucial question concerning the system as a whole: is more satisfaction (relative as always to the existing distribution of political power) gained than lost by the action? If the answer to these questions is no, then the administration cannot continue for long, because it will steadily lose public support. Again, the task is much simpler, and instrumental actions are much more possible, in a system with expanding resources. Also, in a system in which the proportion of resources in the public sector is much lower or higher than optimal, there is great opportunity for a political entrepreneur. If, by a sequence of political borrowing, he can carry out the right policies (a series of actions moving resources either into or out of various parts of the public sector), he should end with a much more satisfied populace, and thus a high amount of political credit. In short, if the system is far from a Pareto-optimal position with regard to the amount and distribution of public expenditures, for whatever reason, then a political entrepreneur can transform conflict into consensus through appropriate use of political credit.

All the above points are consequences of the fact that the collectivity exists through time, and thus that an action cannot be considered in isolation from other possible actions of the collectivity. Power relevant to that action, in the form of a vote, is a commodity – not necessarily to be used for that action, but possibly to be stored as political credit and used on a later action of more importance to the individual, possibly to be used to force immediate consideration of an action that would otherwise arise later.

The fact that power inherent in a vote can be and is used as a commodity in collectivities means that individuals must decide how best to use their votes on the sequence of actions they face. In particular, they must pay attention to the same point they would attend to in economic transitions: *the marginal utility of a vote commitment*. This marginal utility is the increment to the individual in expected utility consequent upon the commitment of a vote favouring (or opposing) the action. The rational individual will examine the marginal utility of a vote commitment not only in deciding whether to commit his vote, but also in deciding whether to seek vote commitments from others, by use of his political credit or by incurring political debts.

In calculating this marginal utility, the critical question is what increment in probability of passage an additional vote commitment will produce. This increment in probability depends greatly upon the number of votes already committed for and against the action. What does the marginal utility (or increment in probability of passage) look like to the individual asking whether he should seek an additional vote commitment?

I will not go into the marginal utility calculations here,[2] but will mention only a few general results. The most important point is that marginal utility does *not* behave like marginal utility in consumption of private goods, which declines with additional quantities held: it is *not* necessarily declining with additional vote commitments obtained, but under certain circumstances may rise sharply. Thus we would expect quite different behaviour in the acquisition of vote commitments than in the acquisition of private goods. In particular, two results are of importance:

(1) Other things being constant, as the number of vote commitments increases and the size of the uncommitted group decreases, the marginal utility of a vote commitment *increases*. Under the 'other things constant', the most important is that the balance of votes necessary from the uncommitted group remain constant as the commitments are made. For example, under a majority voting rule, this proposition holds so long as commitments are made at an equal rate to both sides. Thus as more commitments are made in both directions, the utility of the *next* commitment continually increases.

---

[2] See J. S. Coleman, 'The Marginal Utility of a Vote Commitment', *Public Choice*, Vol. V, Fall 1968, pp. 39–58.

(2) For a given size of the uncommitted group, the marginal utility of a vote commitment increases as the number of votes from the uncommitted necessary for passage is closer to that necessary for defeat. With a majority voting rule, this means that the marginal utility of the next vote is greatest when the numbers committed pro and con are equal.

Putting these two propositions together, the result is that as vote commitments are made, if they are made at an equal rate on both sides, the marginal utility of the next vote increases on two counts. Thus in such a situation, the contest for power over the action should *increase* in intensity over time. If, however, the balance is not maintained, the second effect described above dominates, and the marginal utility of the next vote commitment becomes less and less. The contest for power decreases in intensity, and there is instead a tendency to barter off one's vote commitment for future power before it loses all value. Thus there is a snowballing effect to the decline in intensity.

These are only initial results. The concept of marginal utility of a vote commitment, and its implications for behaviour, are far from having been explored. It appears likely that the implications will aid greatly in the understanding of conditions under which collective decisions erupt into conflict.

One important implication of such marginal utility considerations concerns the 'size' of the units that act as rational individuals in a collectivity. In the discussion so far, I have implicitly assumed that each individual with a single vote acts alone. But there is a special property of collective decisions that make it to each individual's interest to pay special attention to his neighbour's action. This is the fact that if any one individual obtains a vote commitment in favour of the action, this affects not only *his* expected utility, but also that of all others affected by the collective action. In economists' terms, the commitment in favour of the action provides an external economy to all others who will be benefited by the action, and an external diseconomy to all those who will be hurt by it. Suppose, then, that three individuals who favour the action are bound together as an acting unit, in which the costs of obtaining a vote commitment are shared. If they, acting as a unit, obtain a vote commitment, its value to each is just what it was if each were acting alone; but the cost to each in political credit is only one-third the cost of the commitment if he were acting alone. Thus such a combined acting unit, if one can be formed, can afford to obtain vote commitments that no single individual could afford; and the larger the unit composed of individuals favouring or opposing the action, the more it can afford to seek out and purchase vote commitments.

The implications of this are enormous. As a first simple implication, it means that other things being equal, if those on one side of an action are organized, and those on the other side are not, the organized side can always win by offering the uncommitted, or even opposing individuals, more than can any individual on the unorganized side. Perhaps the best example of this is the cases in legislation where 'special interests' can win in legislation even though they are in a numerical minority, because they act as a unit, and consequently can afford the costs, fiscal and political, of obtaining vote commitments that no member of the fragmented opposition can match.

Another important example of this phenomenon is the case of democratic organizations with an administrative hierarchy and an unorganized mass, such as labour unions or professional associations. If there is an issue to be decided by a vote of the mass, and the mass is otherwise roughly evenly split, the side favoured by the administrative hierarchy nearly always wins. The administrative hierarchy can afford to incur costs in obtaining votes that no single member of the unorganized opposition could begin to afford.

This example begins to suggest the crucial role of opposition parties in any collectivity with an organized administrative élite. Such a party can provide the organization which can afford to compete for votes against the already-organized incumbents. But the example raises also the question: why does not organization always occur on both sides of an issue, since it appears to be to the benefit of each individual to so organize? This is where the rub comes: it is to each individual's benefit *not* to participate in the costs of obtaining vote commitments, but to let others pay the full cost – for the external economies of vote commitments mean that he will benefit equally from the commitment whether he is or is not a member of the organization. Thus he will not join an 'opposition party' and contribute money, effort, or political resources to it, if he is rational. Organization in favour of or opposed to the action will *not* occur, unless he is forced to contribute to such organization by virtue of other holds it has over him. This last point, incidentally, has recently been made by an economist, Mancur Olson, in applying the theory of provision of public goods to the question of the conditions under which political pressure groups will form.[3]

This impossibility of organization of the interests on either side of a collective action without some external binding power thus shifts the burden of importance from the political party, which has no binding power for the electorate as a whole (though it does have such power for

---

[3] Mancur Olson, *The Logic of Collective Action* (Cambridge, Mass.: Harvard University Press, 1965).

the legislature, through the use of committee memberships, campaign support, and other devices as rewards, depending upon the legislative structure), to existing organizations in the collectivity, formed on other grounds, that do have such binding power, and are in turn free from the power of the governing hierarchy of the organization.

Nations with highly developed economies do have many organizations of this sort, while nations without developed economies, and voluntary associations such as labour unions, professional societies, and trade organizations, do not. An interesting exception that proves the rule is a trade union whose political system I once studied: the typographical union of the U.S. and Canada.[4] This union has long had a stable opposition parties, making it a curiosity among unions. But the crucial structural elements in the union were the organizations that constituted the source of party power. For one party, these were the large locals, whose officers were independent of the central administration. For the other party, the locals were supplemented by other organizations: mutual benefit societies, and a monotype club that acted as an employment agency for monotype operators. These bases, and not the party system itself, provided the organized resources by which the members could oppose their leaders when they so desired.

This concludes my general exposition of the elements of a theory of collective decisions and collective action. These elements constitute only a beginning, as I hope I have made clear. But their virtue is that they stem from a single theoretical frame of reference: the rational man, acting in such a way as to further his interests, yet doing so not by individual action, but as a member of a collectivity of which he is part. I suggest that this is the most difficult problem of social organization, but the one which, when adequately solved, will be of the greatest importance to our knowledge of social organization.

[4] S. M. Lipset *et al.*, *Union Democracy* (New York: The Free Press of Glencoe, 1956).